QUESTIONS LITURGIQUES

STUDIES IN LITURGY

Revue trimestrielle
A Quarterly Review

Septante-huitième année
Volume seventy-eight

1998

ABDIJ KEIZERSBERG
FACULTEIT GODGELEERDHEID

LEUVEN

Ces études ont aussi paru dans la revue *Questions Liturgiques/Studies in Liturgy* 79 (1998) n° 1-2.
These studies have been published simultaneously in *Questions Liturgiques/Studies in Liturgy* 79 (1998) no.1-2.

ISBN 90-429-0577-8
D. 1998/0602/263

TABLES DES MATIÈRES
CONTENTS

Introduction:
A Colloquium on
Popular Religion, Liturgy
and Evangelization

Jozef LAMBERTS

The importance of our topic

It is probably a cliché to say that while on the one hand participation in
our eucharistic celebration on the Lord's Day as the weekly celebration
of the paschal mystery has decreased, on the other hand some forms of
popular religion have maintained. One of the most remarkable expressions of this fact is apparently the phenomenon 'pilgrimage'.[1] Although
elements like increased transportation, tourism, curiosity, the making of
a tough journey as a challenge, especially to important international
places of pilgrimage, may play an important role, not all can be
explained by these. Religious motives, the search for salvation – whatever way this may be understood –, the experience of a community
which transcends the societal, are other possible elements. The question
then is how we should interpret this and particularly how we should deal
with it. What, for instance, is the reason that in a country like Belgium so
many people visit the Marian place of pilgrimage Scherpenheuvel each
year? Is it only a vague, childlike Marian devotion which can still be
expressed there? Is it because one can still pray the rosary there, or participate in the Way of the Cross or ask for a blessing?[2] Yet, in the meantime, many people participate in the several eucharistic celebrations held
in the basilica, whereas in parish churches with reduced eucharistic
celebrations on Sunday the number of faithful in each celebration is
declining.

The sacraments of baptism, confirmation, and marriage, and a sacramental like the funeral liturgy, which together are sometimes referred to
as the 'rites of passage', 'les fêtes des quatre saisons', or the 'rituals of

---

1. See e.g. Jozef Lamberts, *Op weg naar heelheid. Over bedevaart en liturgie*, Nikè-
reeks 39 (Louvain-Amersfoort: Acco, 1997) with bibliography.

2. André Keppens, "Bedevaartsoord te Scherpenheuvel," *Tijdschrift voor Liturgie* 81
(1997) 103-114.

life'[3] still have relative success, although there is a certain decrease. Indeed, the question is whether what the Church is offering as a sacrament and what people want to express and experience by it are correspondent. The relative success of such celebrations is understandable in a culture where precisely the Church is the only institution which offers people a celebration to mark the key moments in human life. But the question then becomes: is the Church only experienced as a 'religious service-institute'[5] or is there something more? So once again: how should we understand and deal with them? Must we heighten the threshold or rather lower it? Must we decide for a pluriform sacramental pastoral? Do we have opportunities for it or is there rather a specific task of evangelization because of the concrete sacramental praxis? Similar questions arise from reflection on events such as the burial of king Beauduin in Belgium or of princess Diana in Britain. Many people are touched by the intense moment of the celebration of christian initiation amidst a massive experience of popular religion on the occasion of the pope's visit to France in the summer of 1997.

Did one, probably, expect too much from liturgical renewal during the sixties and seventies? For example, one might have thought that by the realization of active participation the liturgy could really become an 'ecclesial liturgy'[6], in other words a celebration with the engagement of the entire local congregation, in such a way that popular devotions, which had proceeded from a period of ignorance, magic, and alienation from the real liturgy, would cease to exist since they were no longer necessary. The 'ecclesial liturgy' is now a possibility we need to realize *hic et nunc* if there were not the fact that the 'ecclesia', the convoked people of God, are present in such small numbers. Some expressions of popular religion, however, continue to inspire many people, but then we are speaking about 'paraliturgy'. This is at least a strange situation: an ecclesial liturgy almost without ecclesia and a paraliturgy with people. Nevertheless, the word 'liturgy' also means: a work of the people. Do we then have to broaden the notion 'liturgy' in such a way that popular

---

3. See the KADOC-project 'Levensrituelen' (Rituals of Life): *Levensrituelen. Het Vormsel*, Kadoc-Studies 12, ed. Karel Dobbelaere, Lambert Leijssen, and Michel Cloet (Louvain: Universitaire Pers, 1991). *Levensrituelen. Het Doopsel*, Kadoc-Studies 20, ed. Lambert Leijssen, Michel Cloet, and Karel Dobbelaere (Louvain: Universitaire Pers, 1996).

4. See as regards the evolution in Flanders (the Dutch speaking part of Belgium) between 1967 and 1993: Anne Van Meerbeeck, "Dopen: waarom niet? Een sociologische verkenning van de betekenis van dopen in Vlaanderen", in: *Levensrituelen. Het Doopsel*, 199-216, 200 and 216.

5. Jozef De Kesel, "De huidige sacramentenpastoraal: een teken aan de wand? Een theologische bezinning," *Tijdschrift voor Liturgie* 75 (1991) 132-145.

6. About the notion 'ecclesial liturgy' see Jozef Lamberts, "Ecclesiale liturgie en het Romeins Missaal," *Tijdschrift voor Liturgie* 68 (1984) 358-373, especially 358-365.

devotions may have their place in it, or should we instead speak about 'worship' where liturgy *stricto sensu* is the inner heart, indeed 'summit and source'? Do not we have to look for new ways to better relate both liturgy and popular devotions so that a cross-fertilization may emerge?

The rediscovery of popular religion may perhaps lead us to conclude that the liturgical renewal incited by Vatican II is not yet completed. It is not because the liturgical books have been revised that all is done. When our liturgy intends to be really of and for the people, we must consider how the expressions of popular religion can be recognized and have their place when the faithful gather together to celebrate.

On the one hand, Pope Paul VI in his 1974 apostolic exhortation *Marialis cultus* criticized

> the attitude of some engaged in the pastoral ministry who, rejecting popular devotions *a priori*, suppress them (whereas in fact, when rightly conducted, they are endorsed by the magisterium). Such people thus create a vacuum they cannot fill. Clearly they forget that the Council did not direct the elimination of popular devotions but rather their harmonization with the liturgy.[7]

On the other hand, he also repeated that

> popular devotions must be subordinated to the liturgy, not intermingled with it.[8]

In short; how can liturgy and popular devotions be balanced? How should we deal with them? Because this is a fact:

> The attitude of the Church to popular religion has varied, in different periods and countries, from a tolerance meant to show receptivity to a weakness that lets itself be overrun or, at the other extreme, a severity that condemns and seeks to purge.[9]

For these reasons, the members of the Louvain Liturgical Institute thought to choose for their thirteenth international liturgical colloquium

---

7. Paul VI, "Exhortatio Apostolica Marialis cultus," *AAS* 66 (1974) 113-158, no. 31. English text in *Documents on the Liturgy, 1963-1979* (Collegeville: The Liturgical Press, 1982) no. 1220.

8. *l.c.*

9. Jean Evenou, "Processions, Pilgrimages, Popular Religion," in *The Church at Prayer. An Introduction to the Liturgy. New Edition. Volume III: The Sacraments*, ed. Georges Aimé Martimort (Collegeville: The Liturgical Press, 1988) 241-262, 256 [Original French edition: *L'Église en prière: Les Sacrements* (Paris-Tournai: Desclée, 1984)]. Remark that the first edition in one volume [*L'Église en prière. Introduction à la Liturgie* (Paris-Tournai-Rome-New York: Desclée, 1961)], except for a short mention of the 'pia exercitia' (p. 9-10) did not have a chapter on popular religion as such, while it had a chapter on processions, pilgrimages, jubillees, and blessings (p. 631-655).

the topic: 'popular religion, liturgy, and evangelization'. Although we have already mentioned the word 'evangilization' we would like to further explain why we have included this word in our title. In the important apostolic exhortation *Evangelii nuntiandi*, which Pope Paul VI promulgated on 8 October 1975, a year after the third general meeting of the Synod of Bishops on evangilazation in the modern world, we read:

> Thanks to the liturgical renewal, the eucharistic celebration is not the only appropriate moment for the homily. The homily has a place and must not be neglected in the celebration of all the sacraments, at paraliturgies, and in assemblies of the faithful. It will allways be a privileged occasion for communicating the word of the Lord.[10]

A little further he explicitly deals with popular religion and devotions when he states:

> These expressions were for a long time regarded as less pure and were sometimes despised, but today they are almost everywhere being rediscovered. During the last Synod the bishops studied their significance with remarkable pastoral realism and zeal. Popular religiosity of course certainly has its limits... But if it is well oriented, above all by a pedagogy of evangelization, it is rich in values.[11]

This increased interest for popular religion that the Pope is referring to was to a large extent the result of the 1968 second meeting of the Latin American Episcopal Conference (CELAM) at Medellín. There the discussion focused on the liberating message of the Gospel on the basis of the dogmatic constitution on the Church, *Lumen Gentium*, and of the pastoral constitution on the Church in the Modern world, *Gaudium et Spes*. Document number six of Medellín dealt with popular religion in the context of popular culture, more precisely the subcultures of marginal rural and urban groups.[12]

The link with the preceding colloquia

The topic of this colloquium can be seen in the line of our preceding colloquia. After having reflected in 1995 on the inculturation of the

---

10. Paul VI, "Adhortatio apostolica Evangelii nuntiandi," *AAS* 68 (1976) 5-76, no. 43. English text in *Origins. NC Documentary Service*. 5 (1975-76) 459-468, 465.

11. *Ibid.*, nr. 48. English text in *Origins*, 466.

12. Jozef Lamberts, "Who Are Our Guests? Some Considerations about Liturgy and Popular Catholicism," *Questions Liturgiques - Studies in Liturgy* 74 (1993) 65-88 with more literature.

liturgy[13], we now had to investigate whether our liturgy is really rooted in popular culture, does the people right, and meets their deepest aspirations? It probably is not a coincidence that Anscar Chupungco's third book on inculturation is titled: 'Liturgical Inculturation. Sacramentals, Religiosity and Catechesis'.[14] Indeed, it examines 'sacramentals': processions, pilgrimages, and blessings which belong to the sacramentals, all of which are an important domain of popular religion. The Philippine Benedictine wrote in this book a chapter with the manifest title: 'Popular Religiosity and Liturgical Inculturation'.[15] In this chapter he does more than only to invite our attention to popular religion.

While in 1993 we studied the current issues in sacramental theology[16], we now can continue the line to the anchorage of the sacraments in the life of the popular faithful, to the tension between what the Church wants to celebrate in its sacraments and what the popular faithful expect when they for instance ask the Church for a celebration at the nodal points of life.[17]

While in 1991 we dealt with the theme 'liturgy and language'[18] as an important element for the active participation of the faithful in liturgy, we now ask whether a translation into the vernacular is enough to guarantee a 'liturgy of the people'. Do not we have to search for other things in order that the popular or the marginal faithful may feel that they really belong?

Further development of the theme

To address our theme more extensively, we called once more upon several specialists who deal with popular religiosity in their scholar investigations and/or their daily practice. The first contribution is by Professor Paul Post of the Theological Faculty at Tilburg (Netherlands), who has become, possibly more then anyone in the Dutch-speaking world, an

13. *Liturgie et inculturation. Liturgy and Inculturation*, Textes et Études Liturgiques XIV, ed. Jozef Lamberts (Louvain: Peeters, 1996).

14. Anscar J. Chupungco, *Liturgical Inculturation. Sacramentals, Religiosity, and Catechesis* (Collegeville: The Liturgical Press, 1992).

15. *Ibid.*, 95-133.

16. *Accents actuels en théologie sacramentaire. Current Issues in Sacramental Theology*, Textes et Études Liturgiques XIII, ed. Jozef Lamberts (Louvain: Peeters, 1994).

17. Already in 1981 the Louvain Liturgical Institute studied the issue of liturgical celebration with marginal christians. See Cor Traets e.a., *Liturgie et marginalité. Baptême, mariage, funérailles*, Textes et Études Liturgiques V (Louvain, 1982) [= *Questions Liturgiques* 62 (1982) 1-84].

18. *Liturgie et langage. Liturgy and Language.* Textes et Études Liturgiques XII, ed. Lambert Leijssen (Louvain: Peeters, 1992).

authority in the field of 'popular culture and liturgy'.[19] He first offers a description of the broad scope of 'religious popular culture and liturgy' and its theoretical approach. Subsequently he discusses a particular case, *in casu* the commotion at the occasion of a liturgical innovation during the celebration of All Souls in a Dutch parish. From theory and praxis he eventually formulates a number of approaches of religous popular culture and its anthropological characteristics. The author also offers an enhanced bibliography, which one can find in the footnotes, concerning the different aspects and topics he is dealing with in his text. Consequently, the interested reader has a great deal of interesting material at his/her disposal when he/she wants to further investigate the different aspects of the immense domain of religious popular culture and liturgy.

Dr. Charles Caspers, coordinator of the Liturgical Institute at Tilburg, is specialized in the history of liturgy and popular religiosity during the middle ages and early modern times.[20] Accordingly, he introduces us into the way popular devotions were experienced in that period, taking the so-called 'agnus dei' as an example.

Times change and we are confronted with new challenges. While Caspers' contribution was situated in early modern times, Professor Lambert Leijssen of the Faculty of Theology of the Catholic University of Louvain, seeks to lead us into was is called 'postmodernity'. Colleague Leijssen, along two other colleagues and two associate researchers has recently started an important research program in order to develop a 'postmodern sacramento-theology'.[21] Moreover, he has been

---

19. As a liturgist he was engaged from the very beginning in the research program 'Christian pilgrimage: shape, functions, and pastoral-theological implications of a phenomenon of popular religiosity', which since 1986 is executed at the (former) Faculty of Theology and Pastoral Work in Heerlen (now part of the Catholic University of Nijmegen). See e.g. *Christelijke bedevaarten. Op weg naar heil en heling*, ed. Marinus van Uden and Paul Post (Nijmegen: Dekker & van de Vegt, 1988). *Bedevaart en pelgrimage. Tussen traditie en moderniteit*, UTP-Katernen 16, ed. Jos Pieper, Paul Post, and Marinus van Uden (Baarn: Gooi & Sticht, 1994). *Oude sporen, nieuwe wegen: ontwikkelingen in bedevaartonderzoek*, UTP-Katernen 17, ed. Marinus van Uden, Jos Pieper, and Paul Post (Baarn: Gooi & Sticht, 1995). Paul Post, "Traditie gebruiken. Sint Hubertus in Muiderberg," in *Bij geloof. Over bedevaarten en andere uitingen van volksreligiositeit*, UTP-Katernen 11, ed. Marinus van Uden, Jos Pieper, and Ernest Henau (Hilversum: Gooi & Sticht, 1991) 191-211. Paul Post, "The Modern Pilgrim: A Christian Ritual Between Tradition and Post-Modernity," *Concilium* (1996) no. 4, 1-9.

20. See Ch. Caspers, *De eucharistische vroomheid en het feest van Sacramentsdag in de Nederlanden tijdens de late middeleeuwen*, Miscellanea Neerlandica 5 (Louvain: Peeters, 1992). *Bread of Heaven. Customs and Practices Surrounding Holy Communion. Essays in the History of Liturgy and Culture*, Liturgia Condenda 3, ed. Charles Caspers, Gerard Lukken, and Gerard Rouwhorst (Kampen: Kok Pharos, 1995).

21. Promotors of this project are professors Lambert Leijssen, Georges De Schrijver, and Lieven Boeve. Associate researchers are dr. Jeff Bloechl, and drs. Stijn Van den Bossche. See Georges De Schrijver, "Experiencing the Sacramental Character of Existence: Transitions from Premodernity to Modernity, Postmodernity, and the Rediscovery of

investigating for some time the relation between Christian sacraments and the 'rites of passage'.[22] After an introduction on postmodernity, he discusses popular religion under the critique of the modernity. Subsequently, he deals with popular religiosity in the Latin American context. In his third section he presents an interpretation of popular religiosity in a postmodern context. Eventually he offers some conclusions about the tension between symbiosis and integration, and the task for inculturation.

In accord with a good tradition, we also invite specialists from disciplines other than theology. Professor Liliane Voyé (Université Catholique Louvain-la-Neuve), a sociologist of religion, is also known and appreciated in European circles of theologians, and particularly of liturgists and pastoral theologians, because of her investigations on the working of rites and the phenomenon of popular religiosity.[23] She presents a sociological approach under the title which clearly confronts the issue: 'Effacement or re-legitimation of popular religion?'.

The three following contributions seek to enter into concrete shapes of popular religiosity and liturgy from one's own experience. Dr. Antoine Rubbens, national chaplain of the Christian Health-Funds of Belgium, informs us about his experiences with and reflections on organized pilgrimages with the sick. Bernard Valentijn Fets, from the Praemonstratensian abbey of Averbode and rector of the Marian pilgrimage-place Kortenbos (Belgium), reflects on the possibilities of co-existence of popular Marian devotion and liturgy. Drs. Stijn Van den Bossche, previously diocesan coordinator of the pastoral care for young people in the

---

the Cosmos," *Questions Liturgiques - Studies in Liturgy* 75 (1994) 12-27. Lieven Boeve, "Een postmoderne theologie van het 'open verhaal'," *Onze Alma Mater. Leuvense Perspectieven* 50 (1996) 210-238.

22. See Lambert Leijssen, "Het vormsel als sacrament van geloof en als overgangsritueel. Een theologische benadering," *Het vormsel*, 217-231. Id., "Sacramentologische reflectie op het kinderdoopsel," *Het kinderdoopsel*, 261-277. Id., "De ziekenzalving als sacrament van geloof en 'rite de passage'," *Liturgie en kerkopbouw*, ed. Ernest Henau and Frans Jespers (Baarn: Gooi & Sticht, 1993) 127-157.

23. Liliane Voyé, "Le rite en questions," *Le rite, source et ressources*. Publications des Facultés Universitaires Saint-Louis 69, ed. René Devisch, Charles Perrot, Liliane Voyé, and Louis-Marie Chauvet (Brussels, 1995) 105-136. Id., "Religion populaire et pèlerinages en Europe," *Marche vers la Splendeur. Ton Dieu marche avec toi*. Actes du Premier Congrès Mondial de la Pastorale des Sanctuaires et des Pèlerinages. Conseil Pontifical pour la Pastorale des Migrants et Itinérants (Rome, 1972). Id., "Les jeunes et le mariage religieux: une émancipation du sacré," *Sécularisation et religion: la persistance des tensions*. Actes de la XIXe conférence internationale de sociologie des religions, Tübingen 1987 (Lausanne, 1987) 57-67. Id., "Les jeunes et le mariage religieux," *Social Compass* 38 (1991) 405-416. Id., "Du monopole religieux à la connivence culturelle en Belgique. Un catholicisme 'hors les murs'," *L'Année sociologique* 28 (1988) 135-167. Id., *Sociologie du geste religieux* (Brussels, 1973). Id., "Over de zondag. Een sociologische bijdrage," *De zondag. Een tijd voor God, een tijd voor de mens*, ed. Ernest Henau and André Haquin (Brussels: Licap, 1992) 8-29.

diocese of Ghent and now associate researcher for the Louvain project 'postmodern sacramento-theology', reflects on the topic 'popular religiosity, liturgy, and young people'. He first describes postmodernity as frame-work. He subsequently investigates the religiosity of postmodern young people, their religious questions and the christian answers. In his third section, he deals with young people's relation to christian liturgy. He concludes with two open questions.

The last contribution by the president of the liturgical institute deals with the need and opportunities for evangilization in relation with popular religiosity and liturgy. He first presents a re-reading of Sacrosanctum Concilium 13 on popular devotions. Subsequently he points to the need for evangilization in relation with popular religion, demonstrates the positive elements emerging from popular religion for the inculturation of the liturgy, gives a critical approach of some overestimations of popular religion, and finally formulates some criteria for a more positive approach to popular devotions.

Final reflection

Since the year 1998, on the road to the year 2000, is in the pastoral field focused on the Holy Spirit, we dare to express our hope that the Holy Spirit, through the contributions which are collected in this book, may inspire and stimulate all those who work in the pastoral field to pay attention to the people they meet at the places of popular religion. In such a way that they may find with them the ways which lead to the Lord who through his human concern revealed God's love. Probably they then will participate in our liturgy to honor and to praise the Father through, with and in Christ, in the unity of the Holy Spirit and strenghtened by the Holy Spirit to cooperate in the building of a world according to God's heart.[24] The Holy Spirit as *vinculum caritatis et unitatis* wants to bind all together in unity and love with each other and with God.

> By the power of the gospel [the Holy Spirit] makes the Church grow, perpetuallly renews her, and leads her to perfect union with her Spouse. The Spirit and the Bride both say to the Lord Jesus, Come! Thus, the Church shines forth as 'a people made one with the unity of the Father, the Son, and the Holy Spirit.[25]

24. See the contributions on an earlier colloquium of our Liturgical Institute: *L'Esprit Saint et la Liturgie*. Textes et Études Liturgiques IX, ed. Lambert Leijssen (Louvain, 1986).
25. *Lumen Gentium*, no. 4.

Religious Popular Culture and Liturgy: An Illustrated Argument for an Approach[1]

Paul POST

Opening remarks

1. A fuss about an All Souls' Day observance

On All Souls' Day, Saturday, November 2, 1996, in Blaricum, The Netherlands (Province of North Holland, Diocese of Haarlem), a change in the repertoire of liturgical hymns stirred up some strong feelings. Although there was also understanding and appreciation expressed for this liturgical innovation, disappointment and indignation predominated among the reactions voiced. An official written reaction from the vice-chairman of the parish council provides a succinct review of the affair:

> Many from far and wide again came to St. Vitus's Church on Saturday evening. The centuries' old tradition in Blaricum of observing All Souls' Day with a sung mass, followed by a procession through the graveyard with most of the graves lighted, is always an impressive event for all concerned. The atmosphere in the church, and especially also in the dark evening procession, and standing by the graves of one's own deceased family members, lighted only by a single lantern, encourages everyone to pause and reflect upon the deceased, the mystery of death and the light of faith.
> This year there was, however, a change in the established tradition, which many found to be objectionable. The text of the closing hymn, 'Uit de diepe boetekolken,' was changed. Immediately after the observance there were many reactions to this, to the pastors, and to members of the pastoral staff and the parish council.[2]

What had happened? As the residents of the town would proudly testify, the closing hymn of the All Souls' observance in Blaricum had "for centuries" been a song of supplication for the deceased of five verses and a refrain, with as its title and opening line "Uit de diepe boetekolken" (From the depths of purgatory). In 1996 the parish council introduced a

---

1. This article is an expanded and annotated version of the opening lecture at the international liturgical colloquium "Volksreligie, liturgie en evangelisatie" (Popular religion, liturgy and evangelism) at Louvain, October 13-14, 1997. I thank Dr. Charles Caspers for his critical reading of an earlier version of this article, and also Pastor Jan Duin, of Huizen, for his kind cooperation. Translated by D. Mader MD.

2. F. Vlak, vice-chairman of the parish council, "All Souls' Day, 1996," in: *Galmgaten. Kontaktblad van en voor de parochiegemeenschap St. Vitus Blaricum* 10,7, December, 1996, 6-9, cited from p. 6ff. See also in this number the reaction by J. Rigter, "Dus toch," 9-10.

new text by Jan Duin, while the tune remained the same.

This is, in my eyes, a striking example of religious popular culture and liturgy. I will shortly expand upon this fascinating case study in this paper. At this point it is sufficient to indicate the terrain to be explored. I would add that there are many other case studies that could also be presented to supplement it. Perhaps, in fact, this is precisely what should be done in order to indicate the spectrum of religious popular culture. Without going into them more deeply, I will only mention the more or less classic cases of weeping Madonnas (in The Netherlands the most recent this past summer (1997) in Volendam[3], followed shortly thereafter by a crying statue of Elvis Presley in Brabant, traditionally one of the most Catholic provinces in The Netherlands), flourishing local and regional pilgrimage sites in Europe, but also all kinds of rising new rites or "emerging rituals," for instance those surrounding AIDS, or in the colorful world of youth culture.

2. Organization

I intend to approach our subject, religious popular culture, thematically (that is, as concrete ritual actions), always in the broad context of a continuing and often surprising dynamic of cultus and culture.

My argument comprises three points. First, there is a theoretical, and chiefly also historical part. Although liturgy and liturgical studies provide the most important perimeters, the central concern there will be to wrestle with the concept of 'religious popular culture,' so deserving of the adjectives 'recalcitrant' and 'complex,' in the light of a series of relevant disciplines in the humanities. This theoretical exploration will close with notice of a remarkable book by the ethnologist Walter Hartinger, in which he proposes, briefly, that the liturgy within the precincts of the church is the chief purveyor of the ideas and forms found in religious popular culture. A second section will deal with the case study. There I will expand on the fuss surrounding the All Souls' observance in the Dutch parish which I mentioned above. In the third and closing section, drawing from theory and practice, I will formulate a number of approaches to and qualities of religious popular culture.

---

3. This Volendam case of a weeping Madonna image was only one of many in Europe over the last years. I will list here only the notable cases in Civitavecchia (Italy) and Brunssum (The Netherlands) in 1995. See now *Bedevaartplaatsen in Nederland. Deel 1: Noord- en Midden-Nederland*, ed. P.J. Margry and C. Caspers (Hilversum-Amsterdam, 1997) s.v. Volendam, 777-780. See the curious J.M. Touw, *[Huilt Maria in Brunssum?] Wenende Madonna's. Kritische analyse van een fenomeen toegespitst op het huilende Mariabeeldje van Brunssum* (Herkenbosch, 1995).

EXPLORING THE TERRAIN:
RELIGIOUS POPULAR CULTURE AND LITURGY

1. General survey: Religious popular culture and liturgy

1.1. Diagnosis regarding interest in the subject

One can ask in a general sense where, and to what degree the subject of religious popular culture stands on the liturgical studies agenda. Two extreme evaluations or diagnoses are then possible.

A first diagnosis is somber. There is, after all, much to indicate that popular culture is hardly a subject for liturgists. It has been that way for a long time. In the surveys of research into religious popular culture in general, and pilgrimage in particular, which I have prepared with some regularity during ongoing research in recent years (the most recent charting the state of affairs in the mid-80s)[4], it is apparent that theology and liturgical studies have played hardly any role, or at best a marginal role, in academic studies into the theoretical, methodological reflection on religious popular culture in general, or in studies of concrete popular cultural subjects such as pilgrimage, the cult of relics, devotions involving statues, feasts and festivals, etc., and indeed that theology and liturgical studies often discover and use developments in other disciplines belatedly, eclectically or inadequately. Recently, in his super-disciplinary review of the literature on the subject of "celebration, feast and festival," Arno Schilson came to the same conclusion.[5] Looking back over the last decade, one could argue that not much has changed in this situation. The general picture is that now and then the subject of religious popular culture is placed on the agenda, often through an impetus from outside the discipline, but that it is not really a dominant subject for study. At the most, the subject is now and then drawn onto the demesne of liturgy, in accordance with policy or from a normative perspective, or it is dealt with as an appendix, a marginal loose end to be caught up for the sake of completeness.

Another more positive diagnosis or weighing of the research situation in and around the field of popular culture and liturgy does certainly catch

---

4. See the bibliography and survey in P. Post, "Onderweg. Tussentijdse notities met betrekking tot bedevaartonderzoek," *Christelijke bedevaarten. Op weg naar heil en heling*, ed. M. van Uden and P. Post (Nijmegen, 1988), 1-38, and Id., "Thema's, theorieen en trends in bedevaartonderzoek," *Bedevaart en pelgrimage. Tussen traditie en moderniteit*. UTP-Katern 16, ed. J. Pieper, P. Post and M van Uden (Baarn, 1994) 253-301.

5. A. Schilson, "Fest und Feier in anthropologischer und theologischer Sicht. Ein Literaturbericht," in *Liturgisches Jahrbuch* 44 (1994) 3-32.

sight of attention being given to the topic. Since the second half of the 1980s, however, this attention has been directed not so much on general and/or theoretical reflection on the subject, but on various themes. As we see in a multi- or even supra-disciplinary overview, from an open and broad practice of liturgical studies, the subject is certainly present in the handling of all sorts of topics in what we might call the popular religious canon. Religious popular culture especially appears to be a series of subjects which by their nature invite overstepping the boundaries of academic disciplines. Popular religious subjects appear especially to always be 'shared subjects.' Subjects, which are also every whit 'our subjects,' are elsewhere basking in interest, and 'our' discipline can not avoid encountering these studies in adjoining disciplines. It would be too much to run through an extensive survey of the literature here, but one can think of the subjects of *image/art and rite*[6], *pilgrimage*[7], *devotions to*

6. H. Belting, *Bild und Kult. Eine Geschichte des Bildes vor dem Zeitalter der Kunst* (Munich, 1990); A. Stock, *Poetische Dogmatik* (Paderborn etc., 1996-): compare now: *Poetische Dogmatik. Christologie. Bd. 2: Schrift und Gesicht* (Paderborn etc., 1996); Id., *Keine Kunst. Aspekte der Bildtheologie* (Paderborn etc., 1996); P. Van Dael, *Tot lering en vermaak. Functies van kunst in de Middeleeuwen* (Kampen, 1997).
    7. See note 4 above; "Pelgrimage. Een historische, antropologische en spirituele belichting van een universeel verschijnsel," = special issue, *Concilium* 32,4 (1996); "Bedevaart en pelgrimage," = special issue, *Communio* 22,3 (1997); Report of the symposium "Bedevaarten zonder grens. Nieuw onderzoek naar bedevaartcultuur in Nederland en Vlaanderen," = *Volkskunde* 97,3 (1996) 269-379. See also the fact that the 12th international congress for Christian archaeology (Bonn 1991) was devoted to pilgrimage: *Akten des XII. Internationalen Kongresses für christliche Archäologie Bonn 1991*, C.d.Vaticano/Münster, 1995, = Jahrbuch Antike und Christentum Erg. Bd. 22,102 / = Studi di Antichità Cristiana 52; *Der heilige Rock zu Trier: Studien zur Geschichte und Verehrung der Tunika Christi anlässlich der Heilig-Rock-Wallfahrt 1996 im Auftrag des Bischöflichen Generalvikariates*, ed. E. Aretz e.a. (Trier, 1995); *350 Jahre Kevelaer-Wallfahrt, 1642-1992*, 2 vol., ed. R. Schulte Staade (Kevelaer, 1992); D. Blackbourn, *Marpingen: Apparitions of the Virgin Mary in Bismarckian Germany* (Oxford, 1993); M. Wingens, *Over de grens. De bedevaart van katholieke Nederlanders in de zeventiende en achttiende eeuw* (Nijmegen, 1994); S. Zimdars-Swartz, *Encountering Mary: from La Salette to Medjugorje* (New York, 1991); W. Christian Jr., *Apparitions in Late Renaissance and Medieval Spain* (Princeton, 1981); Id., *Local Religion in Sixteenth-century Spain* (Princeton, 1981); Id., *Moving Crucifixes in Modern Spain* (Princeton, 1992); Id., *Visionaries: the Spanish Republic and the Reign of Christ* (Berkeley, 1996); P. Margry and P. Post, "Het project 'Bedevaartplaatsen in Nederland': een plaatsbepaling, in: *Volkskundig Bulletin. Tijdschrift voor Nederlandse cultuurwetenschap* 20,1 (1994) 19-59; = "Wallfahrt zwischen Inventarisierung und Analyse. Ein niederländisches Forschungsprojekt in historiographischem und methodologischem Kontext," in: *Rheinisch-westfälische Zeitschrift für Volkskunde* 39 (1994[1995]) 27-65; *Bedevaartplaatsen in Nederland, deel 1: Noord- en Midden-Nederland*, ed. P. Margry and Ch. Caspers (Amsterdam-Hilversum, 1997); J. Lamberts, *Op weg naar heelheid. Over bedevaart en liturgie*. Nikè reeks 39 (Leuven-Amersfoort, 1997). Apart from this, the subject of popular Catholicism and liturgy has been on Lamberts's agenda for some time: see for in-

saints and cults of relics[8]*, celebrations, feasts and festivals ('festivity')* ,
rites surrounding *dying, death and burial*[10]*, marriage rites*[11] *, proces-*

stance Id., "De Constitutie over de liturgie en het volkskatholicisme," *Bij geloof. Over
bedevaart en andere uitingen van volksreligiositeit.* UTP-Katernen 11, ed. M. van Uden,
J. Pieper and E. Henau (Hilversum, 1991), 211-236; Id., "Pius Parsch (1884-1954) en het
'volksliturgisch apostolaat'," in: *Tijdschrift voor liturgie* 77 (1993) 151-162; Id.,
"Bedevaart en liturgie," in: *Bedevaart en pelgrimage* (note 4, above), 201-240.

8. A. Angenendt, *Heilige und Reliquien. Die Geschichte ihres Kultes vom frühen
Christentum bis zur Gegenwart* (Munich, 1994); A. Legner, *Reliquien in Kunst und Kult.
Zwischen Antike und Aufklärung* (Darmstadt, 1995).

9. For the subject of "feast and festival," in addition to Schilson, "Fest und Feier'
(note 5 above) see also: K.-H. Bieritz, "Nächstes Jahr in Jerusalem. Vom Schicksal der
Feste," in: *Jahrbuch für Liturgik und Hymnologie* (1994/95) 37-57; J. Boissevain, *Revi-
talizing European Rituals* (London, 1992); H. Cox, *The Feast of Fools: A Theological
Essay on Festivity and Fantasy* (Cambridge, 1969); B. Kranemann, "'Feiertags kommt
das Vergessene..' Zur Deutung und Bedeutung des christlichen Festes in moderner
Gesellschaft," *Liturgisches Jahrbuch* 46 (1996) 3-22; O. Marquard, "Kleine Philosophie
des Festes," in *Das Fest; eine Kulturgeschichte von der Antike bis zur Gegenwart*, ed. U.
Schulz (Munich, 1988) 413-420; T. Michels and P. Post, "Huwelijk: dynamiek van feest
en sacrament," in: *Tijdschrift voor liturgie* 81 (1997) 327-343; P. Post, "Liturgische
beweging en feestcultuur. Een landelijk onderzoeksprogramma," *Jaarboek voor liturgie-
onderzoek* 12 (1996) 21-55; Id., "Een idyllisch feest. Over de natuurthematiek in
Brabantse oogstdank-vieringen," *Natuurlijke liturgie.* Liturgie in perspectief 6, ed. A
Mulder and T Scheer (Baarn, 1996) 118-139; F. Taborda, Sakramente*: Praxis und Fest*
(Düsseldorf, 1988); see here also the long-running project at Louvain on Christian rites of
passage: K. Dobbe-laere, L. Leijssen and M. Cloet (eds.), *Levensrituelen. Het Vormsel.*
KADOC-Studies 12 (Leuven, 1991); *Geboorte en Doopsel.* KADOC-Studies 20 (Leuven,
1996); see now also P. Post & L. Van Tongeren, "Het feest van de eerste communie. Op
zoek naar de iden-titeit van het christelijk ritueel," *De passie van een grensganger.
Theologie aan de voor-avond van het derde millennium*, ed. K.-W. Merks & N. Schreurs
(Baarn, 1997) 249-266; T. Walther-Sollich, *Festpraxis und Alltagserfahrung. Sozialpsychologische Predigtana-lysen zum Bedeutungswandel des Osterfestes im 20. Jahrh.*
Praktische Theologie Heute 29 (Stuttgart, 1996) = diss. Göttingen, 'Festtheorie' in: 1.1.,
1.2 and 1.3. pp. 17-94.

10. From a real explosion in literature I will list only a handful, consciously including
both good and bad in order to indicate the broad range: *Midden in het leven, staan wij in
de dood. Wat kan de kunstenaar toevoegen aan het uitvaartritueel?*, ed. and coord.
Carpay & Capaan, H. Heynink (Amsterdam, 1996); J. Enklaar, *Onder de groene zoden.
De persoonlijke uitvaart. Nieuwe rituelen in rouwen, begraven en cremeren* (Zutphen,
1995); K. Guth, "Sterben, Tod und Trauer aus volkskundlicher Sicht," *Liturgisches
Jahrbuch* 44 (1994) 237-251; G. Lukken, *Op zoek naar een geloofwaardige gestalte van
de dodenliturgie.* Liturgische handreikingen 19 (Breda, 1995); P. Post, "Iconisering of
ontbeelding? Enkele notities over de ontwikkeling van de beeldzijde van bidprentjes met
de ikoon als invalshoek," *Jaarboek voor liturgie-onderzoek* 4 (1988) 235-277.

11. See J. Pieper and P. Post, "Rituele veranderingen met betrekking tot de huwelijkssluiting: een onderzoeksvoorstel," *Jaarboek voor liturgie-onderzoek* 12 (1996) 136-163;
Michels and Post, "Huwelijk: dynamiek van feest en sacrament" (= note 9).

sional culture[12], the *material culture* of popular religion[13], religious popular culture as it manifests itself in various *domains outside the church*,[14] and the culture of popular religious *hymns and songs*[15].

In addition to this rather classical image of the canon of popular religious expressions, there is also the more open view that in the postmodern era sees the transformation of old forms of religious popular culture and the rise of new forms.[16] In the region covered by the Dutch

12. S. Felbecker, *Die Prozession: historische und systematische Untersuchungen zu einer liturgischen Ausdruckshandlung*. Münsteraner theologische Abhandlungen 39 (Altenberge, 1995).

13. *Antonius. "De kleine en de grote,"* Museum voor religieuze kunst Uden (Uden, 1995); *Clara in de Nederlanden* (ibid., 1994); *Volksdevotie. Beelden van religieuze volkscultuur in Noord-Brabant*, ed. L. Van Liebergen and G. Rooijakkers (ibid, 1990); *L'Almanach des vieus ardennais: Traditions et saints du printemps* (Bastogne: Musée diocésain en Piconrue; Art religieux et croyances populaires en Ardenne et Luxembourg, 1992); *L'Almanach des vieus ardennais: Traditions et saints de l'été* (ibid., 1994); *L'Almanach des vieus ardennais: Traditions et saints de l'automne* (ibid, 1997); *Naître autrefois. Rites et folklore de la naissance en Ardenne et Luxembourg* (ibid., 1993); C. McDannell, *Material Christianity. Religion and Popular Culture in America* (New Haven etc., 1995). See also the catalogues which have accompanied recent Dutch exhibition projects on devotions for saints: *Sanctus. Met heiligen het jaar rond*, ed. L. Van Liebergen and W. Prins (Uden: Museum voor religieuze kunst, 1997); C. Staal and M. Wingens, *Bedevaarten in Nederland* (Zutphen, 1997); *Gouden legenden. Heiligenlevens en heiligenverering in de Nederlanden*, ed. A.B. Mulder-Bakker and M. Carasso-Kok (Hilversum, 1997).

14. *Religie thuis*, ed. P. Post, P. Nissen and C. Caspers = special issue *Trajecta* 4,2 (1995); see further also: P. Post, ""Paysage rituel: liturgie en plein air (I)," *Questions liturgiques-Studies in Liturgy* 77 (1996) 174-190; Id., "Paysage rituel: la liturgie en plein air (II): la visite du pape, action de grâce pour la moisson, rites autour d'une mort subite, *ibid.*, 240-256.

15. J. Smelik, *Eén in lied en leven. Het stichtelijk lied bij Nederlandse protestanten tussen 1866 en 1938*. Series of monograph studies in the "Nederlandse cultuur in Europese context" project, ijkpunt 1900 (Den Haag, 1997) (= dissertation Rijks Universiteit Groningen 1997); A. Vernooij, *Het rooms-katholieke devotielied in Nederland vanaf 1800*. Kerkmuziek en liturgie 4 (Voorburg, 1990); H. Evers, *Pastoraat en bedevaart. Een onderzoek naar het pastorale aanbod in het kader van de devotie tot Sint Gerardus Majella en de bedevaart naar Wittem, met bijzondere aandacht voor het gezangrepertoire* (Etten-Leur, 1993).

16. R. Grimes, *Reading, Writing and Ritualizing: Ritual in Fictive, Liturgical and Public Places* (Washington DC, 1993); N. Mitchell, "Opkomende nieuwe riten in de hedendagse cultuur," in: *Concilium* 31 (1995) 138-147; see also surveys of shifts in this ritual market: P. Post, "Goede tijden, slechte tijden: devotionele rituelen tussen traditie en moderniteit," *Goede en slechte tijden: het Amsterdamse Mirakel van Sacrament in historisch perspectief*, ed. P.J. Margry (Aerdenhout, 1995) 62-80; Id., "Zeven notities over rituele verandering, traditie en (vergelijkende) liturgiewetenschap," *Jaarboek voor liturgie-onderzoek* 11 (1995) 1-30; Id., "Liturgische beweging en feestcultuur" (see note 9); Id., "Liturgische bewegingen: een literatuurbericht," *Praktische Theologie* 24,1 (1997) 59-80; *De Madonna van de Bijenkorf. Bewegingen op de rituele markt*. Liturgie in perspectief 9, ed. P. Post and W.M. Speelman (Baarn, 1997). In this connection, certainly

language, there is growing attention for new, rising rites of this sort on the borders of Christian, general religious or secular/profane domains, an field that, to my mind, may be fully accounted as part of the broad field of research for religious popular culture.[17]

These are the two divergent diagnoses. It is now worth noting that each of these two visions has a different starting point and takes a different standpoint: the one sees the traditional domain of liturgical studies as a closed and subdivided territory; the other is oriented more toward the subject. This difference now enables us to take both diagnoses together and formulate a sort of middle position. On the one side it is indeed still true that the subject of religious popular culture does not stand high on the agenda of international liturgical studies. We see that it has been brought to the foreground in the contributions of certain researchers, but that beyond this it functions on the margins. Moreover, important developments in adjoining disciplines are not taken into account, and thus to an important extent people overlook the fact which we have already pointed out as an important aspect, namely that subjects in popular religion are always shared subjects. We will soon see that the situation in The Netherlands diverges from this general image.

On the other side, it can be stated that subjects from popular religion which also have a great deal to do with the canon of liturgical studies, do enjoy considerable interest in various other cultural studies. Once more

see also: J. Koenot, *Voorbij de woorden. Essay over rock, cultuur en religie* (Averbode-Baarn, 1996) and J. De Visscher, *Een te voltooien leven. Over rituelen van de moderne mens* (Kapellen, 1996). In this connection, reference is often also made to what are termed "New Age rites." This terrain likewise should be approached with nuance and a capacity for making distinctions; for this, see: W.J. Hanegraaff, *New Age Religion and Western Culture: Esoterism in the Mirror of Secular Thought.* Studies in the History of Religions 72 ((Leiden, 1996) (= originally dissertation at Rijks University Utrecht, 1995), and M. Moerland and A. Van Otterloo, "New Age: tegencultuur, paracultuur of kerncultuur," *Amsterdams sociologisch tijdschrift* 22,4 (1996) 682-710. For the situation in Germany, see: A. Schilson, "Das neue Religiöse und der Gottesdienst. Liturgie vor einer neuen Herausforderung?," *Liturgisches Jahrbuch* 46 (1996) 94-109.

17. This interest should in part be placed in a broader interest in rites and symbols. It is striking that in this attention is chiefly devoted to rituals in everyday life. See *Religions and Social Ritual. Interdisciplinary Explorations*, ed. M.B. Aune and V.M. Demarinis (Albany, New York, 1996) [See my review in *Worship* 71,1 (1997) 87f.]; L. Bakker, L. Boer and A. Lanser, *Rituelen delen. Een verzameling ideeën om geloven vorm te geven* (Kampen, 1994), 2nd. ed.; F. Frijns et al., *Rituelen. Rituelen in het dagelijks leven van mensen, in het bijzonder van mensen met een verstandelijke handicap* (Best, 1996); R. Fulghum, *From Beginning to End: The Rituals of Our Lives* (London etc., 1995); R. Grimes, *Marrying & Burying: Rites of Passage in a Man's Life* (Boulder, 1995); C. Rosseels, *Rituelen vandaag* (Antwerpen-Baarn, 1995); J. Roose-Evans, *Passages of the Soul: Rediscovering the Importance of Rituals in Everyday Life* (Shaftesbury etc., 1994); M.P. Somé, *De kracht van rituelen. Wat zij betekenen voor mens en samenleving* (Utrecht-Antwerpen, 1996); De Visscher, *Een te voltooien leven* (see our note 16).

this confirms the importance of multidisciplinary work, and 'cross-border contacts' among academic disciplines. There is also the important challenge of bringing specific dimensions such as liturgical renewal and inculturation, the identity of Christian rituality and sacramentality, theological dimensions and the perspective of the *liturgia condenda*, all so important for our discipline, into the investigation.[18]

1.2. Striking developments

After this general diagnosis, it is fitting to provide a broader historiographic note on the development of the interest in and the study of religious popular culture. This development has been very complex, because the sometimes stormy debates and achievements have definitely not taken place synchronously in various academic disciplines. For my survey sketch, I have selected the following four academic clusters that, down to the present day, have exchanged impulses among themselves: (1) the theological disciplines, for our subject especially the subdisciplines of pastoral theology and liturgical studies; (2) historical studies, or more broadly, the humanities; (3) the social sciences in general, and cultural anthropology in particular; and (4) European ethnology or 'Volkskunde', which we would locate between the previous two clusters, the historical studies and social sciences.

Within these domains, I now want to distinguish four characteristic lines of development:

1.2.1. Liturgical renewal and debates about popular religiosity

Especially if we enter into how the subject came onto (and returns to) the theological agenda, liturgical development itself forms an important orientation point, not only for theology and liturgical studies but for other disciplines as well. The liturgical reforms that took shape after the Second Vatican Council, particularly in the 1970s and early 1980s, were directly or indirectly an impetus for a good deal of reflection and debate over and around religious popular culture. The special issue of *La Maison-Dieu* from 1975, "Religion populaire et réforme liturgique," is

---

18. See *Liturgie en inculturatie*, ed. J. Lamberts (Leuven-Amersfoort, 1996); G. Lukken, *Inculturatie en de toekomst van de liturgie*. Liturgie in perspectief 3, (Heeswijk-Dinther, 1994); Id., "Inculturation de la liturgie: théorie et pratique," *Questions liturgiques-Studies in liturgy* 77 (1996) 10-39; *Toekomst, toen en nu: beschouwingen over de ontwikkeling en de voortgang van de liturgievernieuwing*. Liturgie in perspectief 2, ed. L. van Tongeren (Heeswijk-Dinther, 1994); L. van Tongeren, "Liturgie in context. De vernieuwing van de liturgie en de voortgang ervan als een continu proces, *Tijdschrift voor liturgie* 81 (1997) 178-198.

an illustration of this.[19] There was a fierce debate about popular religiosity going on in France and Latin America at that time, and arising from pastoral theology and the social sciences, from about 1974, but especially after 1977, the subject of popular belief and popular religiosity assumed a place on the theological agenda.[20] From our perspective today, it is striking that in spite of this special issue of *La Maison-Dieu*, liturgical studies were really to all intents and purposes absent from this debate. (Systematic) theologians, pastoral theologians, pastors from parishes and ecclesiastical policy-makers all entered the lists, and so did liberation theologians and 'postmodern culture theologians' like Harvey Cox. In Latin America, North America and France the argument proceeded along very diverse tracks, in the framework of a discussion over the orientation of ecclesiastical action, chiefly about the boundaries of liturgical renewal, the experience and reception of rituality, the often unappreciated anthropological dimensions of rituality, and also the rediscovery of the dominance of a relatively autonomous, lived faith that, as Delumeau argued, at the very least nuances the channeling strategies of the Church.[21]

When I now reread the flaming arguments of men such as Plongeron

19. *La Maison-Dieu* 122 (1975).

20. There are various sources where one can find a survey of this debate concerning popular religion, with extensive bibliographies. I will list only: Evers, *Pastoraat en bedevaart* (our note 15); *Volksreligiositeit: uitnodiging en uitdaging.* HTP-Studies 3, ed. A. Blijlevens, A. Brants and E. Henau (Averbode, 1982); *Popular Religion*, ed. N. Greinacher and N. Mette [= special issue *Concilium* (1986)]; K. Rahner et al, *Volksreligion - Religion des Volkes* (Stuttgart etc., 1979); see also the special issues of *Collationes* 21,5 (1975) and *Tijdschrift voor theologie* 17,4 (1977). Bibliographical surveys can be found in F. Spiertz, "Volksreligiositeit: een literatuuroverzicht," *Volksreligiositeit*, 159-189; Evers, p. 412, n. 15. The subject of religious popular culture in Latin-American, Asian and African contexts will not be further pursued here. It can, however, be noted that because of the interest in inculturation, Western theology and liturgical studies are being asked to consider religious popular culture again from this perspective. Important here are the studies of Anscar J. Chupuncgo. See: *Popular religion, liberation and contextual theology: papers from a congress (Jan. 3-7, 1990, Nijmegen) dedicated to A. Camps OFM.* Kerk en theologie in context 8, ed. J. Van Nieuwenhove and B. Klein (Kampen, 1991); *The Popular Use of Popular Religion in Latin America.* CEDLA Latin American Studies 70, ed. S. Rostas and A. Droogers (Amsterdam, 1993); F. Wijsen, *"There is only one God": a social-scientific and theological study of popular religion and evangelization in Sukumuland, Northwest Tanzania.* Kerk en theologie in context 22 (Kampen, 1993); C. Parker, *Popular Religion and Modernization in Latin America: a Different Logic* (Maryknoll, 1996). See further the article by my colleague Dr. Leijssen in this collection.

21. R. Pannet, *Le catholicisme populaire. 30 ans après 'La France, pays de mission?'* (Paris, 1974) 3rd ed.; *Le christianisme populaire. Les dossiers de l'histoire*, ed. B. Plongeron and R. Pannet (Paris, 1976); J. Delumeau, *Le Christianisme va-t-il mourir?* (Paris, 1977).

and Pannet in what became a real conflict about rites, I find themes constantly recurring there which now, for example, are central to the Dutch national liturgical studies' research programme surrounding the culture of celebration.[22] In our Dutch-speaking region, these issues were brought to our notice by special issues of *Collationes* (1975) and *Tijdschrift voor Theologie*.[23]

1.2.2. 'Volkskunde' or European ethnology

It is likewise striking, and in a certain sense has had tragic consequences down to the present, to see how despite some influences from the social sciences, this theological debate stands almost in isolation from other academic disciplines. Theologians show little or no acquaintance with discussions and reflections in adjoining disciplines which were and are occupied with the same problematic. For instance, in German-speaking countries, the theological debate had been preceded by an interesting theoretical debate about popular culture and its study in the circles of European ethnology / 'Volkskunde'.[24] Unfortunately, it was relatively late – in general, after 1985 – before people in other fields became acquainted with the fruits of this debate which took place over the decade from 1967 to 1977. Briefly, and leaving aside nuance and subtleties, in 'Volkskunde' or European ethnology the issue was an important wrestling with the object of study. The old established canon of popular culture was being left behind. On the one hand, the canon was problematized (see Hermann Bausinger's apposite slogan, "Probleme statt

22. Post, "Liturgische beweging en feestcultuur" (see our note 9).

23. Both special issues employ the term 'volkskatholicisme' (popular Catholicism) rather exclusively. Nevertheless there is also a Protestant religious popular culture: see: R. Weiss, "Grundzüge einer protestantischen Volkskultur," *Schweizerisches Archiv für Volkskunde* 93,1 (1997) 71-84 [= originally 61 (1965) 75-91]; A.Th. van Deursen and G.J. Schutte, *Geleefd geloven: geschiedenis van de protestantse vroomheid in Nederland* (Assen, 1996).

24. See below for the most important theoretical lines in this debate. I will here mention only: H. Bausinger, *Volkskunde. Von der Altertumsforschung zur Kulturanalyse* (Berlin-Darmstadt, 1971); *Antiquaren, liefhebbers en professoren. Momenten uit de geschiedenis van de Nederlandse volkskunde*, ed. T. Dekker, P. Post and H. Roodenburg [= *Volkskundig Bulletin. Tijdschrift voor Nederlandse cultuurwetenschap* 20,3 (1994)]; see therein: P. Post, "Volkskunde in Nederland. Notities over disciplinaire eigenheid," 229-243 and Id., "Belangstelling vergeleken: een actuele plaatsbepaling van de Nederlandse volkskunde," 414-427; a recent, up to date and richly documented survey, tailored to the Dutch situation, is to be found in: W. Frijhoff, *Volkskunde en cultuurwetenschap: ups en downs van een dialoog* (Amsterdam, 1997) [= Mededelingen der Koninklijke Nederlandse Akademie van Wetenschappen afd. Lett. NR 60,3, 89-143 (5-59)].

Fakten"[25]); on the other hand, the canon was being thrown open. In addition to rural areas, the city and the working class now came under the loupe; not only the past was of interest, but also the present. This reconsideration of object and canon concentrated primarily on a fundamental theoretical and critical thinking through of the sustaining concepts of 'people' ('Volk') and 'culture.' In a general sense, as also in the historical disciplines, there was a movement from a normative conception of culture to an interactive concept of culture. By 'popular culture" one no longer referred primarily to certain segments or layers of the society (elite vs. popular), nor primarily to nations or tribes, but rather to general civilization, the culture that people often unconsciously share with one another. One could here speak of the matrix of the culture. Popular culture is like that part of an oak leaf that survives when the rest molders away, the supporting structure that determines the contours of the leaf. This broad, generally shared group culture is culture with a small 'c', not culture of the 'Kleine Leute.' Study of this popular culture brings regional and social differences in a culture into focus, and is oriented particularly to collective, broad, supporting cultural phenomenon that shape daily life. Another important element in the discussion was the insight that the continuity of culture was no longer the starting point and presupposition, but rather its dynamics and development, or, also, contingency. In many respects, the masks of centuries-old traditions fell away. In the debate it became all the more clear how many assumed continuity theses were constructs.

Now, this aspect of continuity touches particularly on religious popular culture and liturgy. Here, after all, one often finds the development schema of superstition, religion and Christianity employed, whereby elements of religious popular culture can then be cherished or decried (according to one's ecclesiastical or ideological standpoint) as remnants of earlier phases of culture and religion.

It is very interesting in this connection to make a comparison with liturgical studies and then refer to insights and practices in the discipline during and since the Liturgical Movement. There too continuity theses are present, which are likewise sometimes ideologically determined, as can be seen in the work of Guéranger and Baumstark, but also in Dix.[26]

25. Bausinger, *Volkskunde* (see our note 24); Frijhoff, *Volkskunde en cultuurwetenschap* (also note 24), 130.

26. In summary, see P. Bradshaw, "The Homogenization of Christian Liturgy - Ancient and Modern: Presidential Address," *Studia liturgica* 26 (1996) 1-15; Post, "Zeven notities over rituele verandering" (our note 16).

1.2.3. The modernizing agenda of historical studies

'Volkskunde' or European ethnology stands between anthropology and the historical disciplines.[27] I turn now particularly to the historical studies because it was via this channel that modernizing impulses reached liturgical studies. Church history served here as the intermediary. The influential programmatic article by Willem Frijhoff from 1981 with the sketch of a 'histoire religieuse' that took the place of the old traditional 'histoire de l'Église' can serve as a model for the modernizing agenda of historiography.[28] Some years ago, in a theoretical essay also precisely oriented to religious popular culture, the Belgian historian Jan Art arrestingly laid out this new approach, the opportunities it offers and its perspectives.[29] In historical scholarship, as it has been modernizing itself, scholars have increasing been raising the most difficult questions that historians can ask, namely, those about everyday life. This is such a favorite subject field for them chiefly because in it they can (perhaps!) rise above the hoary opposition between action and structure or the interplay of objective and subjective factors in history. Thus everyday life becomes a beckoning perspective. Traditional historical research into religious factors in culture, certainly as it has been carried out within the framework of church history, generally avails itself of what can be termed the institutional approach. Religion in everyday life, the sense in which religious popular culture is now being understood, is here approached by investigating what influences a religious institution has in and on daily life. These could be certain pastoral activities, or ecclesiastical prescriptions, etc. Under the influence of the social sciences, re-

27. For the academic 'cross-border traffic' among these three disciplines, see: Frijhoff, *Volkskunde en cultuurwetenschap*; also: Id., "Inleiding: historische antropologie," *Cultuur en maatschappij in Nederland (1500-1850): een historisch-antropologisch perspectief*, ed. P. Te Boekhorst, P. Burke and W. Frijhoff (Meppel-Amsterdam-Heerlen, 1992) 11-38.

28. W. Frijhoff, "Van 'histoire de l'Église' naar 'histoire religieuse'. De invloed van de 'Annales'-groep op de ontwikkeling van de kerkgeschiedenis in Frankrijk en de perspectieven daarvan in Nederland," *Nederlands Archief voor Kerkgeschiedenis* 61,2 (1981) 113-123.

29. J. Art, "Possibilities and Difficulties in Studying the Place of Religion in Everyday Life in the 19th and Early 20th Century," *Experiences and Explanations: Historical and Sociological Essays on Religion in Everyday Life*, ed. L. Laeyendecker, J. Jansma and C. Verhaar (Leeuwarden, 1990) 103-116. Art depends here particularly on C. Lalive d'Epinay; see: "By Way of Introduction: The Flow of Everyday Life, the Reflow of History," *Social Compass* 28,4 (1981) 333-334, as introduction to the special issue (see: *Religion et vie quotidienne. À propos de la 16e Conférence intern. de sociologie des religions*, ed. E. Pace et al. (Lausanne, 1981) [= special issue *Social Compass* 28,4 (1981)]; see further: "Sacredness and Everyday Life," *Recherches sociologiques* 17,1 (1986) 9-64.

search takes a new direction now: the starting point is not a religious phenomenon but rather a general social category, and researchers ask what role religion plays within that framework. This procedure is what I had in mind when I spoke above of an open, broad approach to religious popular culture. Culture, but more pointedly, everyday life, is first broadly and descriptively approached via a group, profession or, most often, a location (a town or city; I am here thinking of the influential work of William Christian, Jr., who defines religious popular culture chiefly as local culture; for him 'popular religion' is 'local religion'[30]), and then the religious factor is brought into focus within this broad cultural and social context. In addition to new questions, this approach, which offers a much greater opportunity for a contextual descriptive research phase than before, especially demands new sources, and new research methods and techniques. In this regard, there is a preference for speaking of 'traces.' The researcher goes in search of diverse traces of actions and actors. In addition to the traces of elites, one also diligently searches now for traces of 'silent groups.' It is here of importance to note how, with this new approach, it is chiefly rituals which come under the lens. Historians who work with this new agenda discover how it is precisely through ritual repertories that the researcher can penetrate deeply and decisively into the network of a culture.

This approach to popular culture as, briefly, the particular design[31] of everyday life then comes to be seen with increasing frequency in the context of appropriation processes.[32] This important research perspective, which can be traced back through Chartier[33] and the Jesuit De Certeau[34], does not focus on how culture and cultural elements are designated from the outside, but defines popular culture as "a specific manner of dealing with culture which is rooted in the social group or community itself."[35] This leads to an essential shift in the accents in research: from

---

30. See the oeuvre of W. Christian, Jr., note 7, above.

31. See A.J. Bernet Kemper's little-noted "Volkskunde en 'bijzondere vormge-ving'," *Bijdragen en mededelingen van het Rijksmuseum voor volkskunde 'Het Nederlands Openluchtmuseum'* 33,2 (1970) 25-52 (= inaugural address, University of Amsterdam, October, 1969). The same author also has a fine study of the palm-branch to his name: Id., *Om een struik die palm werd* (Arnhem, 1966).

32. An outstanding theoretical introduction with regard to appropriation is offered by W. Frijhoff, "Toeëigening: van bezitsdrang naar betekenisgeving," *Trajecta* 6,2 (1997) 99-118.

33. R. Chartier, *The Practice of Everyday Life* (Berkeley, 1984); Id., *Cultural History between Practices and Representations* (Cambridge, 1988); Id., "Popular Culture: A Concept Revisited, *Intellectual History Newsletter* 15 (1993) 3-13.

34. For De Certeau, see: Frijhoff, *Volkskunde en cultuurwetenschap*, p. 10 with bibliography in note 20 (note 24, above), and Id., "Toeëigening".

35. Frijhoff, *Volkskunde en cultuurwetenschap*, 94.

top down to bottom up, from vertical to horizontal, from prescribed order
to lived practice, in which the central locus is the community in which
culture is shaped.[36]

To recapitulate, in the field of historical studies we see an open, broad,
contextual and multidisciplinary approach to culture, directed toward
everyday life, in which rituality plays a key role. It is here, in this specific programmatic context, that the term 'religious popular culture' is
preferred, as is in the title of an influential 1986 collection in which
Gerard Rooijakkers and Willem Frijhoff had a hand.[37] The subtitle of the
collection, "the tension between prescribed order and lived practice,"
shows us that the earlier dichotomy of 'elite' and 'popular' had not entirely disappeared. In addition to the term 'religious popular culture,'
there are several other favored terms, chiefly 'religion in everyday life,'
'everyday religion' and 'lived faith,' and there have been a number of
multidisciplinary conferences held under the title 'Religion in everyday
life.[38]

36. This approach is applied in various Dutch studies. In addition to Frijhoff's work, I
will here mention only: G. Rooijakkers, *Rituele repertoires. Volkskcultuur in oostelijk
Noord-Brabant 1559-1853* (Nijmegen, 1994).

37. *Religieuze volkscultuur. De spanning tussen de voorgeschreven orde en de
geleefde praktijk*, ed. G. Rooijakkers and Th. Van der Zee (Nijmegen, 1986).

38. See *Religion in Everyday Life. Papers Given at a Symposium in Stockholm 1993*.
Konferenser 31, Kungl. Vitterhets Histori och Antikvitets Akademien, ed. N.-A. Bringéus
(Stockholm, 1994). *Experiences and Explanations*, ed. Laeyendecker, Jansma and
Verhaar (see note 29). Further in this connection I would mention the following relevant
titles: U. Altermatt, "Prolegomena zu einer Alltagsgeschichte der katholischen Lebens-
welt," *Theologische Quartalschrift* 173 (1993) 259-271; Bausinger, *Volkskunde* (see note
24); W. Brückner, "Popular culture. Konstrukt, Interpretament, Realität. Anfragen zur
historischen Methodologie und Theorienbildung aus der Sicht der mitteleuropäischen
Forschung," *Ethnologia Europea* 4 (1984) 10-24; Id., "Frömmigkeitsforschung im
Schnittpunkt der Disziplinen. Über methodische Vorteile und ideologische Vor-Urteile in
den Kulturwissenschaften," *Volksfrömmigkeitsforschung*. Ethnologia Bavaria 13, ed. W.
Brückner et al. (Würzburg, 1986) 5-37; Id., "Zu den modernen Konstrukten 'Volksfrömmigkeit' und 'Aberglauben'," *Jahrbuch für Volkskunde* NF 16 (1993) 215-220; I.
Cieraad, *De elitaire verbeelding van volk en massa. Een studie over cultuur* (Muiderberg,
1988) [To be read with the critical reviews by H. Roodenburg in *Volkskundig Bulletin* 17
(1991) 65-67 and G. Rooijakkers, "Volk en cultuur als elitaire misleiders. Het ideeën-
archeologisch pleidooi van Irene Cieraad," *Volkscultuur* 7 (1990) 97-84]; Van Deursen
and Schutte, *Geleefd geloven* (note 23); *Ethnologie des faits religieux en Europe.
Colloque national de la Société d'ethnologie Française, Strasbourg 24, 25 et 26 nov.
1988*. Le regard de l'ethnologue 4 (Paris, 1993); I. Greverus, *Kultur und Alltagswelt.
Eine Einführung in Fragen der Kulturanthropologie* (Munich, 1987); W. Kaschuba,
"Volkskultur: Themen, Publikationen, Perspektiven. Ein Forschungsüberblick aus
volkskundlicher Sicht," *Archiv für Sozialgeschichte* 26 (1986) 361-398; and particularly:
Id., *Volkskultur zwischen feudaler und bürgerlicher Gesellschaft. Zu Geschichte eines
Begriffs* (Frankfurt a.M., 1988); *Religion et vie quotidienne. À propos de la 16e Con-
férence intern. de sociologie des religions, Lausanne, 1981*, ed. E. Pace et al. = special

While, in my experience, some scholars in Dutch church history re-
acted rather defensively to this, it did not take long for this line of research to achieve a prominent place in Dutch liturgical studies.[39] After
all, scholars here had for some time been sensitized to academic 'cross-
border' traffic, and, more particularly, were in search of ways, sources
and methodologies for approaching the newly arisen questions about
reception and experience. Liturgy was no longer a book, but faith as it
was lived and celebrated by people. Moreover, this new wind connected
with the growing interest in the fundamental anthropological dimensions
of liturgy and in completing the 'turn' to the subject. After the mid-
1980s, popular religious themes were abundantly present in Dutch liturgical studies. I will mention here only the annual conferences held by
those teaching in the field of liturgical studies in The Netherlands. In
1986 the one-day conference was devoted to prayer cards[40], in 1991
explicitly to liturgical studies, 'Volkskunde' or European ethnology and
the study of feast, festival and ritual[41]. I would also mention a Palm
Sunday project[42], the festschrift for Herman Wegman in 1990 devoted to
the role of 'the people' in the liturgy[43], the work of Herman Wegman[44]

issue *Social Compass* 88/4 (1981); R.W. Scribner, "Ritual and Popular Religion," Id.,
Popular Culture and Popular Movements in Reformation Germany (London-
Ronceverte, 1987) 17-48; Id., "Volksglaube und Volksfrömmigkeit. Begriffe und
Historiographie," *Volksfrömmigkeit in der frühen Neuzeit*, ed. H. Molitor and H.
Smolinsky (Münster, 1994) 121-138; *Popular Religion in Germany and Central Europe,
1400-1800*. Themes in focus, ed. B. Scribner and T. Johnson (Basingstoke etc., 1996);
Weiss, "Grundzüge einer protestantischen Volkskultur" (see our note 23).

39. This could be seen, for instance, in the mixed reactions to the forward: M.
Monteiro, G. Rooijakkers and J. Rosendaal, "Van hoogaltaar tot tochtportaal," *De
dynamiek van religie en cultuur. Geschiedenis van het Nederlands katholicisme*, ed.
Monteiro, Rooijakkers and Rosendaal (Kampen, 1994) 9-20.

40. See: *Jaarboek voor liturgie-onderzoek* 2 (1986) 1-31.

41. See: *Jaarboek voor liturgie-onderzoek* 7 (1991) 77-184. In this connection, see
also the conference devoted to the reception of hymns, *Jaarboek voor liturgie-onderzoek*
3 (1987) 217-273.

42. P. Post and J. Pieper, *De palmzondagviering: een landelijke verkenning*
(Amsterdam-Kampen, 1992); Id., "De palmzondagviering. Verslag van een landelijke
verkenning," *Tijdschrift voor liturgie* 76 (1992) 365-388.

43. *Omnes circumadstantes. Contributions towards a History of the Role of the People
in the Liturgy*, ed. C. Caspers and M. Schneiders (Kampen, 1990).

44. At the same time, I do not wish to suggest that in all cases academic 'cross-border'
traffic around the subject of religious popular culture was a matter of course. In
Wegman's case one can see how, for instance, fundamental discussions in European
ethnology were still unfamiliar, and thus the classic theme of defining pilgrimage and
making the distinctions within that category were nearly begun again ex nihilo (see H.
Wegman, "Een vragende voetnoot," *Jaarboek voor liturgie-onderzoek* 8 (1992) 333-339;
see also my reaction in: P. Post, "The Modern Pilgrim: A Study of Contemporary Pilgrims' Accounts," *Ethnologia Europaea* 24 (1994) 85-100, here: 95-97. For this problem

and Gerard Lukken[45], and also the ongoing national research project with liturgical movement and the culture of celebrations as its unifying theme[46].

1.2.4. Present state of affairs

After a period of synthesis through collections in the 1980s[47], after about 1990 we enter the phase of thematization which we have already sketched. The theoretical and methodological debate is behind us, and the theoretical achievements and broad, open canon are being applied in specific subject studies. An illustration of this is the fact that in 1986 the international journal *Concilium* devoted a special issue to the topic 'popular religion' (fitting into the synthesis process around 1985)[48], and recently, in 1996, devoted an issue to 'pilgrimage'.[49]

Furthermore – and this is a tendency which has remained almost unremarked thus far – in various adjoining disciplines such as art history, cultural history and European ethnology, a remarkable revaluing of the liturgical factor in the complex of religious popular culture is taking place. In a study by Walter Hartinger there is even discussion of a sort of 'liturgical primacy.' I wish to pause a moment to examine this remarkable work, because various of the lines examined above come together in it.

1.3. Primacy of liturgy: Hartinger

The book *Religion und Brauch* by the German ethnologist Walter

of definition, see: W. Hartinger, *Religion und Brauch* (Darmstadt, 1992) 99-101; Margry and Post, "Het project 'Bedevaartplaatsen in Nederland', (our note 7), 40-45, but particularly the survey in: P. Berbée, "'Bedevaart' en 'Pelgrimstocht' in Nederland. Over oude termen en nieuwe methoden in bedevaartonderzoek,' *In de schaduw van de eeuwigheid; tien studies over religie en samenleving in laatmiddeleeuws Nederland; aangeboden aan A.H. Bredero*, ed. N. Lettinck and J. van Molenbroek (Utrecht, 1986) 167-199, notes on 287-295. See now: *Bedevaartplaatsen in Nederland, deel 1*, ed. Margry and Caspers (see our note 3), 12-18.

45. G. Lukken, *Per visibilia ad invisibilia. Anthropological, Theological and Semiotic Studies on the Liturgy and the Sacraments*. Liturgia condenda 2, ed. by L. van Tongeren and Ch. Caspers (Kampen, 1994).

46. Post, "Liturgische beweging en feestcultuur" (see our note 9).

47. W. Frijhoff (compilation), "Literatuurwijzer," *Religieuze volkscultuur* (note 37, above) 137-171; F. Spiertz, "Volksreligiositeit: een literatuuroverzicht," *Volksreligiositeit* (note 20, above) 159-189.

48. Popular Religion (note 20, above).

49. *Pelgrimage, een historische, antropologische en spirituele belichting van een universeel verschijnsel*, = special issue: *Concilium* 32,4 (1996).

Hartinger came out in 1992, almost without notice.[50] What at first glance appears to be a survey of religious practices in the course of a year and the course of a human life, like so many others which have appeared over the past years[51], when more closely examined is a book challenging thinking precisely in the subject area of religious popular culture and liturgy.[52] Although it would be possible to offer a critical analysis of the book against the historiographic background just provided, I would still opt for a more pointed approach and confine myself to presenting several main lines from the book, focusing on what is said about liturgy. In the way of general criticism, it can be said that Hartinger handles the legacy of the German 'Volkskunde' debate, described above, and the theoretical work surrounding religious popular culture in a thoroughly individual manner. Thus we will see that Hartinger reintroduces precisely the old high/low or elite/popular opposition again in a provocative manner as a model for explaining the design of religious popular culture. On the one side there are the "kultischen Vollzügen der Amtskirche," and on the other the "volksfrommes Brauchtum."

Hartinger, characterized by his German colleagues as "ein solider und zurückhaltender Wissenschaftler," is professor of 'Volkskunde' at Passau, a specialist in religious popular culture, and belongs to what is termed the Munich school, along with great names including Hartinger's teachers Dünninger and Brückner. For his book on religious "habitualisiertes Verhalten," the author sought out an analytical model which could throw light on how religion functions in everyday life as an all-encompassing system – to my mind, a strikingly modern description of religious popular culture.[53] In his approach to this general task,

---

50. W. Hartinger, *Religion und Brauch* (Darmstadt, 1992).

51. See, for instance: Kl. Richter, *Feste und Brauchtum im Kirchenjahr: lebendiger Glaube in Zeichen und Symbolen*. Herderbücherei Bd. 1763 (Freiburg i.Br., 1992), 2nd ed.; A. Schreuders-Derks, *Uit Anna's Santenkraam: volksgebruiken rond heiligen* (Sittard, 1992); H.M. Wolf, *Das Brauchbuch. Alte Bräuche, neue Bräuche, Antibräuche* (Freiburg-Basel-Wien, 1992).

52. To my knowledge, the book received no wide attention in the international arena. With the aid of Dr. Michael Simon (Münster [now (1998) Dresden]) I traced only a handful of reviews or notices in German-language countries: H.M. Wolf, in: *Österreichische Zeitschrift für Volkskunde* 95 (1992) 559-560; W. Seidenspinner, in: *Bayerisches Jahrbuch für Volkskunde* (1994) 297-298; R.-E. Mohrmann, in: *Blätter für deutsche Landesgeschichte* 131 (1995) 498. Although very close to Roman Catholic liturgy and liturgical studies, to my knowledge Hartinger has never entered the domain of liturgical studies. This is in contrast to his close colleagues such as Brückner and, especially, Klaus Guth (Bamberg). The latter has previously presented European ethnological research into the culture of pilgrimage and liturgy for the dead in platforms for liturgical studies such as the *Liturgisches Jahrbuch*. See Guth, "Sterben, Tod und Trauer" (our note 10).

53. See Hartinger, *Religion und Brauch*, Vorwort, 1-3.

Hartinger chooses a very specific perspective, which could also be designated as a very pointedly liturgical perspective, asking which parts of the
extensive selection of religious rituals people have taken on board in
their own lives and internalized, both in terms of form and content. In
addition to focusing on practice, on concrete ritual behavior, he pays
ample attention to theory and method. In a first, theoretical chapter, he
carefully locates and defines the concepts Religion and Brauchtum. The
outlines of modern 'Volkskunde' or European ethnology, as they have
been sketched above, are present here in their entirety: not thinking in
terms of survivals and continuity, but always having an eye for change,
context and dynamics. Drawing upon Dünninger, Hartinger also there
offers a definition of Brauchtum with six elements[54]: (1) communal
actions (2) laid down and passed on in tradition (without that tradition
having to be 'ancient'), (3) "von der Sitte gefordert," (4) with a specific
design (separate language, attitude, clothing, etc.), (5) referential, symbolic in nature and (6) functionally bound to time and place. At the end
of the chapter he defines Brauchtum as "das gemeinsame oder analoge
Handeln von Gruppen und einzelnen in traditionell geprägten und
geforderten Formen, die auf einen hinter ihnen stehende Sinn verweisen
und an bestimmten Situationen gebunden sind."[55] A bit further on, he
fittingly remarks that 'liturgy' too actually fulfills these "Brauch-crite-
ria."[56] He does not develop that further, and turns to ritual actions, which
he locates and characterizes as "liturgienähes Brauchtum."[57] In the book,
that field is mapped out and thematized in a most surprising manner. In
brief, he follows neither the cycle of the year nor the human life cycle,
but considers the following topics: adoration of images[58], domestic religion[59], what he terms "Geistliche" landscape[60] , the use of images and

---

54. Hartinger, 38ff.
55. O.c., 70.
56. O.c., 73.
57. L.c. "Liturgienähes Brauchtum" is the title of chapter 2, 73ff.
58. O.c., 74ff.
59. O.c., "Bilderzones," 81ff.
60. O.c., 83ff. Under this heading he considers roadside and field crosses, arma Christi
crosses, etc. Hartinger employs the term "spiritual landscape" following G. Kapfhammer,
"Geistliche Landschaft. Regionale Marginalien zu einem internationalen Phänomen,"
*Forschungen zur historischen Volkskunde, Festschrift Torsten Gebhard zum 80.
Geburtstag*, ed. I. Bauer, E. Harvolk and W.A. Mayer (Munich, 1989) 231-236. For The
Netherlands, see the fine article: P.J. Margry, "De creatie van heilige ruimten in
negentiende-eeuws Nederland. Het martelveld te Brielle," *Heidenen, papen, libertijnen
en fijnen. Artikelen over de kerkgeschiedenis van het zuidwestelijk gedeelte van Zuid-
Holland van de voorchristelijke tijd tot heden*, ed. J. Okkema, et al. (Delft, 1994) 249-
276. General, with bibliography: Post, *Ritueel landschap*, = "Paysage rituel" (note 14).

symbols[61], pilgrimage and processional cultuŕe[62], the seven sacraments (for which it is not so much the rites of the sacraments themselves that are central, as the circumstances of life in which they are rooted)[63], and theater and drama ("geistliche Spielbrauchtum")[64]. The book closes with a discussion, intended as illustrative, of a series of "Einzelelemente in Kult und Brauch," for which he chooses bread, water and fire.[65]

The book can be placed on the interface of 'Volkskunde' or European ethnology and liturgical studies, and, in addition to being of interest for his surprising new arrangement of the material and the richly documented presentation of material from religious popular culture ("Liturgie-nähes" ritual) and liturgical material, is also of particular importance for the theses that the book carries forward. In brief – and therefore obviously leaving out much of the nuance and the illustrations – these theses are as follows, which I will try to summarize under a series of key words:

1.3.1. Evil

In a general sense, the structure of the interplay of religion and Brauchtum (to speak of it more easily, at this point I will deal with our theme of religious popular culture and liturgy under this term) is determined by a pair of elements: on the one side, the presence of evil in the world, and on the other side the conviction that it is possible to obtain defense and protection through ritual acts and objects. The foundation for the rich repertoire of blessing-seeking behavior and the banishing, exorcizing, averting and protection-seeking dimensions of ritual conduct lies here.[66]

1.3.2. The lay perspective

There is constantly the defining distinction that, in contrast to liturgy, in religious popular culture the lay perspective is dominant: it is the ritual actions or behaviors of, by and for the laity. This lay perspective rises to the surface again and again, as when, for instance in the discussion of the nature of pilgrimage, Hartinger says in summary,

---

61. Hartinger, 87ff.
62. O.c., 99ff.
63. O.c., Chapt. 3, 130ff.
64. O.c., Chapt. 4, "Geistliches Schauspiel/Weltliche Spielbräuche," 194ff.
65. O.c., Chapt. 5, "Beispielhafte Einzelelemente in Kult und Brauch," 223ff.
66. O.c. See particularly Chapt. 1, where among other things the concepts of Religion and Brauch are discussed.

In der Gestalt des Wallfahrtswesens haben wir ein Musterbeispiel vor uns, wie sich im Umfeld der Liturgie, basierend auf Vorstellungen und kultischen Vollzügen der Amtskirche, ein volksfrommes Brauchtum ausbilden konnte, das hervorgebracht wurde durch die Bedürfnisse der Laien nach einer sinnenhaften Erfahrung des Heiles und das im wesentlichen auch in der Eigenverantwortlichkeit der Laien verblieb.[67]

1.3.3. The primacy of liturgy

The main thesis of Hartinger's book is to be found in the above citation regarding the culture of pilgrimage. Hartinger proceeds from a dominant parallelism between ritual design of religious popular culture and that of official liturgy, and of the primacy of liturgy in this. Much more than is generally the case, he recognizes the predominant influence of liturgy in Brauch; for the rest, he employs a narrow and closed understanding of liturgy (liturgy is the official ecclesiastical product, chiefly as set down in books), and at the same time again introduces a variant of the hoary popular cultural dichotomy between popular and elite. The expanded perspective of "liturgy beyond texts" appears to have passed Hartinger by. Actually, in the book Hartinger introduces an inversion of the prevailing perspective. He is not in search of popular cultural elements in Christian liturgical actions, nor is he in search of their non-Christian background and dimensions; no, he turns things around and explains, locates and names customs and rites from the domain of religious popular culture by demonstrating how ecclesiastical liturgy carries over into life outside the walls of the church. Saints' images in the home have the image culture inside the space of the church as its parallel. Pilgrimage, liturgical processions, the rosary all originally come out of the clerical, monastic context. Above all, as evidence of liturgical primacy, there is the constant fascination with the host and eucharist in religious popular culture. It always appears that the structure of any particular "Alltagshandeln" is defined by ecclesiastical, and often sacramental, actions.

Hartinger employs this perspective most emphatically in the final chapter, when he considers three elements that occupy a dominant and ritual place in liturgy (bread, water and fire) in their role in ritual actions in para-liturgy and outside liturgy. In this, he is in search of the cross-connections between liturgy and religious popular culture. The conclusion is always the same: bread rites are not defined by ancient mythic rites of the Aztecs, Mithraic cultus, Germans, Celts, and so forth, but have, as their only ritual analogy, the liturgy. The same is true for fire:

67. O.c. 121ff.

Gegenüber dieser massiven Repräsentanz der Feuer- und Lichtverwendung durch die christliche Kirche muß er Bezug zu vorchristlichen Sinngebungen (Sonnenkult, Fruchtbarkeitszeremonien), der in der volkskundliche Literatur teilweise auch in allerjüngster Zeit noch bemüht wird, als sekundär oder vernachlässigbar bezeichnet werden.[68]

Hartinger is most decided on page 240, where, briefly, he postulates the thesis that the most important force in regulating conduct in everyday life over the past century has been the Christian Church. Sometimes the movement has been from below to above, and from outside to inside, as, for instance, when after initial resistance and subsequently adjustments, certain forms of devotion to images, pilgrimage or drama are received into the Church's liturgy. But generally the movement is the other way around: from inside to outside, from above to below! The Church's liturgy is the most important source of the symbolic conceptual language that we encounter in the multifarious world of religious popular culture. A final citation may serve to further cement this thesis:

Die eminente Bedeutung der Kirche als Ideenlieferant für alles brauchtümliche Geschehen liegt m.E. darin begründet daß sie auf allen denkbaren Ebenen des Brauchkomplexes entscheidend in Erscheinung trat.[69]

4.3.4. Internalization and travesty

This provision of ideas and forms from the liturgy follows definite patterns and varies in respect to its depth and duration. Certain signals can put us on the track of the influence of liturgy, and particularly the depth and breadth of its reach. Various signs point to a profound integration or internalization of liturgical or theological material in the cultural design of celebration and day-to-day life. One such sign, for example, is the inversion of liturgical praxis, or Travestierung, also termed "travestierende Nachahmung."[70] What this refers to are rites such as marriages at harvest celebrations and carnival, the ritual burial of carnival, winter or bachelor life, or the baptism of ships or houses. Rather than seeking the background for these in "ancient" Germanic, Celtic or other pre- or non-Christian cultic usages (namely, in fertility rites, rites of spring, etc.), the Church's liturgy is the model for them. But, according to Hartinger, image culture in the home, and particularly the dominant place of the Holy Family within it, also demonstrates a high degree of internaliza-

68. O.c., 236ff.
69. O.c., 240f.
70. See, among others, o.c., 191.

tion:

> Hier konnten sich fromme Bräuche anlagern, die wesentlich zur Internalisierung bestimmter theologischer Lehrmeinungen beitrugen.[71]

The rule can also be read in the other direction. For instance, the extremely shallow roots of the sacrament of confirmation can be seen in the fact that there are hardly any customs surrounding this 'forgotten sacrament.' Hartinger briefly observes,

> Kurzum, die schwache Verankerung der Firmung im kirchlichen Ritus findet ihre Entsprechung auch im Brauchtum.[72]

Another sign involves the singularity of confirmation:

> Man wird immer dann am ehesten auf kirchlichen Einfluß schließen dürfen, wenn das betreffende Element vorwiegend innerhalb liturgischer Gepflogenheiten verwendet wird und es keine oder wenige Entsprechungen im Alltagshandeln hat.[73]

1.3.5. Sensory perceptibility and drama

Finally, for Hartinger there is an element of sensory perceptibility or sensuality and drastic dramatization that defines and characterizes religious Brauchtum. In regard to this final aspect, Hartinger's thesis merges seamlessly with the subjects of corporeality and liturgy and theater, both now so important in liturgical studies.[74]

---

71. O.c., 83.
72. O.c., 152.
73. O.c., 61.
74. Beside the culture of pilgrimage, drama and stage/theater is one of the main themes in Hartinger's work. For that, see the ample notice of this subject in Hartinger, Chapt. 4, 194ff; see further his bibliography with many titles in this field (cf. Id., "'...nichts anderes als eine zertrunkene Bierandacht..' Das Verbot der geistliche Schauspiele im Bistum Passau," *Volkskultur - Geschichte - Region. Festschrift für Wolfgang Brückner zum 60. Geburtstag*, ed. D. Harmening and E. Wimmer (Würzburg, 1990) 395-419; Id., "Geistliches Schauspiel im Bistum Passau," *Ostbairische Grenzmarken* 31 (1989) 110-140; Id., "Kirchliche Frühaufklärung in Ostbayern. Maßnahmen gegen Wallfahrten und geistliche Spiele in den Bistümern Passau und Regensburg am Beginn des 18.Jahrh." *Ibid.* 27 (1985) 142-157). For the topicality of the subject of liturgy and theater, see among others: J. Bärsch, "Das Dramatische im Gottesdienst. Liturgiewissenschaftliche Aspekte der osterfeiern und Osterspiele im Mittelalter," *Liturgisches Jahrbuch* 46 (1996) 41-66; J. Besemer, "Ieder speelt zijn eigen rol - ieder geeft zijn deel," *Leve(n)de liturgie!*, ed. J. De Wit et al. (Baarn, 1995) 56-67; Id., "Theater en liturgie," *Een ander huis. Kerkarchitectuur na 2000*. Liturgie in perspectief 7, ed. P. Post (Baarn, 1997) , 49-54;

This is sufficient to provide a first acquaintance with this, to my mind most interesting study about liturgy and religious popular culture. As I noted, this is not the place for a critical analysis of this work, an analysis which, for example, might particularly be focused on the point of departure sketched, of the interaction of Brauch on one side and liturgy on the other. Hartinger is very traditional in his use of both terms.[75] The foundation of his surprising and original view in essence lies in an old, and to my mind controversial, use of both ritual domains that, again, corresponds to an idiosyncratic position in the European ethnological debate sketched above. That, however, I will also let rest here. In that regard, it is enough to have both illustrated the earlier historiography and brought it up to date, especially as it is particularly related to the theme of liturgy and religious popular culture.

BLARICUM'S 'DEPTHS OF PURGATORY': A CASE STUDY IN RELIGIOUS POPULAR CULTURE

After exploring the theory, we will now turn to the practice. By means of a case study I wish not only to illustrate a broad and open approach to religious popular culture, but also to indicate how the characteristics of

W.Früwald, "Zwischen Märtyrerdrama und politischem Theater. Vom spannungsvollen Verhältnis der Kirche zur Theaterkultur," *Theologie und Glaube* 85 (1995) 35-46; K. Koch, "Liturgie und Theater. Theologische Fragmente zu einem vernachlässigten Thema," *Stimmen der Zeit* 213,120, 1 (1995) 3-16; R. Kurvers, "Liturgisch drama in de middeleeuwen: lessen voor nu," *Tijdschrift voor liturgie* 79 (1995) 178-196, = *Kunst van geloven, Annalen van het Thijmgenootschap* 84,1 (1996) 13-38, ed. E. Van de Loo, et al. [these contributions further elaborate on his dissertation: *Ad faciendum peregrinum. A study of the liturgical elements in the Latin Peregrinus plays in the Middle Ages* (Frankfurt a.M., 1996)]; *Liturgie en theater = Werkmap Liturgie* 25,3 (Baarn, 1991); G. Lukken, "Wat heeft liturgie met theater te maken? Een verheldering vanuit de semiotiek van de verschillen, overeenkomsten en raakvlakken, *Luisteren tussen de regels. Een semiotische bijdrage aan de praktische theologie*, ed. G. Lukken & J. Maas (Baarn, 1996) 134-166; Post and Pieper, *De palmzondagviering*, sub 6.2.5. pp. 59-63 (see note 42, above); W.M. Speelman, "The Plays of Our Culture: A Formal Differentiation between Theatre and Liturgy," *Jaarboek voor liturgie-onderzoek* 9 (1993) 65-81; V. Turner, *From Ritual to Theatre: the Human Seriousness of Play* (New York, 1982). See also the bibliography in Post, *Een ander huis*, sub 10, p. 100 (above).

75. Essentially, Hartinger begins with the old dichotomy of Brauch on the one side and Liturgie, or particularly Glaube, on the other, which until recently dominated German "Volkskunde" studies. See, for example, the subtitle of a well-known collection on ex votos: "Brauchtum und Glaube" [*Ex voto. Die Bilderwelt des Volkes. Brauchtum und Glaube*, ed. R. Creux (Zurich, 1980)].

religious popular culture listed by Hartinger take shape in practice, and perhaps must be readjusted or supplemented from that practice. I also hope to demonstrate how complex pastoral liturgical practice can be with respect to popular religious rituals.

The case study chosen was already introduced in the opening of this paper. It involves the commotion which arose when, in 1996, there was an intervention into the 'traditional' ritual repertoire for All Souls' Day in Blaricum. The text of the closing hymn was replaced by a new version.

So that everyone understands the situation, and also to indicate why some in and around the parish sought a suitable replacement for the traditional text, we will here reproduce both texts, and English translations which closely reflect them. First, the old hymn which was sung until 1996:

Hymn of supplication for the deceased:
Closing hymn, All Souls' Day Service

Uit de diepe boetekolken
dringt een weeklacht naar de wolken:
al de doden, die dit uur
lijden in het lout'rend vuur.
Heer, ontferm U hunner.

Refrain:
En Gij, Moeder der genade
sla hun smart'lijk zuchten gade,
ach, wil hun tot toevlucht zijn
in hun onuitspreekbare pijn.
Bid voor hen, Maria.

Wil genadig, God, vergeven
wat zij tegen U misdreven:
maak een einde aan hun straf,
wis hun laatste smetten af.
Heer, ontferm U hunner.

Laat, och, hen, die U beminden
laat hen nu ontferming vinden
om het lijden van uw Zoon.
Geef hun 't langverbeide loon.
Heer, ontferm U hunner.

Geef hun, die in kerkernachten
naar uw Vaderblik versmachten
geef hun in uw aangezicht
eeuwig rust en eeuwig licht.
Heer, ontferm U hunner.

Nog eens voor U neergebogen
smeken wij: heb mededogen;
voer hen uit de lange nacht
in de glorie, die hen wacht.
Heer, ontferm U hunner.

[From the depths of purgatory
Soars a cry to You in glory:
Have mercy, Lord, on all the dead
Who suffer now within its dread
Purifying fire.

Refrain:
And You, O Mother of all grace,

To their sighs now turn your face,
That they in You a refuge gain,
In their time of wracking pain:
Pray for them, Maria.

For all wherein they've You offended
Now let their punishment be ended;
O'er all may Your forgiveness reign,

Cleanse them of this their final stain,
God, Whose will is mercy.

Let them in life who looked to You,
Let them now find Your mercies true.
O, for the sake of Your dear Son,
And what He on the cross has done,
Cancel out their debt.

Pining in their dungeon there,
Thirsting for Your fatherly care,

O'er them lift up Your count'nance bright,
Grant everlasting rest and light,
In their darkest hour.

Yet again before Your seat,
We bow us down and repeat:
Lift them out the pur'fying fire
To Your glory; fill their desire!
Have pity on them, Lord!]

In 1996 the following new text was introduced:

Memorial hymn:
Closing hymn, All Saint's Day, Blaricum

Heer en Hoeder van ons leven,
die de doden hebt geschreven
in uw hart, en in uw hand,
erfgenamen van uw land -
Kyrie elei-son.

Refrain:
Vader God en goede Herder,
leid ons door de tijden verder
langs de wegen van uw woord,
tot de dag van Pasen gloort -
amen, - alleluja.

Dat zij op de weg naar vrede
in het voetspoor zijn getreden
van die ons is voorgegaan
uit de tuin des dood vandaan -
Kyrie elei-son.

[Dear Lord, Protector of mankind,
Those gone before are in Your mind,
We living now are in Your hand;
O bring us all to Your promised land
Kyrie elei-son.

Refrain:
Father God and Shepherd true,
Lead us onward, all times through,
And by your word our footsteps guide
'Til we in Easter's dawn abide!

Dat zij in uw schaduw wonen,
vaders, moeders, dochters, zonen, -
in uw huis dat ruimte heeft
aan wie sterft en aan wie leeft -
Kyrie elei-son.

Dat uw licht over hen lichte,
als een lach op hun gezichten -
als de vreugde die Gij schenkt
aan de mens die U gedenkt -
Kyrie elei-son.

Die ons voor de nieuwe aarde
hebt geschapen, zult bewaren -
laat er dan geen dood meer zijn,
en geen tranen, en geen pijn -
Kyrie elei-son.

Amen! Allelujah!
On the way to peace may they
Ever in the footsteps stay
Of He Who for us first was risen
Out of death's dark vile prison
Kyrie eleison.

Under your shadow may they abide,
In your house of many rooms reside -
Fathers, mothers, daughters, sons -
Until we there join our loved ones:

Kyrie eleison.

So may Your light round them embrace,
Like a smile spread upon their face;
Like tides of joy that You confer
On all those whom You remember.
Kyrie eleison.

Your new people, for Your new land,
Created, preserved by Your hand,
O, bring us all to that fair place,
Where death, pain, tears dissolve in grace
Kyrie eleison.

There are three lines along which I wish to develop this case study, as a striking example of the dynamics of religious popular culture. First we will pause to examine the hymn itself, then we will expand our perspective to the ritual context, and finally draw up a brief balance sheet.

1. The hymn

In the various written and oral reactions to interventions in traditional liturgical legacies, the suggestion is often made that we are dealing with 'centuries-old' hymns. In this instance, as is so often the case in 'centuries-old' popular religious traditions, upon further examination it appears the hymn goes no further back than the second half of the 19th century. From further research it also appears that the tradition by which the text and melody have been handed down could be termed dynamic, and decidedly is not a witness to an established tradition. With the help of a specialist in the field of Dutch Catholic devotional hymns, Dr. Anton Vernooij, the following information has been brought to light.[76]

76. The following items can serve as source material with bearing on this hymn (with thanks to Dr. A. Vernooij): P. Van der Ploeg, *Kerkliederen* (Leiden, 1875) 3rd ed. (1st ed.: 1872)) no. XXVII, pp. 58-60; *De Kevelaarsche devotie tot de H. Maagd Maria voor de pelgrims der Utrechtsche Processie gevestigd te Utrecht 1740* (Maarssen, 1890, 1st ed.; 1891, 2nd ed.), no. 21, pp. 240-242; P. Van der Ploeg, M. Lans and W. Jansen, *Marialiederen* (Leiden, 1901: 4th ed.; 1st: 1887), no. 47, pp. 81-84; *Cantate Domino. Gezangen voor het kerkelijk jaar en ter eere der H. Maagd, tevens geschikt voor processiën en in de maanden maart, mei en october* (Oldenzaal, 1912: 3rd ed.), no. 66,

The hymn can be attributed to Msgr. P. van der Ploeg, and in all likelihood was first published in 1872. Van der Ploeg was a priest in the diocese of Haarlem and professor at the central seminary at Warmond. Now, it is interesting that in his time Van der Ploeg was considered to be an influential innovator in ecclesiastical devotional hymns, particularly in the period after 1875.[77] It would appear, from its incorporation in various Kevelaer collections in which other generally popular hymns were included along with the special Kevelar pilgrims' songs, that the hymn very quickly became a favorite after its appearance in 1872.[78] The tune is separate, and a whole different story. The traditional Blaricum setting, which for that matter was maintained for the new version in 1996, was apparently later, and only coupled with the text of "Uit de diepe boetekolken" afterward. Also, probably until about 1900, there were two tunes that could be used for the hymn. Its 'own' tune, from the hand of W. Jansen, appeared in a collection of Marian hymns in 1887, and stood in the context of attempts, arising from the centres of Hageveld and Warmond, to propagate the new hymnody with text AND melody, preferably presented in that form in a hymnbook with all the verses printed under the tune (a format then viewed as a major modernization and improvement). Van der Ploeg worked toward that end together with M.J. Lans and W. Jansen. In general, however, we can say that this musical renewal was not thought of too highly by the men and women in the pews.[79] We can assume that "Uit de diepe boetekolken" was not often sung to the tune that Jansen composed for it. As so often happened with Van der Ploeg's material, it became a contrafract. The people seized upon a more sentimental devotional melody, probably

pp. 104-107. *Misboekje; Eucharistieviering op Allerzielen*, mimeographed booklet, 11pp.; Lied ter gedachtenis. Slotlied bij de Allerzielenviering in Blaricum, Jan Duin, Nov. 1996 (unpublished, laid in with the preceding missal). The repertoire, inventorying, description, classification and analysis of the spiritual, pious and devotional song in The Netherlands, on both the Protestant and Roman Catholic sides, is a field that to an important degree is still fallow. Reference can be made to the following studies, which although they examine diverse periods and genres, taken together offer us a first image of the Dutch hymn repertoire in the 19th and 20th century: Evers, *Pastoraat en bedevaart* (our note 15); F. Jespers, *'Het loflyk werk der Engelen'. De katholieke kerkmuziek in Noord-Brabant van het einde der zeventiende tot het einde der negentiende eeuw*. Bijdragen tot de geschiedenis van het zuiden van Nederland, 78, (Tilburg, 1988); J. Vos, *De spiegel der Volksziel. Volksliedbegrip en cultuurpolitiek engagement in het bijzonder in het socialistische en katholieke jeugdidealisme tijdens het interbellum*, dissertation (Nijmegen, 1993); Vernooij, *Het rooms-katholieke devotielied* (our note 15); Smelik, *Eén in lied en leven* (note 15). For our purposes here, we rely especially on Vernooij, particularly Chapts. 1 and 2.

77. See Vernooij, Chapt. 2, 75ff.

78. See the list in note 76, above. For the role of Kevelaer, see Vernooij, 63ff.

79. On this, see Vernooij, Chapt. 2, 75ff.

from the 18th century, a tune called "O vijf werelds klare lichten." Already in the third edition of *Kerkliederen* in 1875 Van der Ploeg himself gives this reference.

The further transmission of the text is capricious, and only in the course of the 20th century does it solidify into a fixed tradition. The hymn certainly had a double character. It is both a Marian hymn and a song for All Souls' Day. Very quickly, the 1872 version – probably the original – is being reworked. In an 1875 third printing of the first edition, the hymn of supplication takes the form of nine verses and refrain. In the next phase it becomes explicitly a supplication to Mary and the text is further developed into twelve verses and a refrain (see 1887, 2nd ed. 1901). In 1912 it changes again. Two of the verses which had been handed down are replaced, and ultimately the hymn expands to 14 verses. In the final phase of transmission and adaptation a selection is made from these, and the version of five verses and refrain that we presented above arises.

The new version of 1996 is by Jan Duin. If we compare Van der Ploeg's hymn with Duin's, we find that we are dealing with two pioneers, two important exponents of renewal in liturgical music. It is also interesting to see how both text and tune can be viewed independently of each other. Van der Ploeg found himself at the mercy of this 18th century composition, and Duin did not tamper with it. Quite in keeping with the liturgical movement, especially in the second half of this century, Duin wanted to replace the oppressive devotional atmosphere with a tone of hope, future perspective and resurrection. As a compromise, the old, 18th century melody was maintained for it. As we saw, however, this gesture was to no avail.

2. The context

A more dynamic image yet arises if we next expand our perspective. The fuss surrounding the hymn is only one link in a complex process of change. Some of the contours of this can be sketched as follows.

First of all, there is the immediate liturgical context. The hymn is part of a ritual regarded as 'ancient,' which in essence consists of a refined double liturgy, a combination of a ceremony inside the church (at first, the stations of the cross; more recently, a requiem mass) and after that a circumambulation of the graveyard next to the church, where small lights are placed on the graves. This ritual, which indeed can be claimed to be unique for the region, is a cherished remnant of what until the 1960s was a general All Saints' or All Souls' Day observance.[80] Until that time there was a mass in the early morning (6:00 a.m., though a diary from 1895 reports 7:30), followed by another at 9:00 a.m.; confession was then heard throughout the day, except during the stations of the cross at 7:00 p.m. (during WW II this was moved to 3:00 p.m.). We must see an All Souls' observance of this nature not as a local or regional tradition, but as what was initially a general liturgical practice of which there are still remnants to be found in the southern and eastern provinces of The Netherlands. Around 1964/1965 it was decided to replace the stations of the cross with a sung requiem mass. In this way, the present double celebration of mass and cemetery processional arose.

The controversial Purgatory hymn plays a key role in this ritual. Apparently, as a beloved All Souls' and Marian devotional song, at the end of the 19th century it received a place as a fitting closing hymn for the stations (after 1964/1965: requiem mass), but it at the same time served as the marker for the transition into the outdoor observance. As is often the case with liturgical closing hymns, it came to be seen as a musical rite of passage.[81] Later, I suspect chiefly because of this transitional function as a link between the general, ecclesiastical ritual in the church and the local ritual outside the church, the hymn grew into a sort of identifying sign for the whole observance. Another contributing factor, I suspect, was that the old hymn also fit so well with the commemoration of all the deceased members of the parish. 'Their language' resounded through it. Moreover, the hymn was not only an identifier for All Souls', but also for Catholic Blaricum. Thus it acquired a status that could be compared with the well- known St. Jan's hymn that closes the annual St. Jan's procession in Laren.

While elsewhere since the 1950s and 1960s the celebration of All Souls' has been reduced to an evening service and, separate from it, individual visits to graves, the communal indoor and outdoor observance

80. For the observance of All Souls' Day (Commemoratio omnium fidelium defunctorum) in general, see: *Liturgisch Woordenboek* 1, cols. 102ff. s.v.; Ph. Harnoncourt and H. Auf der Maur, *Feiern im Rhythmus der Zeit II/1*. Gottesdienst der Kirche, Handbuch der Liturgiewissenschaft 6,1 (Regensburg, 1994) 157ff and 235; especially instructive for the ritual context intended here is: Guth, "Sterben, Tod und Trauer (our note 10).

81. I find the similarities with the closing hymn in harvest thanksgiving celebrations in Brabant striking. I have elaborated on this outdoor liturgy in two places: Post, *Ritueel landschap*, sub 4.3. pp. 32-42, and the two studies published in *Questions liturgiques / Studies in liturgy* (note 14 and 60); Id., "Een idyllisch feest" (note 9). I would further refer the reader to an important study by G. Kennedy Neville, *Kinship and Pilgrimage: Rituals of Reunion in American Protestant Culture* (New York-Oxford, 1987) which offers relevant comparative material, especially for this All Souls' ritual. For an extensive bibliography on the topic of rite and landscape: Post, *Ritueel landschap*, at note 24.

at Blaricum remained popular and almost unchanged. In order to understand this, we must say something more about the context of the parish, town and region.

From a comparative and diachronic perspective, this parish in the Gooi (in February, 1956, the Gooi – the region which includes Blaricum and lies north and east of Hilversum – was transferred from the archdiocese of Utrecht to the diocese of Haarlem) could be characterized as an oasis of continuity.[82] Until the mid-1980s the classic traditional Roman Catholic patterns of spiritual / pastoral care and liturgy remained almost unchanged. It is telling that to this very day the neo-gothic interior of the church, including the communion rails, has remained almost entirely unchanged. To an important extent, this is connected with the relatively uniform composition of the primarily agrarian population of the parish and town, which has carefully nourished its own identity with relation to surrounding towns and cities such as Laren, Eemnes, Huizen, Bussum and Naarden, and, particularly, to the long presence of two pastors after World War II, namely Jongerius (1935-1961) and Remmer (1961-1983). Particularly the latter, who was known as a conservative, left his stamp on the parish during the important period he was there.

After about 1984, changes came belatedly but at an accelerated pace, from inside the parish and, especially, outside it. Pastor Remmer was followed by Pastor De Gooijer (1983-1989), a more open shepherd, but there was also an increasing influx of 'foreign' ideas coming in, and the ageing and thinning out of priesthood made its effects felt. Movement, change and renewal began. The oasis of Blaricum came under pressure through redevelopment of the church membership, redrawing parish boundaries, changes in parish teams in the immediate vicinity, and particularly through the construction of a large new suburban housing tract on the boundary with the much larger neighboring community of Huizen.

The decisive signal that a new age had dawned was the departure of Pastor Willems (1989-1996), De Gooijer's successor, in 1996, and the arrival not of a priest but of a pastoral worker. In 1996 he moved into the grand and spacious presbytery, attached to the church building, with his wife and three children. For many that was a shock, though often left unsaid. Very belatedly Blaricum was confronted with radical changes and innovations in the Church. The pastor of nearby Huizen became *pastor deservitor*, and this was (and still is at the time of this writing) the liturgical specialist of the diocese of Haarlem, poet and author of liturgical texts, Jan Duin.

Church attendance was declining, although to be fair that is a process

82. See note 85.

which was already underway before the arrival of the pastoral worker. Slowly and cautiously the new team – Duin at a distance, the pastoral worker on site – tried to carry out the changes which they believed necessary, particularly in the ritual repertoire.

This ecclesiastic/liturgical context ran parallel with a broader process of change in community, social, economic and, especially, cultural areas. The close-knit community of the town was changing in character.[83] The face of the town, which had to an important degree been determined by agricultural businesses, changed; the farmers disappeared, old farmhouses came into the hands of well-to-do 'foreigners' as protected historic properties, in the wider area around the town large-scale land consolidation was carried out, a major expressway was cut through the area that lies between Blaricum and Eemnes, and the community acquired, as we noted above, a large suburban housing development which, while governmentally a part of Blaricum, was really oriented to neighboring Huizen.[84] Since then, the very autonomy of the community has come under discussion, and negotiations are taking place regarding the consolidation of what are being termed the 'BEL-communities,' Blaricum, Eemnes and Laren.

In this context, looking now at and from the ecclesiastical ritual repertoire, we can distinguish two movements. On the one hand, there is the line which cherishes the old Roman Catholic ritual repertoire. Under the dominant pastor Remmer, until the 1980s there were no difficulties with this. All sorts of interventions from outside, such as tests of renewed Dutch liturgies, were turned aside or filtered.

But in the 1980s and 1990s there has been another residual interest in this traditional repertoire, now from a more general cultural corner. One might even speak of a revitalization. For instance, the Corpus Christi procession through the spacious parsonage garden, with wayside altar and a band, complete with devotional images placed along the route and the old banners, has been reinstated. I have a suspicion that this has to do with a broader process of historicizing or musealizing, that in turn is connected with the process of change in the town which we briefly sketched above. Thus, many parishioners were closely involved with the founding of a historical society which has since flourished, and many

83. Some figures regarding Blaricum: from a couple thousand inhabitants in the last century, 68% of whom were Roman Catholic, the number grew to over 10,000 in the 1970s after new housing tracts were added to the community: 1948: 4823 residents, 2040 Roman Catholic; 1960: 6203 residents, 2553 RC; 1971: 6342 residents, 2551 RC; 1988: 10,948 residents, 4060 RC.
84. I am referring to the De Byvanck neighborhood.

publications about the history of Blaricum have appeared[85], the old face
of the village is being celebrated, and its retention is the subject of many
a heated discussion in the often chaotic and heated town politics. Tradition, the past and identity go hand in hand in the town and parish communities.

The liturgical repertoire has now become a part of this process of
cherishing the past. In this connection, it is important to note how some
romanticized shots of the All Souls' observance have been included in a
CD-ROM with typical images of history and town life in Blaricum, com-
piled by the Historical Society. Liturgy becomes a part of an all-inclu-
sive process of historicizing and musealizing, a process that, again, as we
know, is closely connected with the creation of identity through con-
structed tradition.[86]

85. See, among others, the *Mededelingenblad van de Historische Kring Blaricum*,
publications in the regional journal *Tussen Vecht en Eem* (see particularly the 1985
special issue, *Het dorp Blaricum*), and *Kroniek*, 1990 and 1995. For the general context
of historical societies in this region, see: J. Kerkhoven and P. Post, "Historische kringen
in de regio tussen Vecht en Eem en hun periodieken. Een landelijk perspectief," *Tussen
Vecht en Eem* 11 (1993) 153-179.

86. With reference to this process, see: J. Boissevain, *Over de toekomst van de antropologie van Europa* (Amsterdam, 1994); W. Frijhoff, "Traditie en verleden. Kritische
reflecties over het gebruik van verwijzingen naar vroeger," *Jaarboek voor liturgie-
onderzoek* 7 (1991) 125-136; *Historische Faszination. Geschichtskultur Heute*, ed. K.
Füßmann, H. Grütter and J. Rüsen (Köln, 1994); A. Heuß, *Verlust der Geschichte*
(Göttingen, 1959); E. Jonker, "De betrekkelijkheid van het historisch besef," *Bijdragen
en mededelingen betreffende de geschiedenis der Nederlanden* 111,1 (1996) 30-46; G.
Korff, "Musealisierung total? Notizen zu einem Trend der die Institution nach der er
benannt ist, hinter sich gelassen hat," *Historische Faszination*, ed. Füßmann, Grütter and
Rüsen, 129-144; H. Lübbe, *Geschichtsbegriff und Geschichtsinteresse. Analytik und
Pragmatik der Historie* (Basel-Stuttgart 1977); P. Nissen, *De folklorisering van het on-
alledaagse* (Tilburg, 1994); P. Post, "Het verleden in het spel? Volksreligieuze rituelen
tussen cultus en cultuur," *Jaarboek voor liturgie-onderzoek* 7 (1991) 79-124; Id., "Traditie gebruiken. Sint Hubertus in Muiderberg," *Bij geloof. Over bedevaarten en andere
uitingen van volksreligiositeit*. UTP-katernen 11, ed. M. van Uden et al. (Hilversum, 1991)
191-208; Id., "The modern pilgrim" (our note 44); Id., "Goede tijden, slechte tijden:
devotionele rituelen tussen traditie en moderniteit," *Goede en slechte tijden: het Amsterdamse Mirakel van Sacrament in historisch perspectief*, ed. P.J. Margry (Aerdenhout,
1995) 62-80; Id., "De creatie van traditie volgens Eric Hobsbawm," *Jaarboek voor
liturgie-onderzoek* 11 (1995) 77-101; Id., "'God kijkt niet op een vierkante meter..' of
Hobsbawm herlezen," *Constructie van het eigene. Culturele vormen van regionale
identiteit in Nederland*. Publicatie van het P.J. Meertens-Instituut 25, ed. C. van der Borgt
et al. (Amsterdam, 1996) 175-200; Id., "De moderne pelgrim: (een) christelijk ritueel
tussen traditie en (post)moderniteit," *Concilium* 4 (1996) 114-125; P. Raedts, *Toerisme in
de tijd? Over het nut van Middeleeuwse geschiedenis* (Nijmegen, 1996); E. Sturm,
"Museifizierung und Realitätsverlust," *Zeitphänomen Musealisierung; das Verschwinden
der Gegenwart und die Konstruktion der Erinnerung*, ed. W. Zacharias (Essen, 1990) 99-
113. Bibliogrpahical survey in Post, "Goede tijden, slechte tijden," 74, note 24.

Seen liturgically, the first movement, attached to traditional ritual, stands in isolation, an often strange isolation. Certain high points of an originally rich and broad liturgical repertoire, mostly those of a festal nature, now stand in a further reorganized and modernized ritual environment. Many people have become 'Ashes and Palms Christians,' ('Feast Christians') coming only for rites which revolve around the family – baptism, First Communion, marriage and burial – or annual celebrations including Corpus Christi processions, midnight masses or Blaricum's All Souls' observance.

Viewed in the broader perspective, the fuss around All Souls' falls into place. The retelling by Jan Duin, specifically oriented to modern liturgy, collided with another discourse of fesitivity and the past. The debate far exceeds the question of using the right words, or, if you will, the right images, for the pascal dimension of All Souls'. The hymn has been appropriated for various purposes. If you follow the debate in the parish newsletter and examine the discussion in which, in addition to individual parishioners, the parish committees of the pastoral group and the parish council took part, you will find evidence of this. Opponents of the change struggle to link the hymn with an 'ancient' tradition, with the identity of Roman Catholic Blaricum. For instance, the ritual for All Souls' is traced back to a pair of 17th century pastors. People create tradition, yearn for continuity and, it is important to realize, consciously or unconsciously connect it with a series of surrounding changes.

3. Balance

Looking back over this example, and throwing a bridge forward to the final, closing section on approaches to and qualities of religious popular culture, in conjunction particularly with the sections of Hartinger's work in which he discusses his research findings, I would point to a series of aspects or qualities of religious popular culture which we can see in this case study. I will develop several of them as a way of closing off the case.

Among the aspects I see in this case is that of evil, the dread that must be allayed by the hymn and outdoor ritual; the debate also demonstrates how deep-rooted a ritual practice can be. The important dimension of how we deal with the past could also be elaborated. We have already made reference to historicizing and musealizing tendencies and to the fact that a bridge is being built in language and music to bygone generations by means of the 'ancient' hymn.

The aspects of double liturgy, of the lay perspective, as well as the related aspects of festivity, drama, emotionality and idyll, and connected with these, the question of the Christian identity of the ritual, all deserve further brief elaboration.

3.1. In my opinion, it is fundamental for an understanding of the case in Blaricum to see that we are dealing there with a double liturgy. Blaricum's All Souls' observance is a combination of a celebration in the church and one outside it. Now, this second ritual component possesses all of the characteristics of liturgy outside church walls that I have elsewhere discussed comprehensively.[87] All of the aspects of outdoor ritual that I have noted are to be found here. In particular, there is the aspect that the celebration in the cemetery is a lay prerogative. It was only during the period 1983-1989 under Pastor De Gooijer that the pastor-celebrant and the acolytes participated in the outdoor observance. "Uit de diepe boetekolken" is more than a liturgical closing hymn. It marks the transition to the outdoor observance for which laity have the final responsibility, and it typifies the local identity of the ritual. With the beginning of the hymn the 'ritual experts' withdraw, and the laity take over the leadership of the ritual. Jan Duin, in his restatement, viewed the song only as a liturgical closing hymn, thereby disruption the subtle balance between the 'clerical' liturgy inside the church and the lay observance outside the church. That in turn touches still other very important aspects of tradition and change, the local, even regional identity that the hymn construed, and the fact that the prerogatives of the laity had been (at least symbolically) eroded. Perhaps the way that some harvest thanksgiving services in Brabant have been handled would have been a better course: there a new hymn is not used *in place of* the 'traditional' hymn, which like the Blaricum song cannot really be seen as a fitting liturgical closing hymn, but *in addition to* it.[88]

3.2. Separately, in connection with this lay aspect, I would also call attention to the aspect of mediation. In the Depths of Purgatory hymn there is the figure of Mary who, as the Mother of Grace, functions as an intermediary: essentially, the hymn is a Marian hymn! It is now important to note how in Duin's version this element has disappeared; his is no longer a Marian hymn.

3.3. In addition to this cluster of aspects of double liturgy, the lay perspective and mediation, I would call to your attention a cluster arising more from the content. On the face of it, in the All Soul's observance as

87. Summarized in Post, *Ritueel landschap* and the two studies published in *Questions liturgiques / Studies in liturgy* (note 14, 60 and 81, above); Id., "Een idyllisch feest" (note 9). See Kennedy Neville, *Kinship and Pilgrimage* (our note 81); Id. & J.H. Westerhoff, *Outdoor worship as a liturgical form*. Learning through liturgy (New York, 1978).

88. See the remarks on the closing ritual in Post, *Ritueel landschap*, 32ff and particularly p. 36. See further the analysis in Id., "Een idyllisch feest".

a whole, and in the supplicatory hymn "Uit de diepe boetekolken" in particular, a curious fabric of celebration, drama, emotion and idyll is being expressed. I suspect that when, in the discussion about the hymn, people defend it by pointing to the 'atmosphere' that it evokes, it is to this cluster that they are referring. In the observance of All Souls', like that other 'celebration' or Good Friday, people particularly value the place given to emotions and experiences such as guilt, failings, sorrow, uncertainty, doubt, fear, pain, death, absence (including the absence of God), and such, in word and action. A number of sources have already noted that it is precisely these components of experience that, in the process of liturgical renewal in the second half of this century, have almost entirely been replaced by a rather emphatic, all-encompassing postulation of hope, prospect of salvation and resurrection. That this has quite correctly placed the Christian/liturgical proprium of Easter in the center of the praxis of celebration again, is beyond dispute. However, one can ask oneself whether since this has happened, the rewritten liturgy offers sufficient place for the dimensions of experience listed above - guilt, failing, sorrow and such. Particularly with regard to the present burial liturgy, the matter of attention for this concern has rightly been raised.[89]

Now, I suspect that Blaricum's All Souls' observance goes a long way toward meeting this need to be able to 'celebrate' these dimensions. As so often, here too that 'festivity' occurs in the confluence of drama, emotion and idyll. It goes without saying that the hymn, in the version by Msgr. Van der Ploeg, can be called dramatic, while, in addition to its drama, the procession around the lighted cemetery conjures up an idyll of an oasis of rest. In many respects, the All Souls' liturgy is a 'feast' whose character is both that of a drama, in which feelings of anxiety, doubt and guilt are expressed, and that of a romantic idyll, a setting with the attraction of an oasis of calm. That which is feared, which raises doubts, that which has been thought lost, as well as that which is dreamed of and hoped for: all this is celebrated in this idyll, in which dark and light come together. I think it is important to draw attention at this point to the psycho-social dimensions of liturgy, as they were recently strikingly analyzed by Walther-Sollich in his dissertation. It is precisely liturgical festal praxis and everyday experiences and feelings, as analyzed in Good Friday and Easter, that are central in this homiletic

---

89. See, for instance, G. Lukken, "Kernvragen rond de christelijke dodenliturgie, *Tijdschrift voor liturgie* 64 (1980) 146-167, particularly 159ff.

study.[90] Here too anxiety, guilt, doubt and sorrow come together with idyll in an emotional and affective discourse. It is remarkable to note how the study issues into a plea, supported with insights from both psychology and pastoral theology, to give full weight to the celebratory praxis of the popular Church ('Volkskirche').[91]

In the case of Blaricum I would second this plea. The liturgical assembly is thus a ritual oasis even as the church and cemetery actually have also become an oasis. We have briefly noted above too that in the case of Blaricum, this oasis aspect definitely possesses a landscape or territorial dimension: in Blaricum there is a disrupted landscape, in which the changes swirling around it (land consolidation, new tract housing, erosion of the town's traditional face, the expressway) make the cemetery a piece of unchanged landscape. The ritual observance is conjoined with this, and is an unmarred moment in which both hopelessness and hope can find a place in a dramatic celebration, in a dramatic ritual. The tune and the words of "Uit de diepe boetekolken" in no small measure define the atmosphere of the celebratory drama, all the more because there is ever less space for these dimensions to be found elsewhere.

Jan Duin's version fails to appreciate this need for drama and emotion. His text follows the accepted modern liturgical hymn repertoire. There is a distinct Resurrection/salvation tenor couched in hopeful Biblical typology and metaphors. The dramatic idyll is literally left behind: "out of death's dark, vile prison..." "...we in Easter's dawn abide."

Do not misunderstand me: this is decidedly no plea for Van der Ploeg's text! But with Walther-Sollich we must bear in mind the multiplicity of 'functions,' implicit or explicit, of the celebratory idyll. Certainly in the case of Blaricum we have described, I suspect that there is the 'regression to the idyll' identified by critical professionals, the aspect of flight and the emotional, aesthetic and folkloristic consumption that is to some degree compensatory. Yet I hope that I have indicated how this repertoire must be situated in an extremely complex, multi-layered context, and offer room for important liturgical dimensions.

3.4. From the perspective of the pastoral functions of liturgy, we here encounter a dilemma which arises in the case of many rites from the popular religious repertoire. It is a matter of avoiding the two extremes. On the one side one must not deliver liturgy into the hands of, or allow it

90. T. Walther-Sollich, *Festpraxis und Alltagserfahrung. Sozialpsychologische Predigtanalysen zum Bedeutungswandel des Osterfestes im 20. Jahrh*. Praktische Theologie Heute 29 (Stuttgart, 1996) diss. Göttingen. For celebration and idyll see also: Post, "Een idyllisch feest".

91. Walther-Sollich, 244-250.

to slide into a folkloristic, museal repertoire of rites which in essence celebrate the idyll of the town life now lost, and thus construct a new identity in which Christian anamnesis evaporates or is compromised. On the other side, innovative and inculturated liturgy must take into account the breadth of conduct and deeply rooted piety which appears to attach itself not to poetic form and number of feet in lines of text, but to the general atmosphere of a 'dramatic' text and melody, to place and to group. From my contacts with Jan Duin, who worked for years in Tanzania, I have come to understand precisely how clearly he sees this dilemma: with regard to popular culture and liturgy, he speaks of constant tension and union.

The question of the identity of Christian rituality and sacramentality certainly must be posed here, but can only be answered and translated into inculturating ritual actions when one has an picture of the tradition and situation that is as complete as possible. Keeping in mind the complex aspect of double liturgy and the transitional function of the Purgatory hymn is very important for this process in this case. One must avoid thinking of the hymn in isolation.

I will shortly return to this aspect in my closing considerations.

RELIGIOUS POPULAR CULTURE: APPROACHES AND QUALITIES

After our series of explorations and attempts to delineate the territory, and especially after our case study from liturgical practice, by way of closing we can try to draw out several lines of synthesis and perspective.[92] To this end, we will first formulate a series of frequently encountered approaches to religious popular culture in combination with liturgy (and liturgical studies!). The first approaches, which are related to one another and can on occasion overlap, are a sort of *via negativa* that lead us to the open, attentive or indicative contextual approach that I wish to denote by using the term 'religious popular culture' as consistently as possible. Subsequently we will formulate some of the 'qualities' of religious popular culture.

92. To a great extent, bibliographical references can be left aside. They may be found by referring to the notes in section 1.

1. Approaches to religious popular culture

1.1. The normative approach

Under this heading I include diverse approaches which all share an ideological, normative concept of culture. Implicitly or explicitly, the old popular/elite dichotomy plays a role in these 'good or not good' approaches. This might be a heavy ecclesiastical approach which, from a nearly rubristic vision of liturgy as a book of prescribed order, sees religious popular culture as a repertoire to be corrected and Christianized, and therefore approaches it in terms of superstition, magic and paganism. But the same one-sided and often militant normative approach can (although with decreasing frequency) be found in people who view religious popular culture as a reservoir of revolutionary symbols for the emancipation of 'the people.' Often, too, either of these two approaches will become linked, consciously or unconsciously, with the continuity theses and views regarding survivals that we already mentioned in our first section.

Two qualifying remarks must yet be made with regard to such normative approaches. First, it is important to note in what diverse and sometimes even contradictory ways religious popular culture can be employed. Remaining in the ecclesiastical context, we can see a spectrum from the most absolutely revolutionary (Gramsci, Latin America) and even outspokenly anti-clerical movements[93] through pronouncedly conservative movements actively seeking to turn back the clock.[94]

Further, the liturgical studies approach, in the form in which we advocate it in this paper, brings with it concern for inculturation and the identity of Christian rituality, its own form of a normative perspective. This is, however, of a different order from the normative approach discussed here. It is, rather, one could argue, a 'relative' normative approach in the sense that the normative attitude of liturgical studies with regard to the peculiar identity of Christian rituality and sacramentality is nuanced by the open and careful analysis of the cultural context.

---

93. Striking examples are to be found in the collection: *Religious Orthodoxy & Popular Faith in European Society*, ed. E. Badone (Princeton, 1990). See also the oeuvre of William Christian Jr. (our note 7).

94. One example of this is to be found in: G. Hersbach, "Westlandse bedevaartgangers als hoeders van het roomse erfgoed," *Bedevaart en pelgrimage. Tussen traditie en moderniteit*. UTP-Katernen 16, ed. J. Pieper, P. Post and M. van Uden (Baarn, 1994) 81-104.

1.2. Traditional canon approach: appendix, paraliturgy

Related, but much less pronounced, is the approach to the repertoire of religious popular culture as an appendix. In addition to the main stream of liturgy, in the past and present there are the side-channels and loose ends. This is the approach that – sometimes unintentionally – is called to mind by the term 'paraliturgy' and the use of lower case letters.

1.3. Competing repertoire approach: reaction, compensation

This is a tenacious and prevalent approach that does not so much thematize and label religious popular culture as explain it. Popular cultural ritual is seen as competing ritual and explained as reaction or compensation. Often once again working unreflectively with perspectives of high and low, this approach proposes that changes (read: reform or innovation, generally) in the traditional main stream of liturgy provoke reactions in the form of competing and compensatory ritual actions. The reach of this approach which sees religious popular culture as reaction is very wide. The clerical liturgy of the monks in the middle ages provoked a colorful popular repertoire, the renewal of liturgy after Vatican II drove believers into popular devotions and pilgrimages, the crisis among the men and women in the pews in this postmodern era is reflected in those searching for meaning in the New Age ritual marketplace, the cold, modern Blaricum liturgy empties the churches and is the reason the celebration of All Souls' outside the church is so attractive. Recently this approach has surfaced principally in relation to contemporary movements in the ritual and liturgical forum.[95]

In a general sense I regard this approach as unnuanced, although though its advocates can approach the popular cultural canon with an open attitude and are fully alive to all sorts of new rites as they arise. With a certain intellectual audacity, this approach suggests it has a potential for explanation which it generally can not live up to. As we have made clear above at many points and in many ways, we are always dealing with very complex place- and time-rooted cultural processes. The suggestion of a simple system of two communicating vessels of rites, inside and outside of the church, cannot do justice to the complex and multi-layered cultural and ritual context. Furthermore, every compensation thesis applied to culture begins from the false assumption that people in a culture, in our case ritual religious culture, always have need of a

---

95. For a summary with extensive bibliography, see: P. Post, "Alle dagen feest, of: de ritencrisis voorbij. Een verkenning van de markt," *De Madonna van de Bijenkorf* (our note 16) 11-32.

fixed 'amount' of input or output.[96] In essence, a veiled continuity construct is here being smuggled in again, with respect to culture, and change, dynamics and contingency are being ignored.

Thorough contextual and empirical research sufficiently demonstrates, to my mind, the lack of nuance in this approach. I refer once again to the Dutch pilgrimage research, from which it appears that when engaging in this popular cultural behavior, the average participant in pilgrimages is not doing so in response to developments in the parish. On the contrary, it is often the satisfied and involved parishioners who go on pilgrimages, in addition to participating in parish liturgy.[97]

Just as seems to be the case in the alternative medicine circuit, one can not speak of separate and competing tracks of cultural and ritual action, but of behavior which is, to a large extent, non-competitive. People visit their family doctor and the clinic at the University hospital in addition to the iridologist, chiropractor or mental healer.[98] There is just as little reason to unilaterally connect the appeal of a psychic like Jomanda or the popularity of healing services with changes past or present in ecclesiastical liturgical repertoire.[99] Recent figures in a report on secularization and alternative sources for personal meaning in The Netherlands by the Sociaal en Cultureel Planbureau, which has otherwise gotten a very critical reception, establish my point.[100]

All of this is not, however, to say that there are no connections to be found between various liturgical repertoires. It is always that the starting point must be open and impartial. The origin, growth and decline of repertoires should continually be carefully charted empirically, a process in which reaction or compensation can fulfill a heuristic function.

96. See P. van Beek and W. Knulst, *De kunstzinnige burger*. Cahier Sociaal en Cultureel Planbureau 86 (Rijswijk, 1991) 96 with note 1 on p. 100.

97. This observation is made chiefly in the context of research into motives made in the course of the long-running "Christian pilgrimage" research programme. See particularly the research report by Pieper and Van Uden summed up in Post, "Thema's, theorieën en trends in bedevaartonderzoek (see our note 4).

98. See *Geloven in genezen. Bijdragen tot de sociaal-culturele geschiedenis van de geneeskunde in Nederland*, ed. M. Gijswijt-Hofstra (Amsterdam, 1991) [= *Volkskundig Bulletin* 17,2 (1991)]. See now also Id., *Vragen bij een onttoverde wereld*. Amsterdams historische reeks, Kline serie 37 (Amsterdam, 1997).

99. See P. Schelling, *Jomanda, heks of heilige? Pastoraal-kritische kanttekeningen* (Kampen, 1995), and a fine example of the compensation thesis in the reaction to this by M. Parmentier in: *Bulletin voor charismatische theologie* 36 (1995) 37-40.

100. J.W. Becker, J. De Hart and J. Mens, *Secularisatie en alternatieve zingeving in Nederland*. Sociale en culturele studies 24, (Rijswijk: Sociaal en Cultureel Planbureau, 1997).

1.4. Nostalgic approach: folklore

This approach to religious popular culture as a remnant of a religious repertoire that has otherwise evaporated is similarly often connected with a perspective that takes the crisis of the so-called 'Volkskirche' as a starting point. In many respects, this approach touches upon the 'appendix' approach noted above. But here something else is at stake. The implicit but undeniable presupposition here is the hypothesis of secularization- and the crisis in rites. The ecclesiastical liturgical repertoire is evaporating and remains of it are nostalgically cherished as popular culture. It is remarkable to see here how all liturgy is here really being defined as popular culture. Liturgical practice in its entirety seems to change context in the broader setting of cultural processes which could well be termed historicization, musealization, touristization and folklorization. In a different context I have already several times discussed the complex and often surprising processes of both folklorization and liturgizing.[101] Some examples of this process might be the popularity of Gregorian chant[102], the remarkable revival of local pilgrimage sites[103] , and the relation between civil and ecclesiastical marriage rituals[104]. Many pastors and liturgists often do not understand how multiple appropriations and conferrals of meaning can exist at the same time.

1.5. Broad, open, attentive/indicative approach: religious popular culture

Over against these approaches, I argue for a different point of departure, which could be characterized as open and attentive or indicative. Through the term 'religious popular culture,' one enters those ritual religious repertoires that are broadly shared throughout the community and as 'particular designs' belong to the various domains of everyday life. This approach is not opposed to what can be termed a 'liturgical' approach, but to some degree coincides with it, qua object. Liturgy can, after all, be described as the whole of the forms of the ritual expression of the faith of the Christian community.

This approach works broadly and contextually. Just as liturgy should

101. See the bibliography in our note 86.

102. For this, see the provocative essay on the "magic" of Gregorian chant: J. Janssen, "Het moduleren van de stilte. De magie van het Gregoriaans," *Streven*, jan. (1996) 11-23.

103. The Places of Pilgrimage in The Netherlands project offers a very instructive overview of the rise, decline and revival of local and regional pilgrimage sites. See part 1: *Bedevaartplaatsen in Nederland* (as in our note 7).

104. See "Rituele veranderingen met betrekking tot de huwelijkssluiting" (our note 11); "Huwelijk: dynamiek van feest en sacrament" (our note 9).

always be seen in a broad cultural and ritual context, so religious popular culture should be placed in the broad context of popular culture. As we have repeatedly seen above, this fundamental expansion of context does not seem to come as a matter of course. By dropping terms such as 'popular Catholicism,' 'popular piety,' 'popular belief' and 'popular religiosity' too, and embracing the term 'religious popular culture,' we are seeking to indicate that programmatic perspective.[105]

By 'open' and 'attentive or indicative' I am also especially pointing to a series of anthropological qualities or characteristics that together define and give shape to religious popular culture, both thematically and programmatically. In place of a diligent search for a comprehensive definition of religious popular culture, we can perceive its outlines through a series of anthropological qualities which can now, as a conclusion to the foregoing discussion, be distilled. In this, we make connection with the more general trend in what are being termed 'ritual studies.' Thus, with regard to classic themes such as ritual and celebration, we find that recent studies in that field also turn their attention, theoretically and methodologically, to qualities rather than comprehensive definitions.[106]

2. Anthropological qualities of religious popular culture

2.1. First of all, there is the important element that religious popular culture is chiefly *group culture*. Here too the very important *lay perspective* comes to the fore: it is a matter of rituality, spirituality, etc., of, by and for the laity. The whole spectrum of this group comes into the picture, men and women, the broad group, including the 'silent groups.' Seeing things from the perspective of the experts in rituals is not sufficient. Here too lies the natural and obvious alliance between the study of religious popular culture and a theology that desires to liberate men and

---

105. I once again emphasize here that this choice and approach is in no sense new in cultural studies. In our first theoretical and historiographic section, I have already made reference to the argument made in the 1986 collection *Religieuze volkscultuur* (as in our note 37). For me, this is now a matter of repeating their plea, now with direct reference to the context of liturgical studies, illustrated and realized through liturgical praxis, and worked out through 'qualities.'

106. See R. Grimes, *Ritual Criticism. Case Studies in its Practice, Essays on its Theory* (Columbia 1990); summarized in: Post, "Liturgische beweging en feestcultuur" (note 9). For the rest, scholars continue to wrestle with comprehensive definitions; witness: A.M. Visscher and J. Stern, "Family Rituals as Medium in Christian Faith Transmission," *Current Studies on Rituals. Perspectives for the Psychology of Religion*. Intern. Series in the Psychology of Religion 2, ed. H.-G. Heimbrock, H.B. Boudewijnse (Amsterdam-Atlanta, 1990) 103-118, here: 104 sub 1.2. General: B. Boudewijnse, "The Conceptualization of Ritual. A History of Its Aspects," *Jaarboek voor liturgie-onderzoek* 11 (1995) 31-56.

women, be relevant to them, to be inculturated. In addition to this lay perspective, much more comes into focus through group culture. I will here list only the aspect of the construction of identity, which surfaced in the Blaricum case study.

2.2. Next, there is the continuing, fundamental element of *connection with place* in religious popular culture. Locality and territoriality are always dominant categories, so important that, as we have already noted, William Christian, Jr. summarily defines 'popular religion' as 'local religion.' In the research in this paper, this category of locality and territoriality is very apropos, which leads me to further refer to the expansion of the concept of the 'holy place' into 'lieu de mémoire,' including the rites of the 'topolatrie.'

2.3. A familiar subsequent dimension is *festivity*. A main artery of religious popular culture is the celebration, with all the dimensions that accompany this category.

2.4. Next, closely related to the category of rituality and locality or space are the anthropological dimensions of *corporeality* and *sensory perceptibility*. It is precisely here that liturgical studies are catching on by devoting more and more attention to the corporeal aspects of Christian rituality.

2.5. As a separate dimension of religious popular culture, but partially connected with this corporeality, the categories of *dramatic expression* as well as *emotionality* enter the picture. Dramatization, performance and theater are salient categories.

2.6. In this anthropological cluster, it should be noted that, as a relatively isolated category, in religious popular culture there is a preference for *mediated religiosity*, ritual communication through intermediaries who are nearby, recognizable and concrete. Relics, saints, angels, images, and objects provide a framework, something to hold onto. Here the role of materiality is extremely important. Of course, this is all closely connected with the qualities of corporeality and rituality already noted.

2.7. Here the role of *nature and landscape*, which is so significant for religious popular culture, also must be listed. Finally, in this context, the element of the *idyll*, so extremely important for religious popular culture, standing next to, and particularly in relation to, the aspects of territoriality and intermediaries listed above, deserves mention.

CONCLUSION AND PERSPECTIVE:
IDENTITY OF CHRISTIAN RITUALITY AND
'CHURCHIFICATION'

By way of closing and perspective, I will briefly take up again an important perspective which was already discussed above. This regards the
specific responsibility of those working in liturgical studies, investigating ritual repertoires of religious popular culture, to ultimately (that is to
say, after careful contextual analysis and diagnosis) also pose the question of the identity of Christian rituality or the Christian identity of rituals. From my argument it should be clear that in my view, this may never
be the first concern, nor be confrontational, but should always take place
after the study is completed, and with circumspection. A good – and to
my mind, exemplary – illustration here could be the final aspect which
we listed, the idyll. In the case of Blaricum we also referred to the importance of this oft-sought quality of religious popular culture, a quality
which at first sight (as a first concern and confrontationally) seems to
coincide with a certain culture of celebration in which the needs of
Christians are superficially and uncritically met, so that the Christian
proprium seems to disappear below the horizon of a folkloristic dream.
But here too caution is advisable. As Walther-Sollich recently suggested,
that which on the surface manifests itself as a regressive celebratory idyll
can be very deeply rooted in human religiosity and piety. The idyll does
not have to be in conflict with the accepted dynamics of Christian tradition and theology.[107] In a recent essay on pilgrimage, Peter Nissen made
the same suggestion. The great challenge set before us by popular religious rites lies in our making an appropriate and balanced estimation of
them. On the one side there is the danger of an exaggerated pattern of
religious expectations. On the other side, there is the threat of underesti-
mating their anthropological/religious potential.[108]

Another and final aspect in which the responsibility of those in liturgical studies can be illuminated in the context of liturgy and religious
popular culture involves the element of domains, which has been repeatedly referred to in this essay, directly and indirectly. The rites of religious popular culture are pre-eminently connected with domains outside
of the church building. We saw how this perspective is the common

---

107. I am here paraphrasing the conclusion of Walther-Sollich's dissertation, which
focuses on sermon material surrounding [the commemoration of] crucifixion and resurrection. See particularly Walther-Sollich, *Festpraxis* (our note 90), 249ff.

108. P. Nissen, "Grenzen overschrijden. Bedevaart als rituele handeling," *Communio*
22 (1977) 189-200, here 190ff.

thread of Hartinger's book and how this perspective enabled us to understand the Blaricum case study and to interpret it to some extent. The postmodern, complex process of shifts in ritual and liturgy, which to a great degree is incorrectly designated as secularization, retreat from the church and the crisis of rites, when seen from another perspective can be characterized as a process of 'churchification.' Ritual repertoires initially spread over various domains of our culture are pushed more and more to inside the walls of the church. In this way, the liturgical repertoire is 'churchified.' With an eye to inculturated liturgy, a relevant liturgy broadly rooted in a culture, this process of churchification however deserves to be considered critically, and it is there, to my mind, that openings must be sought, ways to raise, and continue to raise, the liturgical repertoire in the domains outside the church for discussion. And it is here that the rites of religious popular culture can play an important role. As old or new forms of 'outdoor liturgy,' popular religious rites have not only a symbolic and anthropological potential which is not to be underestimated, but also an indispensable pastoral/liturgical strategic potential for a broad renewal of liturgy.

The Power of Prayer and the Agnus Dei
Popular Faith and Popular Piety
in the Late Middle Ages
and Early Modern Times

Charles CASPERS and Toon BREKELMANS

Introduction

Prayer takes various forms, and one of them is supplication.[1] The one who prays desires something; he or she desires that God should will the same as he or she does, and that it also should come to pass. In this article, we will be concerned with the way in which this happens and the way in which people were expected to express their piety. We will address this on the basis of a very concrete example, namely the use of one of the *sacramentalia*, the *Agnus Dei* (*AD*), an amulet that because of its consecration (by the Pope), the likeness that it bears (the Lamb of God), the material of which it was made (wax), and the very salutary effects that were attributed to it, enjoyed a very important status in religious life for many centuries.

Before beginning this study, however, we wish to yet provide some commentary on the two terms which have already appeared in our title: 'popular faith' and 'popular piety'. The presence of these terms has been declining in Dutch academic literature on this subject, as they are replaced in academic discussions by the term 'religious popular culture', which has more neutral implications and is more inclusive.[2] Both of these 'old-fashioned' terms are of methodological importance for this contribution, however. They will be used in sharp contradistinction to one another.

- We understand 'popular piety' to be inclusive of all conceptions and expressions of faith on the part of the laity which had the approval of the

---

1. For an exhaustive typology of prayer during the late middle ages and early modern period, see 'Prière,' in: *Dictionnaire de spiritualité*, 12/2 (Paris 1986) 2196-2347, esp. 2271-2288 (Jean Châtillon, 'Prière au Moyen Age') and 2295-3217 (André de Bovis, 'L'Église catholique, 16ᵉ-19ᵉ siècles').

2. For a discussion of 'religious popular culture', see the contribution by P. Post to this collection. Cf. W. Frijhoff, "Vraagtekens bij het vroegmoderne kersteningsoffensief," *Religieuze volkscultuur. De spanning tussen de voorgeschreven orde en de geleefde praktijk*, ed. Gerard Rooijakkers, Theo van der Zee (Nijmegen 1986) 72-73.

ecclesiastical authorities, and indeed were possibly encouraged by them.[3] By developing peculiar accents this piety can (or in any case could, with reference to the late Middle Ages) achieve a more or less autonomous character.[4] Because the circumstances in which the laity lived were other than those of, for instance, monks, other accents in piety were permitted. Thus it was not held against the laity if they resorted to all sorts of patron saints as intercessors,[5] where monks in many cases did not have to be so concerned about the revenues from their estates, and therefore honored the established order of saints as that had been given in their own martyrologium for centuries.[6] In the late Middle Ages it was sufficient for the shepherds of the church that their flock obediently followed the church's teaching.[7]

- We understand 'popular faith' to be inclusive of all conceptions and expressions of faith which did not have the approval of these same ecclesiastical authorities, and possibly were discouraged by them because they were not in agreement with, or even contradicted official doctrine. Here we are thinking of possible relics from pre-Christian paganism,[8] but more precisely of the mixture of conceptions, etc., which with superstition arise out of ignorance.[9]

3. For the official standpoint of the Roman Catholic Church, see *Catéchisme de l'Église Catholique* (Paris, 1992) nos. 1674-1676.

4. See, for instance, with reference to the 'autonomous' character of devotion to saints in the middle ages, Charles M.A. Caspers, "'Een stroom van getuigen'. Heiligenlevens en heiligenverering in katholiek Nederland, circa 1500 - circa 2000," *Gouden legenden. Heiligenlevens en heiligenverering in de Nederlanden*, ed. Anneke B. Mulder-Bakker, Marijke Carasso-Kok (Hilversum, 1997) 165-179, esp. 166.

5. Cf. Arnold Angenendt, *Heilige und Reliquien. Die Geschichte ihres Kultes vom frühen Christentum bis zur Gegenwart* (München, 1994) 348; Idem, *Geschichte der Religiosität im Mittelalter* (Darmstadt, 1997) 71-75.

6. E.A. Overgaauw, *Martyrologes manuscrits des anciens diocèses d'Utrecht et de Liège. Étude sur le développement, et la diffusion du Martyrologe d'Usuard* (Hilversum, 1993) 19-78, esp. 51.

7. 'Honor Sundays and holy days; Abstain from meat on Fridays and penitential days; keep fasts; go to confession at least once a year; receive communion around Easter'. See E. Dublanchy, "Commandements de l'Église," *Dictionnaire de théologie catholique* III (Paris, 1923) 388-393. For an old Dutch formulation of the 'vijf geboden der heiliger kercken die alle kersten menschen sijn schuldich te holden', see *Der Christenspiegel des Dietrich Kolde von Münster*, ed. Clemens Drees (Werl, 1954) 124-127.

8. Cf. L. Milis a.o., *De Heidense middeleeuwen* (Turnhout/Kampen, 1992²) with various contributions on the 'paganism' which the authors believe to have been present in the Middle Ages.

9. Marcel Gielis, "The Netherlandic Theologians' Views of Witchcraft and the Devil's Pact," *Witchcraft in the Netherlands from the fourteenth to the twentieth century*, ed. Willem Frijhoff, Marijke Gijswijt-Hofstra (Rotterdam, 1991) 37-52.

The dichotomy between popular piety and popular faith can be drawn still more sharply through the distinction between 'true faith' and 'magic'. In the fifteenth century we see this distinction worked out time and time again, for instance in 'mirrors',[10] or in commentaries on the Ten Commandments (often included in such 'mirrors'), particularly with reference to the First Commandment.[11] The point of this distinction was that in 'true faith' God was left free (the prayer in the Our Father, 'Thy will be done', was respected); in contrast, in magic God was offended by the special rituals through which attempts were made to call upon Satanic powers for help.[12]

In short, ours is a sharp normative distinction, chosen, as we have said, out of methodological considerations; this distinction reflects the standpoint of the official church in the period in question, and particularly, this standpoint resulted in measures and effects.

After these preliminary remarks we will turn to the *Agnus Dei* and its use in the late Middle Ages and early modern era, with particular attention to the situation in The Netherlands. In the course of this we will pay special attention to the way in which the *AD* was employed to combat popular faith and promote popular piety. As a way of becoming acquainted with this *sacramentale*, we shall introduce two authors from The Netherlands who also submerged themselves in the subject, and to whose writings later generations accorded some authority: Joannes Molanus and Augustinus Wichmans.

Joannes Molanus on the *Agnus Dei*

Joannes Molanus (1533-1585), of Louvain, a militant representative of the Catholic Reformation,[13] produced a tract on the *AD*, *De Agnis Dei*

---

10. For the genre of what are termed 'mirrors', see Petronella Bange, *Spiegels der christenen. Zelfreflectie en ideaalbeeld in laat-middeleeuwse moralistisch-didactische traktaten* (Nijmegen, 1986).

11. C. Caspers, *De eucharistische vroomheid en het feest van Sacramentsdag in de Nederlanden tijdens de late middeleeuwen* (Leuven, 1992) 187-188. As an example of a commentary on the First Commandment, see *Der Christenspiegel des Dietrich Kolde von Münster*, ed. Drees, 86-93.

12. For an authoritative description of superstition and magic in the late Middle Ages and early modern times, formulated by Doctors from the Sorbonne, see Carolus Duplessis d'Argentré, *Collectio judiciorum de novis erroribus*, I (Paris, 1728) 154-157. For a discussion of the notion of "magic" in contemporary behaviourial sciences, see Marijke Gijswijt-Hofstra, *Vragen bij een onttoverde wereld* (Amsterdam, 1997) 9-11.

13. R. Van Uytven, "Molanus," *Nationaal biografisch woordenboek*, II (Brussel, 1966) 580-582.

oratio, which was first published in 1587, two years after his death,[14] and appeared most recently in 1861 as part of the famous *Theologiae cursus completus* by J.-P. Migne.[15] The following will provide a point by point summary of Molanus's tract, which is subdivided into 18 chapters.

- The *AD* is unique in that it is blessed by the Pope;[16] such blessings are of particular importance because they derive their power and efficacy from the 'prince of apostles,' from which they also acquire their title as benedictions of St. Peter (Chapt. 5). The effect of the *AD* is more powerful than, for instance, that of Holy Water, which can be consecrated by an ordinary priest; consecration performed by a priest has power in so far as this person acts in the name of Christ, while the Pope is, however, as successor to Peter, the priest par excellence, who acts in the place of Christ (Chapt. 8).

- The *AD* is mentioned as early as Alcuin and Amalarius of Metz; judging from the testimony of Pope Marcellinus II, the consecration of wax lambs was already a custom before the time of Constantine the Great. The *AD* thus enjoys a respectable antiquity (Chapt. 6).

- With regard to the rite, according to the ceremonial the consecration takes place only by the Bishop of Rome, in Eastertide, in the first year of his pontificate and every seven years thereafter.[17] The *Agni Dei* are retained until Low Sunday, and thereafter distributed to dignitaries and others (Chapt. 7).

- The *AD* has many salutary effects. In its consecration the Pope prays for defense against almost all evils. This important adjuration also draws its power from the rich symbolic value of this amulet, owing to the banner of the Holy Cross that is depicted on the *AD*,[18] to the sacrificed lamb

---

14. *Molanus, Traité des saintes images*, I, ed. François Boespflug, Olivier Christin, Benoît Tassel (Paris, 1996) 27.

15. Tome 27 (Paris, 1861) k. 425-454.

16. Compare: Franz Beringer, *Die Ablässe, ihr Wesen und Gebrauch*, I (Paderborn, 1921; 15th ed.) 407.

17. Joannes M. Hanssens, *Amalarii episcopi opera liturgica omnia*, II. *Liber officialis* (Città del Vaticano, 1948) 110; Michel Andrieu, *Les ordines Romani du Haut Moyen Age*, III. *Les textes (ordines XIV-XXXIV)* (Louvain, 1951) 326-327 (ordo XXVI, 7-8) and 349-350 (ordo XXVII, 9-10); Marc Dykmans, *Le cérémonial papal de la fin du Moyen Age à la Renaissance*, II (Brussels/Rome, 1981) 402, nr. 97 ('Quomodo fiunt agnus Dei cerei').

18. For depictions of the *AD*, see for instance Manfred Brauneck, *Religiöse Volkskunst. Votivgaben - Andachtsbilder - Hinterglas - Rosenkranz - Amulette* (Köln, 1978) no. 145; W. Brückner, "Christlicher Amulett-Gebrauch der frühen Neuzeit.

(in the book of Exodus) with whose blood the Israelites in Egypt had daubed their doorposts,[19] and particularly to the sacrifice of the innocent Lamb that was Christ himself (Chapt. 8). We seek our refuge in the Lamb, who being offered up innocent on the cross, has wrested us from the power of Satan. In the mass we also pray, 'Lamb of God, that takest away the sins of the world, have mercy upon us' (Chapt. 9).

- It is also important that these lambs are produced from virgin wax (i.e., from a product from virgin animals),[20] in order to reflect the Christ, who of course was also born of a Virgin (Chapt. 8 and 9).

- In doing so, those who equip themselves with this amulet pray that it may transpire for them as their faith promises and as was asked in the prayers which were spoken by the Pope in its consecration. It is assumed that those who carry the *AD* with them do not pray in isolation. Or to put it in other words: if the bearer's prayer has results, this is on the grounds of the blessing and *the collective prayers of the church*, with which the bearer is united in his or her own devout prayer (Chapt. 8).

- The *AD* also has a 'secondary' meaning. It not only refers to Christ the Lamb, but also reminds us that we, through our baptism, have become as new lambs, whiter than snow, and that we must preserve ourselves thus arrayed until the day of judgement (Chapt. 10; Molanus here refers to the life of St. Agnes and to Rev. 14:4).

- Especially for doubters and unbelievers, it can be pointed our that the *AD* has also worked miracles (Chapt. 12; Molanus here mentions the preservation of a Spanish prisoner of war, see further in this article).

Grundsätzliches und Spezifisches zur Popularisierung der Agnus Dei," *Frömmigkeit. Geschichte, Verhalten, Zeugnisse. Lenz Kriss-Rettenbeck zum 70. Geburtstag*, ed. Ingolf Bauer (München, 1993) 89-134, esp. 102, 103, 105 (Brückner also distinguishes 'secondary' *Agni Dei*: amulets which did indeed carry a representation of the Lamb of God, but contain no wax object and were not consecrated by the Pope, and even 'tertiary' *Agni Dei*: amulets which were called *AD* but which did not even bear a depiction of the Lamb of God); A.H.M. van Schaïk a.o., *Katholiek Nederland en de paus 1580-1985* (Utrecht, 1985) 85.

19. Perhaps this typological concept was in the past part of the reason that prompted people to place *Agni Dei* in the foundations or roofs of buildings, ecclesiastical and otherwise, see D. Buddingh, *Mirakel-geloof en mirakelen in de Nederlanden* (Den Haag, 1845) 83. Cf. Peter Burke, *The historical anthropology of early modern Italy. Essays on perception and communication* (Cambridge, 1987) 181 (note 32).

20. Cf. Ulrich Bock, "Kontaktreliquien, Wachssakramentalien und Phylakterien," *Reliquien. Verehrung und Verklärung*, ed. Anton Legner (Köln, 1989) 154-160, esp. 155-157.

- There are many misunderstandings – often malicious – about this amulet and its use. For example, it is incorrectly said that the Jesuits affirm that, like the blood of Christ, the *AD* can cleanse us of our sins. This suggestion is in any case untrue; the amulet receives all the power that it has from the consecration and prayers that are based on the blood of Christ. But the original power of Christ's blood and that of the *AD* may not be conflated. Similarity and equality may not be here confused (Chapt. 13).

- Parts of an *AD* posses just as much power and efficacy as a whole.[21] Because in their human weakness, however, people prefer complete lambs, happily priests from the Society of Jesus have found a method of repairing broken lambs (Chapt. 17).[22]

- There are many misunderstandings about the question of whether *Agni Dei* may be painted. It is often thought that the laity may not do this, but that priests may. Pope Gregory XIII however has clearly ordained that no one, including clergy, may paint or alter *Agni Dei*, or provide them with red lettering (Chapt. 18).[23]

That completes our account of Molanus's treatise. The assertion that the consecration of wax objects which were called *Agni Dei* can be established with certainty as occurring since the ninth century is far from the greatest shortcoming in Molanus's tract. Even more violence is done to history in his polemically colored text by his assertion that from its origins, the consecration of the *AD* had been exclusively the prerogative of the Pope. One could only say that this was in any sense true after the late Middle Ages, in any case after 1378.[24] It was also only after that date

---

21. For an analogous argument, but with reference to the host, see for instance Louis-Paul Guiges, *Sainte Catherine de Sienne, Le Livre des dialogues, suivi de lettres* (Paris, 1953) 352 (Traité de l'oraison, chap. 110).

22. It is known that during the third decade of the 18th century, Jesuits in Louvain contracted out the refashioning of *Agni Dei* to the nuns of the Convent of Bethlehem there, see Craig Harline, "Reform in the Convent. The Shadow of the World," *Geloven in het verleden. Studies over het godsdienstig leven in de vroegmoderne tijd, aangeboden aan Michel Cloet*, ed. Eddy Put, Marie Juliette Marinus, Hans Storme (Leuven, 1996) 131-146, esp. 136.

23. This ordinance is often repeated, for example in a Council in Naples in 1699, see *Acta et decreta sacrorum conciliorum recentiorum. Collectio Lacensis*, I (Freiburg, 1870) 201 (no. 5).

24. Adolph Franz, *Die kirchlichen Benediktionen im Mittelalter*, I (Freiburg, 1909) 557. For the consecration in the time of the Papacy in Avignon, see Dykmans, *Le cérémonial papal*, III (Brussels/Rome, 1983) 20-21, 235-237, 336-341.

that it was customary to consecrate *Agni Dei* only every seven years.[25] After these measures, the *AD* became really popular; and this popularity rose further after 1471, when Pope Sixtus IV more exclusively reserved the consecration for the Pope. In a certain sense, the time was ripe for this: already during the high Middle Ages the symbolism of lambs had become increasingly important. For instance, during this period images of the Lamb of God were already in general use in connection with the eucharistic interpretation of Christ's sacrificial death.[26] After 1355 the French king, out of considerations of piety, began to issue a new sort of gold coin, the 'mouton'. Several years later, because of the prestige of this coin, there were even double moutons minted in the Duchy of Brabant.[27] It is remarkable that the theft of the host at Enghien in 1369, which was the prelude to the famous Sacrament of Miracle at Brussels (1370) was to be financed (by a Jew) with sixty of these golden 'lambs'.[28]

In the early sixteenth century clergy and laity took ever greater quantities of wax or already produced *Agni Dei* in order to have them consecrated by the Pope. In order to retain some sort of control over this situation, by the end of the sixteenth century it was determined that only the Bernardines (a group of Cistercians) in Rome were permitted to make *Agni Dei*.[29]

Initially the formula of consecration was taken over from the consecration of candles for the feast of Our Lady of Light on February 2.[30] But after the end of the fourteenth century the formula was expanded to an unrestrained degree, with the numerous dangers to be averted specifically named. As regards to tenor, this long formula, and also the texts in the vernacular based on it, recall what are termed the 'fruits of the mass'.[31] For the rest, one of the supplications in this blessing certainly suggests that the *AD* could have the same power as the sacrament –

25. Dykmans, *Le cérémonial papal*, IV (Brussels/Rome 1985) 181-184.

26. G. Schiller, *Ikonographie der christlichen Kunst*, II. *Die Passion der christlichen Kunst* (Gütersloh, 1968) 132.

27. John Porteous, *Aangemunt en nagemunt* (Amsterdam, 1968) 21 and fig. 19 and 20; see also Jean Lafaurie, *Les monnaies des rois de France. Hugo Capet à Louis XII* (Paris-Bâle, 1951) from Philippe IV to Henri V, passim.

28. Illustration in Petrus de Cafmeyer, *Venerable Histoire du Très-Saint Sacrement de Miracle*, I (Brussels: George de Backer, 1720) 3, also with a remarkable explanation of the edge inscription 'Agnus Dei qui tollis peccata mundi'.

29. Franz, *Die kirchlichen Benediktionen im Mittelalter*, I, 560.

30. Dykmans, *Le cérémonial papal*, IV (Brussels/Rome 1985) 23, 185 ("Deinde benedixit, sicut benedicuntur candele in die candelarum, mutatis vocabulis"); see also Franz, *Die kirchlichen Benediktionen im Mittelalter*, I, 561.

31. Franz, *Die kirchlichen Benediktionen im Mittelalter*, I, 573; Caspers, *De eucharistische vroomheid*, 208-213.

something about which Molanus might well have had something to say. This involves the passage "(...) and as that innocent Lamb Who according to Your will was offered on the Cross, even Jesus Christ, Your Son, has wrested our first father from the might of the devil, may so also these virgin lambs, which we present before the countenance of Your divine Majesty for consecration, obtain the same power."[32] Only in 1752 would the formula of consecration be purified dogmatically and considerably abbreviated on the instructions of – who else? – Pope Benedict XIV.[33]

It is precisely this aspect – the 'familiarity' between the Sacrament and the *AD* – which would generate considerable criticism from the side of the Reformers, but despite this criticism – or perhaps because of it? – the *AD* only became more popular among Roman Catholics.[34] The German folklorist Wolfgang Brückner even suggests that the *AD*, because of its great similarity with the white host, had a function in early modern times in rousing spiritual communion.[35]

Augustinus Wichmans on the *Agnus Dei*

If the approach in the tract by Molanus can be characterized as polemic and apologetic, the passage from *Apotheca Spiritvalivm pharmacorvm contra lvem contagiosam aliosque morbus*,[36] a book by the Norbertine Augustinus Wichmans (1596-1661), pastor of Tilburg and later abbot of Tongerlo, deserves instead the epithet of practical theology.[37]

In this book, the chapter on the *AD* is preceded by a chapter on carrying the text of the Gospel of John (or at least the opening verses of it).[38] According to Wichmans, this is no 'new' superstition, but an old and honorable custom, practiced by, among others, the martyr St. Cecilia, and commended by the church father Augustine in his seventh tractate on the Gospel of St. John (John 1:34-2:4). Those who use this or another text as an amulet must certainly be conscious that these have no 'natural'

---

32. Molanus, *De Agnis Dei oratio* (1861) 435-436; Franz, I, 564: "(...) et quemadmodum ille agnus innocens tua voluntate immolatus in ara crucis, Iusus Christus, filius tuus, protoplastum nostrum de diabolica potestate eripuit: sic isti agni immaculati virtutem illam accipiant, quos consecrandos offerrimus in conspectu divinae maiestatis tuae" (see also p. 567-568).

33. Franz, I, 567-568.

34. Franz, I, 568 (note 1).

35. W. Brückner, "Christlicher Amulett-Gebrauch," 114-115.

36. Antwerp: Ex officina Hieronymi Verdussii, 1626.

37. Frans Hoppenbrouwers, "Franciscus Augustinus Wichmans (1596-1661). Kanunnik, zielzorger en abt van de norbertijnerabdij van Tongerlo ten tijde van de vroege Reformatie," *Analecta Praemonstratensia* 70 (1994) 226-293; 71 (1995) 96-149.

38. Wichmans, *Apotheca* 340-348.

power because of the precise formulation of the words, for instance, or the way in which they are written out, the material out of which they are made, or the number of crosses introduced onto them. If there is a salutary effect which proceeds from them, this can only be attributed to a supernatural cause. With reference to a passage from Peter of Navarre, any use of amulets is forbidden which does not fulfill the following conditions:
- the text must come from the scripture or the writings of one saint or another;
- no other figures may be used besides the cross or other holy symbols;
- nothing deviant may be included, and certainly no invocations to demons;
- no hope may be placed in the way in which they are written, or worn, etc.;
- one may not blindly believe that thanks to the wearing of such amulets no danger whatsoever can befall one.

In the following chapter, it is Wichmans's intention to show that the same effect that is attributed to the amulets already discussed can be attributed to the *AD*.[39] He begins with a reference to the 'ancient papal' custom of consecrating *Agni Dei*. In order to clearly reflect the prestige of the *AD*, he refers to the gift of three *Agni Dei* made by Pope Urban V (1363-1370) to the Byzantine Emperor Johannes; the Emperor came out to meet the bearers of the gift with a procession, and for the rest of his life he would remain fervently devoted to these amulets.[40] Much earlier, Charlemagne had received an *AD* from Pope Leo with similar reverence. Wichmans dates the custom of wearing these amulets from the time of Pope Gelasius (c. 500). In the time of the early church, the *AD* had a very welcome use; only by exchanging them for an *AD* could new converts so easily discard their pagan amulets.[41] The image, the lamb, does not only symbolize Christ, but also refers to his humility, and this is also thus a constant reminder to those who wear it to practice humility of heart. Next, Wichmans can not forbear relating several miraculous occurrences

39. Wichmans, *Apotheca* 349-355.

40. Regarding to Pope Urban, see Dykmans, *Le cérémonial papal*, III (Brussels-Rome, 1983) 77, 341. For a curious illustration of the *Agnus Dei* with the French translation of the poem by Pope Urban, see David Herrliberger, *Heilige Ceremonien und Kirche-Gebräuche der Christen in der ganzen Welt (...) die Ceremonien der Römisch-Katholischen Kirchen* (Zürich, 1745) planche 18. Molanus also discusses this poem by Pope Urban in his tract regarding the *AD* (Chapt. 13).

41. Cf. H. Dünninger, "Amulette," *Marienlexikon*, I (St. Ottilien, 1988) 131.

(with a further reference, though, to Martin Delrio[42]) in which the *AD*
played a central role, such as the unmasking of a circle of witches in the
diocese of Trier in 1585, and many cases in which fires were suddenly
extinguished after an *AD* had been thrown into them.[43] He expresses his
greatest astonishment at the Spanish soldier who was taken as a prisoner
of war in 1568 in Jülich by the Dutch rebels, and was sent before a firing
squad. After he appeared to be invulnerable to the protracted rain of
bullets, he was stripped because it was suspected that he was wearing
some sort of armor under his clothing. The only unusual thing which was
found, however, was an *AD* which he wore around his neck:[44] his faith
had saved him, albeit for only a short time, because thereafter one salvo
put an end to his life.[45] The salutary functions of the *AD* are manifold, at
least *if the church asks* for them in the consecration: freedom from all
that is bad and enjoyment of all that is good. More specifically, these
include protection from storm,[46] hail, floods, earthquake, thunderstorms,
plague, untimely death, fire, ambush by enemies, spirits and other dan-
gerous things and beings, and particularly dangers at childbirth.

This completes our description of Wichmans's views on the *AD*.

A first evaluation

From the above reflections, in this article particular attention should be
given to the stress that both authors place on the *prayer of the church*,
and that doctrine which is allied with it, the church as the sole conduit
salvation. It was during their period (circa 1550-1650) that the Cate-
chisms gave the following description of 'superstition': "the ungodly use
of any words or symbols for any work, for which these possess no
power, neither from their nature, nor from God, nor through the institu-

42. Martinus Delrio, *Disquisitionum magicarum libri sex* (Louvain: Ex officina
Gerardi Rivii, 1599/1600). This book had seen no less than 25 editions by 1755. For a
survey of the examples regarding the *AD* collected by Delrio, see Edda Fischer, *Die
"Disquisitonum magicarum libri sex" von Martin Delrio als gegenreformatorische
Exempel-Quelle* (Frankfurt am Main, 1975) nos. 122, 154, 222, 251, 253, 254, 256-262.

43. For the miraculous power of the *AD* to extinguish fires, Wichmans refers to the
Magnum Speculum Exemplorum (Douai: Ex officina Baltazaris Belleri, 1603).

44. The location of choice for wearing an *AD* was around the neck; cf. Franz, I, 575 (a
provision on this subject by a Synod at Prague, 1605).

45. For the use of amulets during the Dutch Revolt, see also Brückner, 112, 128.

46. Cf. Jonathan Spence, *The Memory Palace of Matteo Ricci* (London, 1985) 78 (in
rounding the Cape of Good Hope in 1578, Ricci and his confrères threw several *Agni Dei*
in the angry waves).

tion of the Holy Church."[47] Put in other words: any religious practice must be acceptable in the eyes of God, or in the eyes of the Church. To be correct dogmatically, it must be noted diffidently that the salutary effect of *sacramentalia* such as the *AD* (see Molanus's tract, Chapt. 13) is less than that of the sacraments, but immediately thereafter it must be added that if those who place their trust in the *AD* unite their own prayer with 'the prayer of the church' (see the phrases in italics in the above discussions of Molanus and Wichmans), they have the greatest chance of their prayer of supplication being heard successfully.

In order to make their arguments come across more convincingly, both Molanus and Wichmans refer to miracles which were evidently accomplished by means of *Agni Dei*. Several of these, such as the fate of the Spanish soldier at Jülich, are also told again and again in other texts.[48] The glorious high point in the history of the *AD* is perhaps the connection between this *sacramentale* and the battle of Lepanto in 1571. Before the Christian fleet sailed out on September 15 of that year for the decisive sea battle against the Turks, which would take place on October 7, the crews were visited by the Papal legate, Cardinal Odeschachi. He presented a large piece of the Holy Cross to the commander in chief, Don Juan of Austria, and all the Christian combatants – there were tenthousands of them – received an *AD*. Here the prayer of the church had a spectacular result, because the Turks, who until them had controlled the Mediterranean Sea, were crushingly defeated.[49]

47. Hans Storme, "Dommer als de staeken zelve. Pastoraal pessimisme over gelovigheid en geloofskennis van het 'gelovige volk'," *Geloven in het verleden*, 203-222, esp. 210. The Mechlin catechism appeared for the first time in 1609, see Marcel Gielis, "De leer over natuur, zonde en genade. Een lacune in de contrareformatorische catechese?," *Geloven in het verleden*, 65-87. One encounters this same formulation in the *ritualia* of the day, see Charles Caspers, "Duivelbannen of genezen op 'natuurlijke wijze'? De Mechelse aartsbisschoppen en hun medewerkers over exorcismen en geneeskunde, ca. 1575 - ca. 1800," *Grenzen van genezing. Gezondheid, ziekte en genezen in Nederland, zestiende tot begin twintigste eeuw*, ed. Willem de Blécourt, Willem Frijhoff, Marijke Gijswijt-Hofstra (Hilversum, 1993) 44-66, esp. 51. For the contemporary view, see *catéchisme de l'Église Catholique*, nos. 1667, 1670.

48. For these and other accounts of miracles involving the *AD*, see for example Antonius Dauroultius, *Flores exemplorum, Sive catechismus historialis* (Köln, 1616) 171-175 (16 examples); Laurentius Beyerlinck, *Theatrum vitae humanae, hoc est rerum divinarum humanarumque syntagma catholicorum, philosophicum, historicum* (Köln, 1631) 409-410.

49. Margaret Yeo, *Don Juan van Oostenrijk* (Amsterdam, 1938) 211; doubts about the facts are found in Brückner, 128. In 1573 Pope Gregory XIII fixed October 7 as the feast of the Holy Rosary, see M. Müller, "Lepanto," *Marienlexikon*, IV (St. Ottilien, 1992) 103-104.

**The place of the *Agnus Dei* in religious life
in the 16th and 17th centuries**

We have drawn above from the writings of two authors from the Southern Netherlands, and have already mentioned several remarkable occurrences involving the *AD*. Above the great rivers, too, already, before the Dutch Revolt, the *AD* had acquired a *sitz*. Thus, in the account books of Utrecht's Buurkerk for the administrative year 1504-1505, among the reports of acquisitions of church furnishings are to be found:[50]
- one small *pater noster*, with an *agnus dei* to be hung around the neck of Jesus.
- a coral *pater noster* with an *agnus dei*, to be hung around the neck of Our Lady when in procession.
- an *agnus dei* with crystal, to be hung around the neck of St. Andrew.
With regard to the year 1551, we know that in Utrecht during the Corpus Christi procession the image of the Virgin from the Buurkerk was included in the procession, adorned with a costly rosary and an *AD*.[51] If we think of Molanus's exposition, this is appropriate attire: the virgin wax, after all, refers to the virgin birth of Jesus. Also, the inclusion of the image with the amulet in the procession on precisely this feast day makes clear the connection which was made between the eucharist and the *AD*.[52]

The *AD* also 'participated' in the Dutch Revolt, as we have already seen above with the Spanish soldier who was executed only with considerable difficulty. In 1572 the protestant rebels stole the ornaments from the image of Our Lady in the church in Zutphen. In 1573, after the city had once again returned to the hands of the Catholics, the image was restored to its place of honor and provided with "a necklace of coral and a beautiful gilded *AD*, to be hung around the neck of Our Lady as ornament."[53]

Beyond the reach of the perils of war, in the territory of the Dutch Mission, the *AD* was an attribute which was chiefly propagated by the Jesuits. The Jesuit Gerard Carbonel, who from 1613 to 1627 worked in the Mission in Friesland, found in the Frisian countryside the custom of

50. "Oude kerkrekeningen," *Magazijn voor roomsch katholijken* 13 (1847) 25. According to Brückner, *Agni Dei* already appear in lists of valuables as early as the 14th century, see Brückner, 92.

51. J.A.F. Kronenburg, *Maria's Heerlijkheid in Nederland*, II (Amsterdam, 1904) 356; regarding the adoration of Our Lady in the Buurkerk, see Frans Rikhof, "Utrecht, O.L. Vrouw ter Nood Gods," *Bedevaartplaatsen in Nederland*, I. *Noord- en Midden-Nederland*, ed. Peter Jan Margry and Charles Caspers (Amsterdam/Hilversum, 1997) 753-757.

52. Cf. Brückner, 111 and 95.

53. Kronenburg, *Maria's heerlijkheid*, II, 336.

trying to prevent fresh milk from turning sour with notes inscribed with fragments from Paul's epistle to the Ephesians, which were first read aloud and subsequently affixed to the milk buckets. Carbonel disapproved of this custom, because no original connection could be demonstrated between this means and keeping the milk sweet; the notes could, however, be replaced by *Agni Dei*, whose protective effects were acknowledged *by the church*.[54] There is the almost touching story of an eleven-year-old French orphan boy who was caught in Leiden in 1642 in possession of a rosary, a prayer book and an *AD*.[55] The protestant preacher Jacobus Trigland[56] ripped the *AD* from his neck, but could not succeed in changing the mind of the lad, who remained true to what a Jesuit father had taught him in his forbidden catechism lessons. Willem Estius wrote a poem in praise of the *AD*,[57] and from 17th century property lists from Weesp and Doesburg it appears that the *AD* was not uncommonly found as a family heirloom – at least in part as jewelry – in Catholic families.[58]

The Enlightenment

During the 18th century and the beginning of the 19th century, the period of the Enlightenment, it was particularly the devotional aspects of religion which came under fire from the trend-setting intellectual elites. Particularly in France, supported by the government and important academic institutions, in their skeptical writings Enlightenment authors (including priests) shredded popular faith and popular piety. For instance, the custom of wearing amulets was shown no mercy in abbé Jean-Baptiste Thiers's monumental work on superstition.[59] It was particularly Thiers, who dismissed things to which earlier authors such as Molanus and Wichmans had attached great value, who would later be

54. Gerrit Vanden Bosch, "Jezuïetenpastoraat in Friesland. Gerard Carbonel als missiepater in Leeuwarden en omgeving (1613-1627)," *Geloven in het verleden* 345-360, esp. 354.

55. J. Barten, "Catechismusonderricht en eerste communie bij de jezuïeten te Leiden gedurende de zeventiende en achttiende eeuw," *Archief voor de geschiedenis van de katholieke kerk in Nederland* 1 (1959) 244-245.

56. Regarding Trigland's significance, see G.P. van Itterzon, "Trigland, Jacobus," *Biografisch lexicon voor de geschiedenis van het Nederlandse protestantisme*, III (Kampen, 1988) 355-358.

57. Buddingh, *Mirakelgeloof*, 83.

58. My thanks to Dr. Gerard Rooijakkers, who provided this information from property lists preserved at the Meertens Institute in Amsterdam.

59. J.-B. Thiers, *Traité des superstitions qui regardent les sacrements (...)*, I-IV (Paris, 1741).

accused by representatives of the Romantic movement of having desired the elimination of the whole of religious life. Although interest in the *AD* decreased in comparison with the period of the Counter-Reformation, the production and distribution of *Agni Dei* continued as before.[60] In the catechization of the populace, the Catholic Church also continued undaunted with the task of combating popular faith in the familiar ways, including, among others, offering orthodox substitutes such as the *AD* for amulets which were not approved by the church.[61]

Restoration

The restoration which began around the middle of the 19th century was accompanied by renewed attention to stimulating devotional life.[62] With reference to the *AD*, this is strikingly illustrated by the book of the French canon Barbier de Montault, running through several editions and translated into various languages, which to this day is the most extensive survey study on this subject.[63]

Beginning with the end of the 19th century, considerable attention was also devoted to the *AD* in Dutch Catholic journals.[64] Several passages from *Het Offer*, from 1904, deserve particular attention here. After first giving a description of what the salutary powers of the *AD* are – which, however, entirely rest upon the prayers of the church – it is emphatically pointed out that we may not think that if we just venerate or possess an *AD*, that nothing can happen to us:

If one venerates an *AD*, in order to be protected against thunder and lightning,

---

60. See Van Schaïk a.o., *Katholiek Nederland en de paus 1580-1985*, 85 (examples of *Agni Dei* from the 17th, 18th and 19th centuries are preserved in the Museum Catharijneconvent in Utrecht).

61. Storme, "Dommer als de staeken zelve," 210. It was particularly after the temporary abolition of the Society of Jesus that the prestige of the *AD* declined. For criticism of the use of *Agni Dei* around 1800, see Brückner, 129-131.

62. See, for instance, the notable writings of an important figure in the renewal of the liturgy in the 19th century, Prosper Guéranger, *Bedeutung, Ursprung und Privilegien der Medaille oder des Kreuzes des heiligen Benedikts* (Einsiedeln,, 1863; transl. from the French). In this booklet, the author reacts vehemently against Thiers, particularly the passage in *Traité des superstitions*, I, 338-359.

63. X. Barbier de Montault, *Traité liturgique, canonique et symbolique des Agnus Dei* (Rome-Paris, 1865; 3th ed.).

64. *De Volksmissionaris* 10 (1889) 208-215, 312-321, 359-365; *Het Offer* 13 (1904) 81-85, 97-99; *Nederlandsche Katholieke Stemmen* 11 (1911) 155-158; *Het Schild* 4 (1922) 15-16, 30-31. See also the discussion of the *Agnus Dei* in a German manual which was also used in The Netherlands for training priests, Michael Benger, *Pastoraltheologie*, II (Regensburg, 1862) 189-192.

against water and fire, then it isn't simply a matter that one can climb a tower or a windmill sail during a heavy thunderstorm, or throw oneself into the sea or into a burning oven, because neither thunder nor lightning, nor water nor fire can harm you. Rather than piety, that would be superstition; rather than trust, recklessness (...). To be sure, prayer is an unfailing means of receiving from God what we ask of Him, but you know that all which comes through prayer happens because it is unfailingly heard. And for that to take place, it is necessary that it be godly prayer, persistent prayer, and that one ask something that is necessary or at least useful for salvation (...). In particular with regard to asking for temporal favors and advantages through the veneration of the *AD*, the Church has always desired that we ask these as subordinate to our eternal well-being (...). Now, God, who is a loving Father for us, knows better than we ourselves do what is useful for our eternal well-being, and thus it can happen that we, although we pray, and although we venerate the *AD* with true piety and great trust, that we still do not receive that for which we ask, for the reason that God foresees that the temporal favors for which we turn in supplication to Him, would not be beneficial to our salvation, but rather work to our spiritual disadvantage.[65]

As an example, the author imagines a sinner who has just purified his soul with contrite confession, and prays that he may live for many years to come. Would not God, who foresees that this person will again sin greatly, render this person a greater service by allowing him die quickly, than by letting him die much later, but laden with sin? Thus, the prayer has not been idle, and indeed has been heard, and is rewarded above expectation and above measure – at least according to the author. Within a metaphysical world view, this is indeed a conclusive rationale. We can certainly, however, ask ourselves to what extent readers of that day, who knew full well that they were far from perfect, may have shrunk back from the *AD*, which had become, in a certain sense, a sort of Russian roulette.

As is the case with many customs which gradually become less important, it is not easy to establish whether the consecration of *Agni Dei* passed away quietly, or was terminated. The section on blessings in the manual *Gottesdienst der Kirche: Handbuch der Liturgiewissenschaft* is utterly silent on the question.[66] The entry for *AD* in the recent third edition of the *Lexikon für Theologie und Kirche* wisely speaks only of the past – even distant past.[67] According to Ulrich Bock, the custom of repeating the consecration every seven years ceased under Pope Paul VI.

---

65. Citations from "Het 'Agnus Dei'," *Het Offer* 13 (1904) 97-98.

66. Reiner Kaczynski, "Die Benediktionen," Bruno Kleinheyer, Emmanuel von Severus, Reiner Kaczynski, *Sakramentliche Feiern*, II (Regensburg, 1984) 233-274.

67. Andreas Heinz, "Agnus Dei als Sakramentale," *Lexikon für Theologie und Kirche*, I (Freiburg etc., 1993; 3th ed.) 244.

In 1965, the second year of his pontificate, and also the final year of the Second Vatican Council, *Agni Dei* were consecrated and distributed for the final time.[68]

Constants and changes

On the basis of the *AD*, are there possible constants or even mechanisms that can be discovered within the late Middle Ages and early modern times, a period so turbulent and subject to such great changes, and/or, on the other hand, can this *sacramentale* function as an indicator of renewals in piety?

- We would regard the thread which runs through this paper as one such constant: namely that, in respect to intention and form, what the people believe must follow the norms of the Church. Put in other words, during the whole period, the efforts of the institutional church were directed toward replacing popular faith (or forms of popular faith) by popular piety (or forms of popular piety).

- As a change, we would note that after the coming of the Reformation, popular piety not only had to be Christian, but also Catholic. It was no longer sufficient that the faithful merely fulfilled the commands of the church. Much more than before, the institutional church made efforts to interpret devotional customs to the people by coordinating these customs and making them subordinate to the prayer of the Church. It is true that devotion to saints, which had already long existed, pilgrimage practices, the wearing of amulets and other customs were still maintained, but more intensively than during the Middle Ages, it was explained to the members of the Church that, for instance, they should not worship the saints themselves, but must exclusively approach them to pray on their behalf. To be quite clear: one does encounter such instruction already in the thirteenth century, but it was then often left to the initiative of the mendicant friars in their missions and preaching,[69] while bishops and parish clergy made little effort in this direction.

- A second change which took place within this period is related to the first which we have mentioned: namely the clarification regarding the power of prayer (discussed above under 'A first evaluation'). Not only is

---

68. Ulrich Bock, "Kontaktreliquien," 156.

69. Cf. Franz Göbel, *Die Predigten des Franziskaners Berthold von Regensburg* (Regensburg, 1929) 422-423 (Berthold points out that participation in the mass was more important than going on pilgrimage).

it emphasized that prayer or other forms of pious activity have results thanks to God, thanks to nature (and natural law), but also thanks to *the prayers of the church*. Henceforth the church assists and supports the faithful, further than merely with regard to certain times and at certain sacred places. Just as within the church building, most sacraments had their salutary effect because of their divine institution, so outside the church building the *sacramentalia* had their salutary effect as a result of the prayer of the church.

The above constant and changes only serve to confirm and illustrate what is already known from the current state of historical research. In our opinion, this survey of devotion to the *AD* allows us to reach further conclusions.

Pope and people

Two more points also appear from the diachronic survey of the veneration of the *AD*: on the one side the restrictions which always surrounded the consecration, production and distribution of the *AD*, and on the other the ever greater popularity of this *sacramentale*.

- The popularity of the *AD* reminds one of a mechanism that appeared during the Gregorian Reformation in the high Middle Ages. During this movement Western Christianity became transfixed by the 'legitimacy of the sacraments'. The liturgy had to be performed in the sacred language, and, particularly, the priest must be a consecrated person (for example, he must be unmarried), because people feared that otherwise the mediation of salvation would be ineffective. The Gregorian Reformation was in many respects a popular movement that played into the hands of the institutional church and, among other things, led to the definitive, strict legislation around celibacy (Lateran III).[70] The people demanded even absolute perfection on the part of priests, at which the church was forced to emphasize the distinction between office and charisma, because otherwise too few good priests would be left. Something similar apparently happened with regard to the *AD*. The chief reason that people wanted to possess the *AD* was that there were so many restrictions placed upon it. It is striking in this regard that in the time of the Dutch Mission once again a sort of 'little Gregorian Reformation' seems to have taken place: in the years before the Dutch Schism (1723) the Catholic segment of the population in the Northern Netherlands turned en masse to the faction

70. Edward Schillebeeckx, *The Church with a Human Face. A New and Expanded Theology of Ministry* (London, 1985) 167-174.

true to Rome. As an explanation for this, it has recently been proposed that these Catholics were especially interested in having 'legitimate' priests, that is to say, priests approved by the Pope, because they doubted the capacity of the other party to mediate salvation.[71]

In respect to the *AD* a fixation on 'legitimacy' likewise is to be seen. Salutary effects were ascribed only to those amulets – the *AD*, above all – which were approved by the church and consecrated by priests. Although the *AD* chiefly only became popular after the Middle Ages, we in fact are dealing with a mechanism which had already existed for a long time.

- One difference from the preceding period – clearly to be seen in someone like Molanus – is that in the early modern era the direct involvement of the papacy clearly comes to the fore in the history of the *AD*. Of course, it is true that the Pope was also the head of the church in the late Middle Ages, but ecclesiastical and religious life was still more locally or regionally oriented, a situation in which one can think of the more or less closed urban cultures that considered themselves as a body of Christ (indeed, a complete body of Christ), with all citizens as members.[72] To be sure, after the Middle Ages the disappearance of such urban cultures, yielding the stage to nation states (and sometimes also national religions) is a general phenomenon in Western Europe, and within the dynamics of the Catholic Reformation it was obvious that 'Rome' would came more directly into the field of view of Catholic subjects (or subjects of Catholic states), but it is still true that the *AD* was the very *sacramentale* which was most fundamentally tied to the Pope, more than, for instance, scapulars or rosaries. Also with reference to the period of the Restoration we have seen that the 'rebirth' of the papacy and its prestige brought with it the 'rebirth' of the *AD* too.

In connection with this, one can also point to the role of the Jesuits. They played a crucial role in the Dutch Mission, in the Southern Netherlands and with the Spanish rulers in Southern Europe. But they were also present elsewhere: in Germany in the time of the witch persecutions, it was particularly Jesuits who made it their special concern to have those

71. Theo Clemens, "Kerkscheuring op lokaal niveau. Petrus van der Maes van Avenrode en de voorgeschiedenis van het schisma van 1723," *Geloven in het verleden*, 413-430, esp. 424.

72. See f.i. B.A.M. Ramakers, *Spelen en figuren. Toneelkunst en processiecultuur in Oudenaarde tussen Middeleeuwen en Moderne Tijd* (Amsterdam, 1996) 49; Xavier Rousseaux, "Du cotrôle social et de la civilisation des moeurs. Pratiques judiciaires et représentations religieuses à Nivelles aux temps des Réformes," *Geloven in het verleden* 89-109.

who were arrested on suspicion of witchcraft put on an *AD*.[73] The Jesuits' promotional activities for the *AD* were often regarded as a way of bringing 'popular faith' under the wing of the Church, but one should not lose sight of the fact that with their promotion of precisely this amulet they showed themselves as the Pope's crack regiment. It is therefore also not surprising that we find *Agni Dei* reported in the lists of property from the Roman Catholic conventicles in The Netherlands, but not in similar lists from Old Catholic churches.[74]

Conclusion

In this paper, the history of the veneration of the *AD* functions as a possible approach for obtaining greater insight into the constants and changes in the religious popular culture of the past, and more specifically into the shift from 'popular faith' to 'popular piety'.

Retracing the history of this *sacramentale* indeed offered a certain perspective, although the imbalance of the approach chosen impels us to relativize the meaning of this amulet. Thus, we have seen that the wearing of the *AD* was once again thought of more highly in the 19th century, but in this we must not lose sight of the fact that since then this amulet increasingly had to share attention with other, new *sacramentalia*, such as the miraculous medal. The *AD* did not become for the laity what the turned collar was for the priest. Rather, the rosary has fulfilled that function[75] – although those Catholics who were 'more Catholic' than other Catholics were pleased to hang an *AD* from their rosary.[76]

How should we now evaluate the *AD*, and more specifically the way in which it was used to transform 'popular faith' into 'popular piety'? On the one hand, it can not be denied that for a long time the history of the *AD* was a success story in this respect. Accepting the existential religious need that people have to win over the divinity for themselves by their supplications, the *AD* functioned as a welcome substitute for other means not approved by the church. On the other hand, reference must be made to the considerable tension between the power of the prayer on the one

---

73. H. Freudenthal, "Agnus Dei," *Handwörterbuch des deutschen Aberglaubens*, I (Berlin-Leipzig, 1927) 218. For Friedrich von Spee, see Brückner, 126. Cf. ibid. 119.

74. In the 17th and 18th century lists of the property of conventicles in Gouda which were administered by seculars and that later went over to the Old Catholic Church, there are, as one might expect, no *Agni Dei* reported; see Xander van Eck, *Kunst, twist en devotie. Goudse katholieke schuilkerken 1572-1795* (Delft, 1994) 195-219.

75. Here, among other things one can reflect on the encyclicals that Pope Leo XIII issued annually. However, there were certainly periods in history when nearly all Catholics in certain regions wore an *AD*; see Brückner, 118, 122.

76. Cf. Walter Hartinger, *Religion und Brauch* (Darmstadt, 1992) 122-129, esp. 126.

side, which, as Wichmans stressed, does not depend on the form or material of any amulet, and on the other side the strong emphasis which was everywhere laid on the legitimacy gained through the consecration, form and material of the *AD*. The way in which the *AD* was dealt with, particularly by the Jesuits, leaves room for doubt with regard to the dichotomy between 'popular piety' and 'popular faith' which was maintained by the institutional church of that era (and taken over in this paper for methodological reasons). Was the distinction between these two really so fundamental, or could the term 'popular piety' in many cases be replaced by 'clerical popular faith'? Whatever the case, for anyone who labors today for 'the faith into which we were baptized', there will be little reason to regret the quiet death in the 20th century of this *sacramentale*, which for centuries was promoted on the basis of absurd typology, uncritical apologetics and a thirst for the miraculous.

Religion populaire et postmodernité

Lambert LEIJSSEN

Dans cet exposé le phénomène de la religion populaire sera décrit et lu à partir d'un cadre interprétatif qui prend appui sur des concepts-clés de la modernité et de la postmodernité. Quelle que soit la complexité de la matière,[1] chemin faisant le terme de postmodernité, tel que nous le comprenons ici, s'éclaircira. On s'accordera facilement sur le point de départ suivant: la raison, la *ratio*, est le rudiment conducteur de toute explication et interprétation des phénomènes culturels. Ceci vaut tant pour la modernité que pour la postmodernité. Comme première définition (personnelle) de la postmodernité, on peut poser, en guise d'introduction, que la postmodernité contient une réflexion critique sur la *ratio*, sur le *rationnel* de la modernité.

Dans la partie centrale de l'exposé, l'horizon sera élargi vers une réflexion sur la religiosité populaire dans le contexte latino-américain. Sur ce continent, le progrès des recherches scientifiques concernant ce phénomène est plus considérable.[2] Le mode d'approche en vigueur là-bas peut jeter une lumière sur l'interprétation des développements à l'Ouest.

Dans la partie finale un bilan sera dressé qui mettra en avant la tâche de l'évangélisation de la religion populaire, afin de préserver celle-ci des excroissances du nationalisme et de l'ethnicisme d'une part, et du fondamentalisme et de la magie de l'autre.

1. La religion populaire sous l'appréciation critique de la modernité

Par le terme de 'modernité', nous entendons dans cet exposé le mode d'approche des dites 'Lumières', plus précisément en ce qui concerne les résultats d'une application poussée de l'analyse rationnelle de la culture. Typique de cette modernité est la place centrale du sujet, de l'individu pensant, qui, à partir d'une interprétation purement rationnelle, tente de

---

1. L'article s'inscrit dans le projet plus large de 'la sacramento-théologie', qui s'élaborera de 1996 à 2000 à la faculté de théologie de la Katholieke Universiteit Leuven. Voir Jeff BLOECHL et Stijn VAN DEN BOSSCHE, "Postmoderniteit, theologie et sacramentologie. Een onderzoeksproject toegelicht", dans *Jaarboek voor Liturgie-onderzoek* 13 (1997) 21-48.

2. Dans A. BLIJLEVENS, A. BRANTS et E. HENAU (réd.), *Volksreligiositeit: uitnodiging en uitdaging* (HTP-Studie 3), Averbode, 1982. Le numéro thématique de la revue *Concilium* (1986) n°4: "Volksgodsdienst. Een kritische bezinning op de vele vormen van volksgodsdienst en hun betekenis voor het pastoraal handelen" contient diverses contributions situées dans ce contexte culturel.

comprendre les développements de la société selon un système de la pensée, ce qui a donné lieu à la construction des idéologies, des dits 'grands récits' (le marxisme, par exemple), où le mythe du progrès s'est constitué. Une deuxième définition conçoit alors la 'postmodernité' comme le mode d'approche qui procède de la déception de la modernité, de la fin des grands récits, de l'écroulement du mythe du progrès, de la prise de conscience issue de l'insuffisance du sujet individuel à se construire une vision du monde cohérente.

Ici la postmodernité ne signifie pas que la *ratio*, la raison, l'intelligence de l'homme soit écartée: dans la postmodernité une suite est donnée à la réflexion sur les résultats de la modernité: qu'est-ce qui est venu après (post) la modernité et comment l'homme, dans cette nouvelle situation culturelle, peut-il de nouveau prendre conscience de son identité? Il est vrai que la postmodernité active d'autres facteurs encore que la seule raison, comme le sentiment, l'émotion, l'expérience esthétique, le sens de la communauté. À nos yeux, la postmodernité, ainsi qu'on la conçoit dans cette contribution, donne l'occasion de glisser la place centrale de l'individu vers la communauté qui l'entoure, de relativiser la perception purement subjective et de l'insérer dans un réseau de relations plus large, qui ne pourra pourtant pas devenir un nouveau 'grand récit', mais qui, fragmentairement, d'une façon particulière, donnera accès à une appréhension caractéristique de la réalité. La modernité a débouché à la reconnaissance que la conception de la vie chrétienne n'en est qu'une parmi d'autres. L'individualisation et la modernité ont convergé vers une fragmentation, une pluralisation des conceptions de la vie. Dans la postmodernité on ne peut pas revendiquer l'hégémonie d'un seul point de vue particulier. Comme troisième définition de la postmodernité ceci siginifie: 'modernité radicalisée', ou modernité 'plurielle' et 'réflexive'.[3]

À l'égard du phénomène de la 'religion', la modernité a en outre réduit la relation de l'homme au transcendantal à une simple fonction du besoin subjectif religieux qui dépendrait d'une vision du monde prémoderne (le *homo religiosus*, cf. Mircea Eliade, Claude Lévi-Strauss, Sigmund Freud)[4]. La vision du monde 'moderne' a expliqué la relation au transcendental comme une projection injustifiée de sentiments subjectifs de dépendance (cf. Friedrich Nietzsche) par rapport à une instance divine, qui dans les différentes religions est nommée de diverses manières. Dans

3. La définition de la postmodernité, et les manières dont on la désigne sont expliquées davantage par L. BOEVE, "Erfgenaam en erflater. Kerkelijke tradities binnen de traditie", dans H. LOMBAERTS - L. BOEVE (réd.), *Traditie en Initiatie. Perspectieven voor de toekomst* (Nikè 36), Leuven-Amersfoort, 1996, 43-77, citations p. 60 et 63.

4. Voir l'avant-propos de Mircea Eliade et David Tracy qui accompagne le numéro thématique de *Concilium* (1980) n° 6: "La chrétienté, une religion?".

la tradition chrétienne cette instance, dans la lignée de la conception monothéiste juive, est l'unique Dieu, révélé de façon particulière dans les actions de l'homme Jésus reconnu comme Fils de Dieu, dans la force du Saint-Esprit. Ainsi la religion chrétienne s'est développée au travers de la foi en la trinité unique de Dieu le Père, le Fils et le Saint-Esprit. Dans ce contexte il est important de garder sous les yeux la distinction que maintient Paul Ricoeur, à l'exemple de Karl Barth, entre religion, foi, et culture.

Dans la religion, les sentiments subjectifs se constituent dans le cadre d'une certaine culture. L'attitude religieuse proprement dite pourtant, est toujours une réponse à une révélation spécifique (voir l'idée de Karl Barth à l'égard de Schleiermacher). La spécificité du christianisme réside précisément en la critique exercée sur la réduction moderne de la religion aux sentiments de dépendance.

Le christianisme est devenu une religion mondiale, en tant que modelage spécifique (particulière) de la dimension religieuse dans l'expérience humaine, mais il ne saurait être assimilé à une religion pure et simple: certes, le christianisme peut être décrit en termes des fonctions qu'exerce une religion, mais son être fondamental est déterminé par la prédication d'un récit de révélation particulier et par une réponse consciente, inspirée par la foi.

Ainsi, le terme de 'religion populaire' qu'affiche le titre de la présente contribution, reçoit déjà un certain éclaircissement: dans la religion populaire sont opérants des facteurs et des fonctions qui couvrent un domaine plus vaste que ce qui appartient spécifiquement aux dogmes chrétiens. La religion populaire apporte des éléments culturels qui ont fait leur entrée dans la société à partir de la tradition précédente, mais qui n'appartiennent pas pour autant au noyau de la foi chrétienne. À ce noyau appartiennent la reconaissance de Dieu comme origine (créateur) du monde, la foi en l'incarnation du Fils de Dieu et en la rédemption par sa mort à la croix et sa résurrection, et en l'espérance de son retour à la fin des temps. Ces credos de la foi sont considérés comme les métaphores de base de la religion catholique.[5] Dans la liturgie ces métaphores de base sont célébrées rituellement et commémorées afin de permettre aux croyants de s'identifier comme chrétiens. Dans la religion catholique la célébration rituelle est indissolublement liée à l'engagement concret pour le prochain (l'éthique).

Dans la religion populaire il y a des éléments au travers desquels se

---

5. Nous traduisons le terme anglais 'root metaphor' par 'métaphore de base'. Voir Georges S. WORGUL, "Inculturatie en basismetaforen", dans J. LAMBERTS (ed), *Liturgie en inculturatie* (Nikè 37), Leuven-Amersfoort , 1996, 57-74 [= ID., "Inculturation and Root Metaphors", in *Questions Liturgiques-Studies in Liturgy* 77 (1996) 40-51].

traduit la religiosité communément humaine consistant à exprimer une relation à l'instance transcendantale (divine) par le biais de rituels.

Suivant l'approche de la modernité, il n'y a guère de place pour ces expressions de la religion populaire: elles étaient liquidées comme restes d'une foi du peuple prémoderne, naïve ou primitive, et où l'élément 'populaire' est synonyme de 'non intellectuel', de 'non rationnel'. Aussi écarte-t-on trop facilement les pèlerinages, les novènes, la récitation des chapelets, le fait de brûler des cierges, etc. comme des rituels magiques visant à influencer l'instance divine afin de s'en emparer ou d'en tirer profit. Quand, suivant la tradition familiale, les parents demandent le baptême de leur enfant, bien qu'ils ne soient pas vraiment impliqués dans le noyau de la foi chrétienne et qu'ils ne participent pas à la célébration du dimanche, un tel rituel appartient aussi à la catégorie de la religion populaire. À l'égard des célébrations des 'rites de pasage' (le baptême, la confirmation, la communion solennelle, le mariage et les obsèques) à l'attention des croyants qu'on a appelés 'les chrétiens festifs' ou 'les chrétiens des quatre saisons' – appelation due à l'absence d'engagement chrétien dans la vie de tous les jours – une forte critique est à noter dans l'approche de la modernité. Qu'en subsiste-t-il dans l'approche de la postmodernité? Y a-t-il encore de l'espace pour ces expressions de la religion populaire dans une interprétation postmoderne?

2. Religiosité populaire dans le contexte latino-américain

Afin de répondré à cette question, les expériences et les réflexions théologiques concernant la religiosité populaire ainsi qu'elle est vécue dans la chrétienté latino-américaine, peuvent être extrêmement pertinentes pour la chrétienté occidentale. La théologie de la libération, qui a trouvé ses origines sur le continent latino-américain, a également critiqué foncièrement le phénomène de la réligiosité populaire, surtout en ce qui concerne sa pertinence éthique. Cette critique peut être considérée – certains théologiens le font explicitement d'un point de vue marxiste – comme exponentielle de la modernité. Or, en même temps et de plus en plus, l'on constate auprès des théologiens des développements qui indiquent que l'appréciation du phénomène de la religiosité populaire s'achemine vers une redécouverte de l'identité chrétienne, ancrée non seulement dans des expressions universelles religieuses, mais également dans des façonnements culturels qui sont propres à un 'peuple'. À ce moment, le terme 'peuple' n'évoquera plus des sens péjoratifs tels que 'sous-développé' ou 'non intellectuel', mais il évoluera dans un sens positif, qui est celui de la 'particularité', d'une communauté réelle où l'individu trouve son identité dans la fraternité (solidarité).

Lors de la conférence CEHILA en juillet 1995 à Sâo Paulo, l'interprétation de la religiosité populaire était le thème d'une discussion menée en groupe. Nous avons participé au débat et nous traduirons dans cet exposé les idées des principaux intervenants[6]. De plus, nous nous concentrerons sur les thèses cardinales dans l'oeuvre du Brésilien Fransisco Taborda, s.j., (Université de Belo Horizonte) et de l'Argentin Juan Carlos Scannone, s.j.. Nous mentionnerons également l'optique d'Orlando Espin (Université de San Diego) ainsi qu'il l'a développée lors du congrès CTSA en juin 1997 à Minneapolis, et qui traitait la religiosité populaire des hispano-chrétiens, établis dans une Amérique du Nord sécularisée.[7]

2.1. Typologie

Dans la religiosité populaire de l'Amérique latine Enrique Dussel, historien et philosophe (Mexique)[8], distingue trois composantes de base qui seraient le fruit d'un processus historique séculaire:
1. La religiosité populaire hispano-lusitanienne ou ibérique, qui s'est développée à partir de la christianisation qu'ont imposée les oppresseurs espagnols et portugais; la célébration du vendredi saint en est un exemple. 2. La religiosité indienne, qui prend appui sur des traditions des plus anciens habitants de ce continent, les Aztèques, les Mayas, les Chibchas, les Incas,...; nous pensons aux fêtes saisonnières et aux processions aux endroits saints. 3. La religiosité africaine, qui a permis aux esclaves noirs de rester en contact avec leur origine, exprimée par exemple dans les danses (Candomblé). Dans la situation présente ces trois composantes de base se sont souvent enchevêtrées comme types de la religiosité populaire des 'opprimés', ou, selon la terminologie biblique, des 'pauvres'. Dès lors, le 'peuple' représente les 'pauvres d'esprit'.

Dans l'interprétation d'Enrique Dussel, cette religiosité populaire doit être vue dans le cadre de la culture populaire, qui, en tant que culture spécifique, se distingue de la culture impérialiste des classes dominantes et de la culture de la masse.[9] Dussel reconnaît que ces formes de religiosité populaire ont fonctionné comme instruments d'oppression des groupes de la population mentionnés, comme instruments aussi de ce qu'il appelle la 'manipulation populiste'. À trois niveaux la manipulation peut être opérante: 1. la tricherie des sorciers, la guérison obtenue grâce aux

6. CEHILA est l'abréviation de la Commission d'étude de l'histoire de l'église en Amérique latine, sous la direction de José Oscar Beozzo (Université catholique pontificale, PUC, São Paulo). Les actes du congrès seront publiés en 12 volumes par la maison d'édition Vozès, Petrópolis.

7. CTSA: The Catholic Theological Society of America.

8. Enrique DUSSEL, "La religion populaire, oppression et libération. Hypothèses sur son histoire et son présent en Amérique latine", *Concilium* 206 (1986) 105-119.

9. *Ibid.*, 106.

herbes médicinales ou grâce aux bénédictions, la 'magie noire', qui sont démasquées par Dussel comme un phénomène décadent au sein de la tradition; 2. l'emploi de la religiosité populaire par des leaders politiques populistes, soi-disant charismatiques, qui en profitent pour contrôler le peuple; 3. l'église catholique également, qui, en fermant les yeux sur ce phénomène, a accordé à la religiosité populaire et à ses pratiques particulières droit d'existence à côté de la liturgie officielle; "Cependant, la hiérarchique église catholique surveille de près les pèlerinages et les lieux de pèlerinage, et ne perd pas de vue la concordance des deux éléments – c'est donc de la 'manipulation'"[10]. À la manipulation populiste de l'oppression, Dussel oppose une autre attitude possible, à savoir celle du caractère libérateur de la religiosité populaire. Une telle attitude ne peut être réalisée qu'au sein des communautés chrétiennes de base qui sont ancrées dans le peuple. Dans ces communautés, les anciennes expériences sont placées dans un contexte historique nouveau, un nouveau horizon de foi consciente, de pratique justifiée et d'action politique.

2.2. Caractéristiques de la religiosité populaire

Comme caractéristiques spécifiques de la religiosité populaire latino-américaine, Enrique Dussel mentionne les cinq éléments suivants: 1. la consécration du temps par les fêtes; 2. la consécration de l'espace par les pèlerinages aux sanctuaires; 3. la consécration du rythme, du mouvement accompagné de musique, de la danse jusqu'à l'extase, Ubanda, Candomblé, Vudu; 4. les destinataires: le Dieu des pauvres, les maints christs (l'enfant, le Christ patient – assis, avec la couronne d'épines –, et surtout le Christ crucifié), la figure de Marie mère de l'eau, les patrons, les décédés, et, surtout dans la religiosité populaire afro-américaine, les esprits; 5. l'ethos de la religiosité populaire qui, typique de la situation latino-américaine, est marqué par une certaine fatalité, par l'acceptation passive de l'oppression, de la souffrance, de la maladie, de la mort, car "telle est la volonté de Dieu"[11].

Le Christ crucifié est un symbole très profond dans cette religiosité populaire, et c'est pourquoi la célébration du vendredi saint est plus importante que la célébration de Pâques. C'est précisément dans la procession traversant le village, un chemin de croix avec un Christ souffrant sur la croix, souvent représenté de manière très piétiste, que le peuple se reconnaît dans la situation du Servant souffrant, de l'Homme des douleurs, tel qu'il est décrit dans le Deutéro-Jesaja. L'identification du Christ souffrant et le peuple souffrant n'est pas seulement un thème chez

10. *Ibid.*, 109.
11. *Ibid.*, 112-113.

tous les théologiens de la libération latino-américains, mais elle est aussi mise à l'avant pendant les grandes réunions de la conférence épiscopale latino-américaine (Medellín 1968, Puebla 1979, Santo Domingo 1992). Il est indéniable que cette figure, plutôt que le Christ ressuscité, est plus au goût du peuple, pour la simple et bonne raison que le peuple subit toujours l'oppression. Pourtant, pendant les dernières décennies de nouveaux accents occupent le devant de la scène: à côté de la résignation devant la misère et la pauvreté, il apparaît de plus en plus de signes de plainte, de protestation contre la violation des droits de l'homme, de banderoles figurant des prisonniers disparus ... et l'on ose peindre des visages contemporains comme des 'Pilates serviles' laissant passer sous silence ce cortège, et qui n'oseront éventuellement plus exercer une nouvelle répression.[12] Ainsi, l'on obtient un chemin de croix de l'espoir, un signe *sub contrario* où transparaît l'espérance de la libération, avec en toile de fond l'image de la souffrance. C'est une évocation de l'utopie, qui n'a toujours pas atteint le statut de réalité.

2.3. Revirement dans l'expérience et l'interprétation de la religiosité populaire

Le peuple pauvre, qui autrefois faisait l'objet d'une évangélisation, devient lui-même porteur de l'évangélisation. Les premiers habitants deviennent les sujets de l'évangélisation, et ils délivrent un message au monde sécularisé. Ce revirement dans l'expérience et l'interprétation de la religiosité populaire, qui selon Gustavo Gutierrez doit être situé entre les années 60 et 70, et grâce auquel les pauvres acquièrent une place au sein de l'église en tant que sujets d'évangélisation, est précisément la période où s'annonce dans le monde occidental la dite postmodernité. Selon l'idée de Mariano Puga (Santiago, Chili) une dimension nouvelle s'instaure petit à petit dans les expressions de la piété, des dévotions et des processions, qui va plus loin que la résignation et le fatalisme. En fin de compte, ce revirement est le fruit d'un processus de prise de conscience, où l'émancipation des 'pauvres' se constitue. Le fait que l'engagement de tant de personnes, des évêques, des prêtres, des religieux et des laïcs, qui soutenaient les pauvres, a été confirmé jusqu'au bout par un martyre, est enfin couronné de succès. Selon Mariano Puga ce continent se réveille maintenant et commence à découvrir la dimension pascale, libératrice de la foi. "On commence à remplacer les symboles de la mort, de la résignation, du fatalisme (Dieu le veut) de cette foi, ou à les compléter de symboles de la vie, de l'homme nouveau, du pays nouveau,

---

12. Mariano PUGA, "La mémoire collective dans la liturgie des communautés de base d'Amérique latine", dans *Concilium* 259 (1995) 91-99.

du peuple eschatologique. La dimension sociale et politique de la foi commence à doter les projets révolutionnaires de l'époque d'une dimension transcendante. L'expérience de la communauté et de la collectivité commence à donner une nouvelle dimension à la religiosité individualiste et fataliste".[13] Mariano Puga, qui, après ses études à l'Institut Supérieur de Liturgie et son travail dans la paroisse universitaire de Santa Ana à Santiago, suit les communautés de base chrétiennes dans les quartiers populaires marginaux depuis vingt ans maintenant, est un témoin fiable du revirement dans l'expérience de la religiosité populaire. C'est avec raison qu'il remarque que la reconnaissance officielle et l'approbation de la religiosité populaire par la conférence épiscopale dans les documents de Medellín (1968) et de Puebla (1979) sont en fait seulement une confirmation de ce qui bénéficiait déjà d'une présence latente et de ce qui s'affirme un peu plus maintenant. C'est l'expérience de tant de théologiens et de prêtres, également lors de la conférence de Santo Domingo (1992), que parfois l'église officielle continue à éprouver des difficultés à apprécier les développements concrets à leur juste valeur, et à les conduire.[14] Cependant, il y a également des signes prometteurs annonçant que le clivage entre d'une part l'église officielle, hiérarchique avec sa liturgie, et, d'autre part, la liturgie et la religiosité populaires avec ses expressions diverses, ne s'élargit pas, mais, au contraire, qu'il se réduit. L'inspiration de l'évêque-martyr Oscar Arnulfo Romero du Salvador, dont le proverbe 'Gloria Dei, vivens pauper', inspiré sans doute par le Saint-Esprit, est une continuation des paroles d'Irénée: 'Gloria Dei, vivens homo', restera une gageure pour tous les responsables de la communauté des fidèles.[15]

Comme exemples de cette liturgie populaire 'style nouveau', Mariano Puga signale, outre les chemins de croix mentionnés, les célébrations eucharistiques comme remémoration dangereuse de la mort à la croix du Christ et de sa résurrection (qui ne penserait pas à J.B. Metz), les formes collectives de jeûne et de veillée, les mouvements de non-violence, les veillées illuminées, les cordons autour des quartiers où il y a eu violation de domicile, les collectes devant les maisons de prisonniers, l'arrêt des métros et de la circulation, des manifestations devant les palais de justice et des ministères... Puga est convaincu que l'appel à l'inculturation de la liturgie, lancé lors de la conférence de Santo Domingo, (1992, n° 43 et 248) est très urgent, car la liturgie de la population opprimée, qui a ses propres symboles, est en fait un enrichissement pour l'église. Si l'église

---

13. *Ibid.*

14. Voir José Oscar BEOZZO, *A Igrega do Brasil. De Joâo XXIII a Joâo Paulo II, de Medellín a Santo Domingo*, Petrópolis, 1994.

15. PUGA, *a.c.*, 94.

officielle n'intégrait pas cette liturgie, le peuple continuerait à la réaliser "dans l'extra-muros de la religiosité populaire".[16] Mariano Puga est d'avis que le fait que l'église hiérarchique reconnaît cette liturgie est d'importance primordiale pour éviter que "l'option préférentiel en faveur des pauvres" ne se réduise à une affirmation creuse.

3. Interprétation de la religiosité populaire dans un contexte postmoderne

Comme cadre interprétatif de ces développements dans l'expérience de la religiosité populaire, l'approche postmoderne peut être utile.

Lors du congrès CEHILA à Sâo Paulo en 1995, la majorité du groupe réuni autour du thème de la religiosité populaire était d'avis qu'une intégration de certaines formes de la religiosité populaire culturelle est impossible: ces formes ne peuvent exister qu'à côté des autres. Porte-parole de ce courant est le théologien bolivien Diego Irarrazaval qui opte pour un modèle de symbiose, plutôt que pour un modèle de synthèse ou de syncrétisme. Il vaut mieux que ne s'effectue pas un enchevêtrement de pratiques religieuses d'origine diverse: qu'elles coexistent, en même temps, simultanément, l'une à côté de l'autre. Irarrazaval pense à un paysage religieux biculturel, ou éventuellement triculturel, et où les tentatives d'inculturation du message chrétien n'auront (peu ou) pas (l'ombre d') une chance. Selon ce modèle, il est clair que la religion catholique reçoit un caractère particulier: c'est une religion "circonscrite" par les autres, définie au milieu des autres.

Le théologien brésilien Roberto Matta (Recife) considère qu'une intégration à la religion populaire afro-américaine est impossible. Dans les formes d'expression des Candomblé par exemple (Salvador de Bahia) ne s'ouvre finalement pas une perspective de libération: c'est une religion d'esclaves qui ne produit pas de véritable libération. Certes, il y a là une expérience mystique établissant une relation entre l'individu et les éléments de la création (la terre, l'eau) – qui, selon une conception animiste, sont personnifiés en dieux et déesses –, et provoquant une fusion avec les forces primitives par le biais de la transe. Or, la perspective eschatologique, fondamentalement liée au message catholique, manque dans ces formes d'expression. De même, les rites des Macumba (Rio de Janeiro) ne font qu'affirmer la simple mystique du sacrifice sans qu'il y ait possibilité de libération. En guise d'exemple, on peut se référer aux ingénieurs agricoles de l'université de Rio, dotés d'un développement intellectuel éminent, mais qui font pourtant toujours des sacrifices aux dieux de la rivière, dans l'espoir de réussir leurs techniques.

16. *Ibid.*, 98-99.

Peut-on se contenter du modèle de symbiose? Les théologiens de la liberation postmodernes continuent à réfléchir à la revalorisation de certains facteurs de la religion populaire comme voies d'accès vers le transcendantal et le sacré. À cet effet, il faut se distancier du paradigme de l'oppression.

Laënnec Hourbon (le Haïti, les Caraïbes) rejette ce paradigme du passé où la religiosité des esclaves noirs était méconnue. Dans cette religiosité (le Vudu, par exemple) on met surtout l'accent sur le culte de la mort et de l'oppression: en évoquant des esprits, on veut représenter le passé marqué par la souffrance. Dans le temps, l'église (coloniale) a expliqué la souffrance du peuple noir comme une punition de la rébellion, et cette attitude est toujours présente dans la religiosité populaire: les vestiges en sont le fatalisme, la résignation devant la souffrance. C'est une caractéristique typique qu'Eddy Stols, dans sa description de l'âme brésilienne, désigne d'une manière significative par le terme de "soulagement de la religiosité"; terme qui rappelle le sentiment mélancolique de la *saudade*.[17] C'est une hypothèse explicative qui s'inspire de la 'modernidad', de la modernité. Dans son compte rendu de cet ouvrage intéressant d'Eddy Stols, Johan Konings, s.j. (Belo Horizonte), fait observer que d'autres explications, plus fondamentales encore, subsistent.[18] L'ancien paradigme est intégré à un horizon plus large, où le rôle que jouent les communautés de base et la lutte pour la justice sociale corrigent une interprétation trop simpliste. Selon cette interprétation plus récente, le respect de la particularité et de la dignité des cultures et traditions noires et indiennes est présent, et, toujours selon cette interprétation, la domination de la culture blanche est condamnée à juste titre. L'inspiration du concile de Vatican II a également incité à une tentative d'intégration et d'inculturation, dont les résultats sont toujours peu visibles pourtant. En effet, on en reste à une évaluation péjorative de toutes les formes de syncrétisme.

De nouveaux paradigmes

1. Fransisco Taborda, s.j. (Belo Horizonte), a dans sa théologie un bon élan vers l'intégration d'une partie de la culture indienne: comme chaînon entre les formes fatalistes de la religion populaire (la résignation) et la lutte pour la justice sociale, il développe une sacramentologie basée sur la catégorie centrale de la fête, de la *fiesta*. Il cimente ses idées à l'aide d'une solide philosophie de l'expérience du temps: le *chronos* est

---

17. Eddy STOLS, *Brazilië. Vijf eeuwen geschiedenis in dribbelpas*, Leuven-Amersfoort, 1996, 431-448.
18. *Streven* (1997) 760-761.

interrompu à des moments déterminés par le *kairos*: échapper à la vie opprimante dans le chaos, grâce à la distanciation que permet la danse. La manière dont le Brésilien (pauvre) fête le carnaval, comble une dimension qui échappe à l'observation de l'Occidental réaliste. Dans cette expérience de la fête, dynamisée par le *kairos*, des couches plus profondes de la religiosité se font jour et ici encore il est possible de scander le message spécifiquement chrétien sur le rythme des fêtes religieuses et d'en imbiber les 'rites de passage'.[19]

2. De même, Orlando Espin (San Diego) donne, dans son analyse de la survie de la religiosité populaire hispanique dans la culture nord-américaine, une appréciation positive et n'exclut pas l'intégration. La moitié des catholiques aux États-Unis consiste en ces Américains d'origine hispanique. Espin s'appuie sur la donnée que ces vieilles traditions contiennent une 'faith-full intuition', un riche contenu de foi (plein de foi) qui exprime le *sensus fidelium*. C'est la foi du peuple. Le cadre interprétatif que choisit Espin – dans une inspiration postmoderne – est une théologie sapientale, une théologie pas uniquement rationelle (modernité). Dans une herméneutique sapientale, la sagesse qu'ont héritée les fidèles peut être ramenée à la surface. Cette herméneutique s'exécute par le biais de trois confrontations: 1. la confrontation à la parole biblique; 2. la confrontation aux textes écrits de la tradition; 3. la confrontation à la culture historique. Espin considère une attitude de foi relayée par la culture comme solution de rechange possible pour la symbiose. Une telle expérience religieuse qui s'enracine dans la propre culture est plus concrète et plus réaliste qu'un système de symboles et de vérités imposé. Selon le point de vue d'Espin, il est évident que l'église prend une option préférentielle pour les pauvres. Or, Espin inverse les pôles de cette affirmation: "combien de temps encore pourra-t-on dire que les pauvres garderont une option préférentielle pour l'église?". Il n'est pas improbable que les pauvres tournent le dos à l'église et qu'il ne s'intéressent plus à la liturgie officielle et à l'église hiérarchique. Les actions de diverses sectes, des Pentecostals par exemple, qui promettent également du support matériel aux pauvres, constituent une sérieuse menace à l'égard de l'église catholique.[20]

3. Comme troisième modèle d'un nouveau paradigme, c'est la théologie

---

19. Voir Francisco TABORDA, *Sakramente: Praxis und Fest*, Düsseldorf, 1988.

20. Voir Orlando O. ESPIN, *The Faith of the People: Theological Reflections on Popular Catholicism*, Maryknoll, N. Y., 1997.

du jésuïte argentin Juan Carlos Scannone qui entre en ligne de compte.[21] Scannone a étudié à Innsbruck, e.a. sous la direction de Rahner, et a analysé les phénomènes religieux selon le canevas de la théorie du symbole et de l'herméneutique de Paul Ricoeur. Ainsi, la pensée occidentale contribue à l'interprétation de la situation latino-américaine. La période de la chrétienté (la 'christianidad') est définitivement passée. Le concile de Vatican II a reconnu l'autonomie du monde et la spécificité des différentes cultures. Il est possible d'y voir un phénomène typique de la modernité. Il n'y a aucune occurrence du mot 'religion populaire' dans les documents du concile. Dans les développements propres au continent latino-américain, surtout depuis Puebla (1979) où la religiosité populaire a reçu une appréciation positive, Scannone a consacré le langage poético-symbolique de la sagesse populaire et les expériences de la religiosité populaire comme *locus theologicus* doté d'une indéniable rationalité que le théologien doit ramener à la surface. Aussi, Erik De Vreese qualifie-t-il le point de vue de Scannone comme suit: "la religion populaire comme partenaire du théologien". La sagesse de la religion populaire n'y est pas présentée en tant que *semina Verbi*, germes de la parole de la révélation – telle était l'expression de l'ancienne missiologie – mais elle apparaît comme *fructus Verbi*, fruit bien mûr provenant de l'ancienne évangélisation. Afin d'interpréter cette sagesse, il y a quatre attitudes possibles: 1. l'attitude tradionaliste, qui tolère une dévotion populaire occasionnelle, d'une part en sa fonction d'arme idéologique au service des régimes coloniaux et dictatoriaux, et, de l'autre, en tant qu'instrument dans la lutte contre les sectes protestantes, ce qui va dans le sens de ce qu'Enrique Dussel a dit à propos de la manipulation populiste de la religiosité populaire; 2. l'attitude progressiste, typique de la modernité, qui oppose la religion populaire comme une foi passive, rituelle, à l'engagement socio-éthique, et qui, partant, devra être soumise à un processus d'épuration intellectualiste; – les exemples que mentionne Scannone sont e.a. Juan Luis Segundo († 1996, l'aile uruguayenne de la théologie de la libération) et Segundo Galilea –; 3. l'attitude des théologiens de la libération dits 'authentiques', qui réagissent contre les inclinations élitaristes des progressistes; selon leur approche, le peuple devient, en tant que sujet collectif, porteur des valeurs qui lui sont propres dans la culture; toutefois, Scannone leur reproche une conscience

---

21. Nous suivons ici la description du point de vue de Scannone par Erik DE VREESE, "Volksreligie als partner van de theoloog", dans *Intersectiones* (1995) n° 2, 2-14. Erik Devreese prépare une thèse de doctorat sur Scannone dans le 'Centrum voor Bevrijdingstheologie' à la Katholieke Universiteit Leuven. Parmi les nombreuses publications de Scannone, nous ne mentionnons que *Weisheit und Befreiung: Volkstheologie in Lateinamerika*, Düsseldorf, 1992.

trop ahistorique, trop mythique, qui perpétue la résignation fataliste dont nous avons déjà parlé plus haut; 4. l'attitude de Scannone, qui est devenue 'l'école argentine' au sein de la théologie de la libération, et suivant laquelle Scannone plaide pour une approche historico-culturelle de la religion populaire; ceci signifie aussi que les situations intolérables de tout ordre, aussi bien socio-économiques que culturelles, sont considérées comme des excroissances de la crise de la modernité et de sa foi en la validité universelle de la rationalité technique, c'est le discrédit de l'ethos moderne, qui, selon Heidegger, est imbibé de l'obsession du pouvoir.[22] L'appréhension exacte de la religiosité populaire refuse les excroissances idéologiques du marxisme, ainsi que du libéralisme, à travers le chérissement d'une nouvelle conscience historique de la dignité du peuple; et c'est précisément dans son analyse de la spécificité du peuple latino-américain que Scannone reconnaît, outre les valeurs de l'unité et de la fraternité, la tendance à s'ouvrir au transcendantal, selon lui inhérente au centre même de l'ethos culturel. Ainsi, il opte pour un paradigme de l'humanisme social qui ne reste pas fermé à la réalité transcendante: il traite la religion non pas comme une donnée culturelle à part entière, mais, avec la culture en toile de fond historique, comme sens ultime qui traverse la pratique culturelle totale. Dans ce contexte Scannone se réfère au paradigme de Chalcedon: la religion et la culture en Amérique latine, quoique différentes, ne sont pas distinctes.[23] Avec la religiosité populaire comme *locus theologicus*, on pourrait atteindre à une véritable 'théologie du peuple' axée sur une communauté située de manière historico-culturelle. Par rapport à ce point de vue de Scannone, Devreese a soulevé à juste titre la question de savoir si l'unité entre la culture et la religion n'est pas posée trop facilement. Il formule cette remarque en se référant au substrat catholique issu de l'évangélisation originelle, fondatrice, auquel le pape Jean-Paul II a fait appel à Santo Domingo, et récemment encore: la théologie du peuple est dotée d'un instinct évangélique, d'un flair prérationnel des valeurs chrétiennes, qui sont en fait également le résultat des traditions transmises. Quoique Scannone qualifie l'unité de la culture et de la religion en Amérique latine de 'pluraliste' et d''analogue', l'accent est mis pourtant sur cette même unité. Non sans raison Devreese pose ici la question de savoir si l'unité survivra, étant donné l'urbanisation qui prend de plus en plus d'ampleur et la sécularisation qui s'ensuit.[24] Ainsi, nous reprendrons dans nos considérations finales les modèles interprétatifs occidentaux qui rendent compte de la sécularisation au sein de la postmodernité.

---

22. DE VREESE, *a.c.*, 8-9.
23. *Ibid.*, 11.
24. *Ibid.*, 13-14.

4. Réflexions finales: la tension entre la symbiose et l'intégration, la tâche de l'inculturation

Il reste donc une grande tension entre la symbiose et l'intégration. Dans la recherche de nouveaux paradigmes, le schéma interprétatif de Paul Post, qui contient trois cercles roulants ou agglomérats fonctionnels qui s'enchevêtrent partiellement, (culturellement - rituellement - culturellement), peut être un instrument utile.[25] Nous avons présenté ce schéma lors du congrès de Sâo Paulo en 1995 et il a 'accusé' une bonne 'réception' en tant qu'approche occidentale, rationnelle du phénomène de la religiosité populaire, qui différencie de façon compétente les différents agglomérats: ce qui provient de la culture traditionnelle (le cercle à droite), ce qui appartient à l'amosphère spécifiquement culturelle (le cercle à gauche), et, en sa qualité de médium entre les deux, l'agglomérat rituel, le besoin de l'expression religieuse via des symboles et rituels universels, qui suivent les trames des expériences humaines. Ceci peut être constaté dans toutes les grandes religions et leurs rituels de la vie respectifs, et où les façonnements typiquement chrétiens constituent des expressions particulières au sein de ce champ plus large. Le schéma peut toujours être appliqué afin de faire une distinction, selon l'approche rationnelle de l'Occident, entre les fonctions religieuses primaires et les formes traditionnelles déterminées par la culture, et dans le but de décider finalement quelle est la part de cette foi épurée, émancipatrice de la société sécularisée, qui serait en état de survivre comme liturgie. Selon ce schéma, le paradigme de la fête, la *fiesta*, acquiert valeur suffisamment probante pour interpréter le phénomène de la religiosité populaire dans le contexte postmoderne.

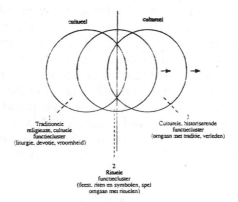

25. Paul POST, "Volksreligieuze rituelen tussen cultus en cultuur", dans M. VAN UDEN - J. PIEPER (réd.), *Bedevaart als volksreligieus ritueel* (UTP-Teksten 16), Heerlen, 1991, 47-76.

1. Agglomérat fonctionnel traditionnel, religieux, culturel (la liturgie, la dévotion, la piété)
2. Agglomérat fonctionnel rituel (la fête, les rites et les symboles, le jeu, l'appréhension des rituels)
3. Agglomérat fonctionnel culturel, historisant (l'appréhension de la tradition, du passé)

Un deuxième schéma interprétatif intéressant se trouve dans la sacramentologie postmoderne de Louis-Marie Chauvet, où celui-ci défend l'évangélisation des 'rites de passage' transmis.[26] En réalité, beaucoup d'éléments de la religiosité populaire ont pour fonction de réaliser l'intégration dans un groupe social et de reproduire un système de valeurs culturel. Les dogmes de la foi proprement dits ne sont pas toujours vécus de façon consciente. Chauvet opte pour une pastorale de l'accueil qui peut mener les fidèles d'une part à une confrontation avec le message de l'Évangile, et, de l'autre, à une conversion plus profonde. Il signale la tension paradoxale qui existe entre les deux pôles de la foi: le pôle 'attestataire' et le pôle 'contestataire'. Au pôle de l'attestataire appartient le fait de reconnaître les pratiques de la religion populaire comme des actes qui font partie d'un héritage socio-culturel, d'une tradition historique et d'un milieu d'identification spécifique. Par contre, une intériorisation personnelle de la foi, une entrée consciente dans le mystère du Christ et le fait de définir l'identité en fonction de l'appartenance à une communauté de l'Église qui reste ouverte à l'universalité du Royaume de Dieu, rejoignent le pôle du 'contestataire'. Si l'on privilégie trop l'aspect 'attestataire', la foi sera réduite à un héritage culturel, l'église à un dispositif religieux et la chrétienté à une forme de la civilisation. En revanche, si l'on favorise trop l'aspect 'contestataire', les indispensables points d'appui culurels, sociaux et institutionnels pourraient être compromis, et, ainsi, on pourrait tomber sous l'emprise de l'illusion d'une foi 'pure', qui n'existe que dans l'imaginaire. La foi est toujours incrustée dans une culture donnée. Le 'contestataire' indique une distinction à faire entre la foi et la superstition. Chauvet plaide ainsi pour une confrontation avec le message évangélique.[27] Voilà aussi la tâche de

---

26. Louis-Marie Chauvet, *Les sacrements. Parole de Dieu au risque du corps*, Paris, 1993, 189-216. Nous avons appliqué ses idées à la demande du baptême pour enfants: voir Lambert LEIJSSEN, "Sacramentologische reflectie op het kinderdoopsel" dans ID., M. CLOET, K. DOBBELAERE (réd.), *Levensrituelen. Geboorte en Doopsel*, (Kadoc-Studies 20), Leuven, 1996, 261-277, p. 274-276.

27. Voir aussi, dans le contexte de la pastorale des jeunes, le plaidoyer pour un rapport véritablement analogique entre la foi et la culture, à réaliser via une approche plus contrastive de la culture inspirée par la foi, in Stijn VAN DEN BOSSCHE, "Youth, Liturgy and

l'église au niveau du catéchuménat.

Les rituels et pratiques transmis doivent être convertis de l'intérieur par la promulgation de la Parole évangélique et par l'accomplissement intérieur du rite, ce qui implique un mode de vie éthique. Dans la sacramentologie postmoderne l'aspect de la contestation et de la protestation contre le mode de vie profane courant se met à l'avant plus qu'autrefois. Le rite se profile alors comme un signe du témoignage, de la confrontation et de l'engagement. C'est un moment du 'kairos', une interruption du 'chronos', à travers lesquels le récit ouvert du Seigneur ressuscité, par la prédication et le témoignage, appelle à l'homme de nos jours, le convoque aussi.

Dans l'approche postmoderne le choix personnel est respecté, mais ne doit pas nécessairement aboutir à une forme de liberté narcissique, individualiste; au contraire, ainsi la voie pourrait être ouverte à la conscience commune d'appartenir à une tradition plus large, quoique toujours particulière, qui a permis à la foi de se développer sans quitter les traces de la culture. Toutefois, il faut veiller à marquer la frontière entre d'une part une saine conscience de la particularité et, de l'autre, les excroissances de l'absolutisme particularisant (le nationalisme et l'ethnicisme). Une autre borne est celle du fondamentalisme et de l'interprétation magique du rituel, qui, suivant l'esprit capitaliste ou la manipulation populiste, souligne le dia-bolique, la dissociation qu'exprimerait le sacrement, plutôt que l'aspect sym-bolique du sacrement, sa force unificatrice, qui signifie l'unification de la culture et de la religiosité, la redécouverte de la dimension transcendante de l'existence.[28]

Nous sommes issus de la modernité, de la pensée des Lumières. Non sans la 'suspicion of reason', et après la déconstruction des grands systèmes et des grands récits, beaucoup reste à être 'pensé', afin de donner à l'homme qui croit, à l'homme croyant actuel, une identité construite au sein du réseau des symboles, et façonnée par la pluralité des conceptions de la vie dans la postmodernité actuelle.

(Traduction: Geert Missotten, K.U. Leuven)

Postmodernity" dans le présent volume.

28. Sur le diabolique et le symbolique dans le sacrement, voir Leonardo BOFF, *Sacramenteel denken en leven*, Averbode, 1983, 85-91.

Effacement ou relégitimation
de la religion populaire

Liliane VOYÉ

Utiliser les termes d'effacement ou de relégitimation pour parler de la situation actuelle de la religion populaire n'évoque pas, à notre avis, de façon tout à fait adéquate la situation de celle-ci en ce qui concerne aujourd'hui, en Europe, les pratiques reprises sous cette expression et qui sont, à des degrés divers, essentiellement associées au catholicisme. Qu'en est-il en effet de celles-ci?

Tout d'abord, il convient de rappeler que, durant les années soixante et septante, il y a effectivement eu, de la part de l'institution ecclésiale, un projet d'effacement, d'éradication plus ou moins profonde de la religion populaire. Dans la mouvance du désir ambiant de rationalité qui touchait tous les domaines, il s'agissait de 'purifier' le religieux de ses aspects profanes et de ses connotations magiques. Ainsi à l'époque a-t-on vu les églises se dépouiller de nombre de statues de saints au bénéfice d'une recentration sur les images de Dieu – geste qui voulait signifier l'essence monothéiste du catholicisme et vider celui-ci des relents polythéistes qu'y voyait Max Weber[1] (1971). En même temps, la 'communion solennelle' s'est vu rebaptisée du nom de 'profession de foi'; loin d'être anodin ce changement d'appellation prétendait mettre l'accent sur l'adhésion intellectuelle volontaire et explicite et évacuer les dimensions festives et profanes – banquet, cadeaux, vêtements luxueux – perçues à ce moment comme détournant du sens réel et profond du rite. C'est aussi à la même époque que des pratiques telles que les bénédictions – des maisons, voitures, animaux, ... –, les pèlerinages, les processions, ... furent soit radicalement abolies, soit entachées d'illégitimité; souvent dès lors, ceux qui voulaient y recourir ne trouvaient pas de ministre disposé à répondre à leurs demandes. Cette dénonciation des pratiques de religion populaire qui s'inscrivait de la sorte dans la ligne d'une virulente prétention à la rationalité, se voyait en outre fortifiée par l'incidence d'une autre caractéristique de cette période: celle qui, sous l'influence du marxisme, voyait nos sociétés traversées par le conflit de deux classes, fondamentalement antagonistes et entre lesquelles il s'agissait de prendre clairement position. Cette vision n'a pas manqué

---

1. M. WEBER, *Économie et société*, Paris, Éd. Plon, 1971.

elle non plus de marquer profondément l'Église catholique dans des pays comme le nôtre: il s'agissait en effet de 'politiser' celle-ci ou, plus exactement, de la contre-politiser dans la mesure où elle avait été jusque là, malgré de remarquables exceptions – Mgr Cardijn ou l'abbé Daens – essentiellement associée à la bourgeoisie. Ainsi apparurent les prêtres ouvriers ou encore des initiatives telle celle du 'groupe de Blankenberge', qui durant tout un temps rassemblait chaque année en ce lieu des prêtres, des religieux et des laïcs soucieux de réorienter la pastorale vers un agir social intramondain, au service des hommes exploités. Ce type de projet semblait lui aussi mal s'accommoder d'une religion populaire vue à la fois comme centrée sur soi et égoïste, comme totalement éloignée des questions sociales et comme recourant volontiers à l'argent et à ses usages pour 'négocier' avec Dieu protection et grâces. Si l'acteur institutionnel du champ religieux, comme celui de tous les autres champs, fut ainsi influencé par la conjonction de ces deux visées – rationaliser et politiser – et conduit par là à déprécier fortement les diverses formes de religion populaire, il n'en alla pas nécessairement de même du côté des 'fidèles', de la 'base': nombreux restèrent ceux qui souhaitaient continuer à recourir à celles-ci mais ils ne pouvaient bien souvent le faire que de façon cachée, honteuse et sans d'ailleurs toujours trouver un répondant à leurs demandes, de nombreux prêtres se refusant alors à se compromettre dans de telles pratiques. On peut donc dire que s'il y a eu à un moment donné une tendance à l'effacement institutionnel de la religion populaire, celle-ci n'a jamais été abolie dans les pratiques de très nombreuses personnes qui, malgré la stigmatisation dont elles risquaient d'être l'objet, ont toujours persisté à y recourir.

Pas plus que l'on ne peut ainsi pleinement parler d'un effacement, on ne peut davantage aujourd'hui évoquer sans nuance l'idée d'une relégitimation de la religion populaire. Certes, il est correct de dire que celle-ci n'est plus aujourd'hui victime de l'ostracisme qui, tout un temps, parut vouloir l'extirper. Nombre de ses formes bénéficient à nouveau d'une évaluation positive, le pape étant sans doute le premier à contribuer à ce changement, notamment en insistant sur le culte de la Vierge et des Saints – dont il accroît d'ailleurs très rapidement le nombre! – et en témoignant d'un souci particulier pour les pèlerinages et pour les grands rassemblements festifs. Cette relégitimation de fait par l'autorité suprême de l'Église n'apparaît cependant pas déterminante, à un moment où, même lorsqu'elle se dit explicitement catholique, la population est aujourd'hui largement caractérisée par un déclin du croire institutionnel: soucieuse de son autonomie à l'égard de toute autorité, elle ne se soucie guère de l'avis de celle-ci, en ce domaine comme en tout autre, et son recours à des pratiques de religion populaire ne dépend pas de la légitimité dont cette autorité les qualifie ou les prive. Dès lors, même si l'on assiste à une certaine relégitimation de la religion populaire par l'autorité institutionnelle de l'Église, ce n'est pas à cela qu'il faut significativement attribuer la vitalité qui caractérise aujourd'hui ces pratiques. Car vitalité il y a bel et bien et nous allons tenter d'en comprendre les raisons. Mais auparavant, il convient sans doute de préciser ce que nous entendons par religion populaire.

1. Des composantes de la religion populaire

Nous avons déjà évoqué les pratiques concrètes qui constituent celle-ci: les bénédictions – de personnes, d'animaux, de lieux, d'objets, d'activités –, les pèlerinages, le port de médailles, le culte des Saints et celui de la Vierge dans ses versions diverses, 'localisées et spécialisées', la vénération d'objets ou d'images les représentant … en constituent les modalités les plus courantes. Au-delà de la diversité des formes matérielles qu'elle revêt, la religion populaire présente un certain nombre de traits qui en font la spécificité.

Le premier d'entre ceux-ci consiste sans doute dans le fait qu'elle ne repose pas sur un corpus élaboré de règles écrites et consignées, cautionnées comme telles par l'autorité religieuse. Sans être exclues, de telles règles ne sont aucunement centrales pour le 'pratiquant', pas plus que ne l'est la caution de l'institution. Certes, celle-ci y apporte souvent la légitimité que donnent la durée et la confirmation de la relation avec la transcendance mais elle n'est pas obligatoirement comme telle à la genèse de ces pratiques, dont elle n'a en outre pas nécessairement le contrôle et qui peuvent se développer avant et en dehors de toute reconnaissance officielle, voire en dépit de l'absence de celle-ci. Ce sont bien souvent les 'pratiquants' eux-mêmes qui, par leur pratique même, en élaborent les détails, les reproduisent ou les transforment.

Autre caractéristique significative de la religion populaire: elle ne donne pas priorité à la parole intelligible ou au discours construit. Certes, elle n'exclut pas la parole mais lorsque celle-ci est présente, ce n'est pas la cohérence intellectuelle du message qui importe: la parole tire davantage sa valeur de ce qu'elle accompagne le 'faire', avec redondance et rythme, prenant souvent la forme d'incantations répétitives, voire de glossolalies. Ceci ne va pas sans troubler le logocentrisme occidental, exacerbé par le rationalisme positiviste au point de confondre verbal et langage et d'oublier ou de refuser d'admettre, que le geste est en lui-même langage et que, comme le souligne Jousse "le sens se grave dans le corps, charnier de signes"[2]. Les gestes inhérents à la religion populaire viennent de la sorte rappeler qu'il n'y a pas dichotomie radicale entre le dire et le faire: le langage est de

2. M. JOUSSE, *Anthropologie du geste*, Paris, Éd. Gallimard, 1974.

nature corporelle et la pratique corporelle est de nature discursive. Nous y reviendrons

Ne requérant ainsi ni règles définies par l'autorité, ni parole intelligible – sans toutefois les exclure – les pratiques de religion populaire supposent par contre souvent une certaine référence à la nature: l'aubépine de Beauraing, la grotte de Lourdes, ... mais surtout l'eau, que l'on retrouve fréquemment dans les ablutions, les aspersions et les absorptions. La nature se voit ainsi utilisée dans une des deux significations qu'elle revêt dans toute culture: celle qui l'associe à la pureté, à la vérité mais aussi à la non-maîtrise par l'homme et, par là, à des forces qui lui échappent et qu'il s'agit dès lors de tenter de se concilier.

La nature ainsi présente contribue par ailleurs à un autre trait de la religion populaire: l'esthétique. Certes, celle qui accompagne celle-ci ne répond pas nécessairement aux canons des académies, ni même aux critères distinctifs du 'bon goût'. Il n'empêche: ces pratiques requièrent en général une sorte de 'mise en scène' – architecture, décor, fleurs, musique, ... – qui contribue à les démarquer des gestes quotidiens, même lorsqu'elles en empruntent les formes. Cette dimension esthétique se retrouve également dans la fête qui parfois accompagne diverses pratiques de religion populaire. La fête – celle des grands rassemblements en particulier – suppose – par définition pourrait-on dire – une 'mise en scène' qui sorte du quotidien et qui fasse sentir l'existence d'un autre temps, d'un autre lieu, d'une autre réalité[3]. En effet, loin qu'il ne faille voir dans ces aspects esthétiques "une inutile concession aux valeurs de ce monde"[4] il s'agit en quelque sorte d'y lire le projet de les extraire du monde profane pour manifester la qualité sacrée de leur destinataire et pour leur donner, si ténue soit-elle, une portée métaphysique. Car, même lorsque – comme c'est le plus souvent le cas – elles sont centrées sur l'existentiel (recouvrement de la santé, obtention d'un emploi, protection contre les accidents, harmonie familiale, ...), ces pratiques et ces fêtes tendent à exprimer tout à la fois une peur, une angoisse, une souffrance face à des situations difficiles de la vie quotidienne et la mise en doute de la capacité des instances profanes – en particulier la science médicale – de résoudre ces problèmes.

Cet accent mis sur l'esthétique et sur la fête par la religion populaire souligne par ailleurs combien celle-ci est volontiers en connivence avec le matériel et le ludique. Elle suppose en effet très souvent l'acquisition,

---

3. A. VILLADARY, *Fête et vie quotidienne*, Paris, Éd. Ouvrières, 1968.
4. J.P. ALBERT, 'Les belles du Seigneur', dans: *Communications*, EHESS, Beauté, Laideur, Éd. Du Seuil, n° 60, 63-74, p. 73.

le port, l'exposition d'objets divers: médailles, images, statues, … Ses pratiques s'accompagnent aussi fréquemment d'intervalles gastronomiques et leur régulière association actuelle avec des activités touristiques en fait souvent l'étape d'un itinéraire au long duquel elles côtoient visites de châteaux, de musées ou de sites naturels (le cirque de Gavarnie à Lourdes), shopping divers, activités sportives et culturelles ou même parfois gueuletons et beuveries. Si d'aucuns sont tentés de voir dans cette mixité du profane et du sacré une condamnable altération de ce dernier, il nous paraît qu'une hypothèse au moins aussi valable peut être avancée: celle qui détecte là une affirmation de la totalité de l'homme – corps, esprit, âme – et un refus d'en dissocier artificiellement ou idéologiquement les composantes.

Mais plus encore peut-être que ces différents aspects, ce qui caractérise avant tout la religion populaire, c'est qu'elle requiert des gestes. En général, elle suppose en effet une implication plus ou moins complexe du corps, dans sa motricité et dans ses dimensions sensorielles. Mouvements et gestes, marche et démarche en sont des composantes importantes, tout comme l'est aussi la mise en oeuvre de divers sens: le toucher, qui creuse la colonne centrale du portail de gloire de Saint-Jacques-de-Compostelle, patine les marbres et les bronzes des statues et en décolore les stucs peints; l'ouïe, qu'émeuvent chants, musique et incantations psalmodiées; la vue où se grave l'image du lieu, du Saint, des cérémonies, des participants et que, parfois, la carte postale, le 'souvenir' ou la photo perpétue ou rappelle; l'odorat, qui inhale le parfum des fleurs, la senteur des bougies; et par son entremise, le goût qui en discerne les saveurs. La bougie précisément illustre bien l'importance de ces dimensions sensorielles dans la religion populaire. La recherche atteste en effet de la nette préférence pour la bougie de cire, dont les atouts ne se retrouvent pas dans la bougie électrique. Allumée mécaniquement et 'au hasard' par la pièce de monnaie insérée dans l'orifice de commande, celle-ci ne donne pas le sentiment qu'on l'a soi-même allumée, en la choisissant du regard et du toucher puis en déterminant son emplacement qui, si la chose est possible – et parfois en y forçant – la dispose de préférence au centre et face à la statue, à l'objet sacré, au lieu nodal de la dévotion. À la bougie électrique font en outre défaut le crépitement de la mèche qui s'embrase, l'hésitation irrégulière de la flamme qu'oriente le vent, la fumée et l'odeur qui contribuent à la réalité de la 'vraie' bougie. Ainsi que l'a souligné Castoriadis[5], tous les détails sont importants, aucun n'est superflu ni insignifiant dans le symbolique et ce, d'autant moins que "celui-ci comporte presque

---

5. C. CASTORIADIS, *L'institution imaginaire de la société*, Paris, Éd. Du Seuil, 1975, 159-230.

toujours une composante rationnelle-réelle: ce qui représente le réel ou ce qui est indispensable pour le penser ou pour l'agir[6]. C'est en ce sens que tous les 'détails' qui distinguent la 'vraie' bougie de son succédané électrique composent les conditions de la croyance en son efficacité symbolique et constituent une voie d'accès à l'intelligibilité de la relation que veut manifester ce geste. Thomas d'Aquin n'avait-il pas lui-même souligné que les hommes appréhendent l'intelligible par le sensible, chose que sont venues confirmer bien plus tard les avancées de l'anthropologie et de l'éthologie, lesquelles montrent de plus en plus clairement que le sens se grave dans le corps.

À toutes ces caractéristiques, la religion populaire ajoute encore le fait qu'elle s'inscrit généralement dans un développement de don et de contredon: ainsi que la chose a été soulignée, ces pratiques sont en effet le plus souvent orientées vers une demande, ce qui conduit le demandeur à entrer dans une relation d'échange où il s'agit de donner – des prières, des fleurs, de l'argent, des ex-votos, des promesses, ... – pour recevoir ou pour remercier d'avoir reçu. Cette demande qui, très souvent, sous-tend les pratiques de religion populaire, concerne en toute priorité soi-même et ses proches – famille et amis – pour qui il s'agit de solliciter protection, rétablissement, amélioration d'une situation dégradrée ou encore réalisation d'une attente, d'un souhait ou d'une espérance. Ces pratiques s'inscrivent par là dans une perspective fortement marquée par l'émotionnel et l'affectif, par la relation aux autres proches. "Moi et les miens" sont en effet au coeur de ces pratiques qui prétendent en quelque sorte ainsi négocier avec Dieu: il s'agit d'une tentative visant à obtenir la protection des êtres auxquels on tient émotionnellement et des relations que l'on entretient avec eux, tentative d'autant plus requise qu'existe le sentiment de la fragilité de ces liens et de l'incertitude de leur avenir et de leur durée[7]. Ainsi se retrouvent diverses fonctions associées au rite: celle de communication et d'échange; celle aussi d'apprivoisement évoquée par Ariès[8]; celle enfin d'accompagnement de situations critiques face auxquelles ces pratiques apportent un sentiment de (re)mise en ordre potentielle et affirment la continuité. À ce propos toutefois, il est important d'apporter une précision. Dans une recherche réalisée auprès de jeunes hollandais, Janssen[9] montre que la prière de demande qui

6. *Ibid.*, 178.

7. L. VOYÉ, 'Religion populaire et pèlerinages en Europe', dans: *Marche vers la Splendeur. Ton Dieu marche avec toi.* Actes du Premier Congrès Mondial de la Pastorale des Sanctuaires et des Pèlerinages. Conseil Pontifical pour la Pastorale des Migrants et Itinérants, Rome, 1992.

8. Ph. ARIÈS, *L'homme devant la mort*, Paris, Éd. du Seuil, 1977.

9. J. JANSSEN e.a., 'A Content Analysis of Praying. Practices of Dutch Youth', dans *Journal for the Scientific Study of Religion* 29 (1990) 99-107.

accompagne nombre de pratiques de religion populaire est ambiguë: proche de la prière primitive en ce qu'elle est porteuse de l'attente d'une réponse à un problème concret – maladie, échec, chômage, ... –, elle se distingue toutefois de celle-ci dans la mesure où, en général, l'attente porte moins sur la résolution effective du problème que sur l'espoir de trouver dans le geste et dans la demande qui l'accompagne la force d'accepter la situation ou la capacité de la résoudre ou de la surmonter par soi-même. Ainsi, alors que, se soumettant à divers rites et priant pour la pluie, le primitif attend effectivement qu'il pleuve, l'homme 'moderne' chercherait le plus souvent dans ces pratiques une sorte de thérapie, de force morale d'acceptation ou de dépassement qui le poserait lui-même en acteur de son devenir.

Un dernier aspect doit encore être évoqué lorsque l'on parle de religion populaire ou, tout au moins, de certaines manifestations de celle-ci comme les pèlerinages ou le culte de la Vierge ou de certains saints. Ces pratiques revêtent en effet souvent un caractère polysémique. Nous avons déjà évoqué le fait qu'elles s'inscrivent souvent dans une logique de demande mais elles répondent parfois aussi à d'autres fonctions. Parmi celles-ci, retenons-en trois, plus ou moins fréquentes.

Tout d'abord, certaines de ces pratiques se veulent ressourcement de foi; tel peut par exemple être le cas de pèlerinages en Palestine ou à Rome: il s'agit alors d'aller au-delà du temps à la rencontre des acteurs et des événements fondateurs de sa religion dans les lieux historiques ayant vu l'origine et l'établissement de celle-ci. N'est-ce pas un tel ressourcement qu'attend l'autorité de l'Église catholique des grandes manifestations qu'elle prépare pour l'avènement du troisième millénaire? Si cette motivation ne sera pas celle de tous les pèlerins, on ne peut douter de ce que tel sera effectivement bien le cas de certains d'entre eux qui trouveront là une occasion exceptionnelle de "faire mémoire" et de réactiver leur sentiment d'appartenance.

Certaines pratiques de religion populaire revêtent parfois aussi le caractère d'une activité pénitentielle; il en va ainsi, par exemple, de certains dons ou encore de certains pèlerinages – et dans ces cas, il n'est pas rare d'associer à ces gestes un élément de sacrifice (se priver pour donner ou pour réaliser un voyage) ou de souffrance (avancer sur les genoux, marcher des heures durant, ...) à titre de compensation ou de 'paiement' pour 'racheter' la faute commise. Certes cette signification paraît en fort déclin, à la mesure de celui qui touche aujourd'hui le sentiment de culpabilité. On ne peut toutefois qu'être frappé par le fait que souvent, sur les lieux de pèlerinage, les confessionnaux sont nombreux et largement fréquentés – contrairement à ce qui se passe habituellement dans les églises. Peut-être faut-il voir en cela un effet de l'ambiance particulière de ces lieux qui, à des degrés divers, évoquent un 'sacré', si flou soit-il, ne serait-ce que parce qu'ils éloignent des lieux des activités quotidiennes. Il semblerait en outre que ce phénomène de confession ne touche guère les participants de pèlerinages organisés par l'un ou l'autre acteur de l'Église alors qu'il paraît caractéristique des pèlerins isolés et/ou touristes; une telle différence pourrait s'expliquer par le rejet au moins implicite des premiers de tout contrôle par l'autorité institutionnelle, particulièrement lorsque celle-ci n'est pas absolument anonyme.

Enfin, c'est une affirmation identitaire qui parfois l'exprime dans certaines pratiques de religion populaire. Outre que la multiplicité des saints permet à chaque ville ou région de se doter d'un 'patron' qui lui soit propre, le culte de la Vierge est souvent celui d'une Vierge particulière, associée de façon préférentielle à un pays, à une région ou à une ville – comme en témoigne par exemple ce vitrail de la cathédrale de Quimper représentant une douzaine de Vierges locales spécifiques. Il en va de même des différents métiers qui se sont eux aussi dotés d'un saint patron. Même si, aujourd'hui, ces cultes ont souvent perdu de leur vigueur, ils sont nombreux à subsister et même à reprendre force ou à être rétablis – comme, par exemple, en Belgique, le pèlerinage des sportifs à Notre-Dame de Chèvremont. Certes, il ne s'agit pas d'automatiquement voir en cela un 'retour du religieux' comme d'aucuns le suggèrent – nous y reviendrons – mais il est incontestable que l'on a affaire là à des pratiques qui recourent à des éléments de religion populaire pour dire une identité, c'est-à-dire aussi une frontière et une altérité.

Telles sont donc à nos yeux les caractéristiques majeures de la religion populaire. Avant d'aborder la question de savoir ce qui peut permettre de comprendre leur actuelle vitalité, une remarque s'impose encore. L'expression 'religion populaire' conduit volontiers à considérer qu'il s'agit là d'un mode d'expression propre à certains milieux sociaux, dont la pauvreté intellectuelle expliquerait la naïveté. En fait, il n'en est rien. Certes les différents milieux sociaux ont leurs modalités, leurs temps, leurs lieux,... privilégiés d'expression de cette forme de religiosité mais, au-delà de leur savoir et de leur richesse, tous y recourent, à l'un ou l'autre moment, tous y retrouvent des gestes proches, des émotions voisines. Cette transversalité sociale de la religion populaire se comprend essentiellement en référence aux intentions qui la motivent et dont on a vu qu'elles consistaient prioritairement en une demande de protection de 'moi et les miens' – en cas de problèmes divers qui n'épargnent aucun milieu et qui laissent les proches désemparés, en quête de tout espoir d'aide et de soutien. L'expression 'religion populaire' doit donc être entendue dans un sens qui, excluant toute connotation sociale, renvoie à la diversité des composantes qui viennent d'être évoquées et, en particulier, au fait qu'elle ne dépend prioritairement ni des régulations ni du contrôle des clercs et qu'elle repose plutôt sur des pratiques concrètes en relation avec la vie quotidienne que sur une élaboration intellectuelle et théologique. Et sans doute, comme nous allons le voir, ces caractéristiques participent-elles à son actuel succès.

2. Des causes de sa résurgence

Posons d'emblée une chose: s'il y a résurgence de la religion populaire – et, selon nous, tel est bien le cas, – il serait peu fondé d'y voir la fin de la sécularisation et les prémisses d'un retour de la religion institutionnelle dans ce qu'elle suppose d'adhésion dogmatique, d'obéissance éthique et d'observance rituelle. Sans qu'elle ne suppose nécessairement une pleine et entière autonomie à l'égard de celle-ci, la religion populaire a sa propre logique qui lui permet tout aussi bien de s'inscrire dans la mouvance de la religion institutionnelle que de se développer en complicité avec des forces qui éloignent de celle-ci. Et en l'occurrence aujourd'hui, il nous paraît que c'est plutôt vers ce deuxième versant de l'alternative qu'elle tend à se diriger dans la mesure où l'institution ecclésiale paraît peu sensible à différents 'signes des temps' de la modernité avancée. Selon nous, en effet, c'est du côté des caractéristiques de cette dernière qu'il convient d'aller chercher les causes de la résurgence de la religion populaire. Parmi ces caractéristiques, certaines nous paraissent déterminantes et nous allons les explorer quelque peu.

Bien qu'elle soit rabâchée à tort et à travers, la première de ces caractéristiques ne nous en paraît pas moins décisive en la matière: il s'agit de l'affirmation de l'autonomie individuelle et de la revendication à la liberté de choix et au primat de l'expérience personnelle qui en découle. En effet, dans nos pays, le contexte contemporain a porté à son apogée une individuation amorcée depuis des décennies sinon des siècles et favorisée entre autres par le développement de la consommation et les habitudes de choix qui y sont associées et par un État-providence qui a réduit l'importance (utilitaire) des liens de famille et de voisinage en substituant ses services bureaucratiques à la solidarité affective qui caractérisait ceux-ci. Choisir en toute indépendance et vouloir ne dépendre d'aucune relation personnalisée qui risquerait d'entraver la liberté d'agir et de penser sont ainsi devenus des composantes majeures de la vision contemporaine du monde et de soi. Toutefois, ce n'est là qu'une face – de loin la plus évoquée – de l'individuation: celle-ci ne se caractérise pas automatiquement par l'isolement, l'égoïsme voire le narcissisme comme d'aucuns le suggèrent. S'il s'agit là de traits effectivement présents dans nos sociétés, ils ne sont pas exclusifs. En effet, l'individuation telle que nous l'avons décrite, s'accompagne fréquemment d'un souci intense de relation à d'autres – amis, partenaires, famille, ... – mais désormais, il s'agit d'autres choisis et non ascriptifs (c'est-à-dire donnés d'emblée par les liens du sang ou du territoire). N'est-ce pas en ce sens qu'il s'agit de comprendre l'importance majeure des amis, relevée dans l'enquête européenne sur les valeurs[10] – celle-ci montrant même que dans certains pays, ceux-ci viennent avant la famille. N'est-ce pas aussi ce dont attestent diverses recherches montrant que les couples ont d'autant plus de chances d'être stables qu'ils intègrent des relations d'amitié (c'est-à-dire d'égalité et de négociation) entre les partenaires. Et n'est-ce pas enfin ce dont témoigne cette affirmation récente d'un jeune, résumant de façon frappante un avis largement partagé par beaucoup de ses contemporains: "C'est plus que ma soeur, c'est mon amie". Ainsi le souci de choisir se retrouve-t-il ici comme ailleurs, attestant tout à la fois et de la revendication à l'autonomie, et du besoin de relation à d'autres mais qui soient des relations électives.

Ces caractéristiques constituent un premier élément de compréhension de l'actuelle résurgence de diverses formes de religion populaire. Tour d'abord, celle-ci est faite avant tout de pratiques discontinues, intermittentes qui visent davantage à 'contraindre les dieux' qu'à vénérer ceux-ci – ce qui, dans le vocabulaire de l'idéal-type de Weber, la rapproche plus de la magie que de la 'religion'[11]. Sans les exclure, les pratiques de religion populaire ne nécessitent donc pas l'intégration dans une 'communauté' ni une relation de quelque durée avec celle-ci et ses responsables (les prêtres). Il s'agit avant tout de pratiques individualisées, n'impliquant impérativement aucune relation d'obédience à une quelconque autorité. Nous avons vu par ailleurs que ces pratiques sont le plus souvent orientées vers une demande de protection ou d'aide "pour moi et les miens proches" – ce qui s'avère en connivence avec ce qui a été dit concernant l'importance des relations électives pour l'individu contemporain.

Un autre trait qui caractérise celui-ci se voit lui aussi rencontré par ces pratiques. En effet, nous avons insisté sur l'importance de la dimension corporelle de celles-ci: le geste est au coeur de la religion populaire et les sens participent au sentiment de légitimité et d'efficience qu'elle suscite. Or la culture contemporaine a largement revalorisé un corps que, il faut en convenir, la religion chrétienne avait déprécié, voire diabolisé au bénéfice exclusif de l'âme et de l'esprit; dans les années soixante, le catholicisme avait en outre raffermi son mépris du corps, dans la mouvance d'une tendance à la rationalité, d'une part, (il s'agissait de

10. L. Voyé, K. Dobbelaere e.a., *Belges, heureux et satisfaits. Les valeurs des belges dans les années 90*, Bruxelles, Éd. De Boeck, 1992.
11. Weber, 450-452.

dépouiller la religion de tous ses débordements profanes) et à l'engagement social, d'autre part, la solidarité concrète avec les travailleurs étant considérée comme l'expression la plus claire et la plus importante de la foi profonde.

Ce double projet s'est aujourd'hui fortement estompé – tant d'ailleurs dans l'ensemble de la société que dans le champ religieux. La résurgence de la religion populaire traduit, dans ce dernier, le déplacement des préoccupations du 'social' vers 'moi et les miens' – comme nous l'avons déjà souligné – et d'une rationalité froide, désincarnée, "désenchantée", comme le dit Weber, vers une reprise en compte de l'émotionnel et du sensible. Ce faisant, elle semble s'inscrire dans la mouvance générale qui accorde au corps une place majeure (que l'on pense à l'insistance mise sur son entretien, son souci, sa mise en valeur ..., par de multiples services des plus divers, allant du sport aux soins de beauté en passant par tant de thérapies qui insistent sur l'importance du bien-être corporel et s'activent à le développer). Elle cadre également avec la montée actuelle du non rationnel (nous ne disons pas de l'irrationnel), dont témoignent par exemple nombre de livres récents à succès (sur les anges et le diable, notamment), nombre de programmes de télévision faisant grimper l'audimat (sur des visions, des prémonitions, des 'expériences' sur-naturelles entre autres). Un non-rationnel qui semble ne connaître aucune frontière comme le montre par exemple ce livre de Brun[12] révélant sa percée jusqu'au coeur d'entreprises parmi les plus modernes et les plus performantes et comme en atteste cette récente révélation, prouvant que certains dirigeants de la BERD (Banque Européenne pour la Reconstruction et le Développement) ont recours à des astrologues pour les aider à prendre leurs décisions...

Se focalisant ainsi sur l'individu et ses relations électives et accordant une grande place aux manifestations corporelles et au non-rationnel, les pratiques de religion populaire sont en outre essentiellement orientées vers l'immanence, vers le monde concret ici et maintenant: c'est en référence à des événements de la vie quotidienne, aux espérances et aux problèmes qui traversent celle-ci qu'elles se manifestent. Ainsi loin de se référer d'abord à des dogmes ou à de grands discours théoriques et abstraits, ces pratiques répondent avant tout à l'ordre du pragmatique et la validité des croyances qui y sont associées renvoie à l'attente de leur utilité et non à leur signification théologique ou à leur reconnaissance institutionnelle.

Cette immédiateté et ce pragmatisme des pratiques de religion populaire s'inscrivent sans doute dans d'autres caractéristiques du contexte actuel – à savoir la relativisation de la confiance en la science et

---

12. C. BRUN, *L'irrationnel dans l'entreprise*, Paris, Éd. Balland, 1989.

la perte de crédibilité en l'État-providence, avec tout ce que cela entraîne comme incertitudes.

Alors que, il y a trente ou quarante ans, la science apparaissait comme la source intarissable de tous les espoirs – elle allait résoudre à terme tous les problèmes: la misère et l'ignorance, la maladie et la souffrance, … – désormais, sans qu'elle ne perde toute crédibilité, la science voit relativiser ses potentialités: elle est en effet loin d'avoir résolu tous les problèmes et rien ne laisse supposer qu'elle va rapidement progresser en ce sens; par ses avancées mêmes, elle crée elle-même de nouveaux problèmes qui ouvrent sur des questionnements éthiques fondamentaux (les progrès de la génétique n'inquiètent-ils pas de plus en plus, par exemple); enfin, la science est de l'ordre du général et du long terme et, comme telle, elle est impuissante face aux problèmes qui se posent ici et maintenant à des personnes particulières (ainsi les progrès en matière de connaissance du cancer et la diminution statistique des décès résultant de cette maladie ne soulagent-ils guère les personnes qui vivent aujourd'hui ce problème). Tout comme sa confiance en la science se délite, celle de l'homme contemporain en l'État-providence se réduit. D'une part, celui-ci ne cesse de rogner ses prestations et d'en appeler à la suppléance des initiatives privées (par exemple, en matière de sécurité sociale, où il incite les citoyens à prendre des assurances 'libres' pour compenser les réductions de leur couverture par les assurances 'sociales'). D'autre part, cet État apparaît de peu de poids face à un acteur économique mondialisé et sans frontières (ainsi ne peut-il empêcher les 'délocalisations' d'entreprises et les 'restructurations' qui se traduisent par de drastiques et brutales réductions d'emplois, parfois en outre illégalement conduites comme récemment dans 'l'affaire Renault'). De plus, dans sa double volonté de rationalité et d'égalité, l'État qui a multiplié les règles et les normes abstraites et entend les voir appliquer telles quelles, laisse bien des problèmes irrésolus et bien des détresses non prises en compte par "la cage de fer" de la bureaucratie (comme l'appelle Weber) qui réduit la complexité du monde et laisse ainsi échapper nombre d'appels le plus souvent silencieux. Et tout ceci sans parler de la perte de crédibilité dont l'État est l'objet suite aux scandales, aux 'affaires', aux malversations qui, depuis des années, dans tous les pays européens, entâchent la réputation de la plupart de ses instances.

Conjugués avec les graves difficultés économiques que connaissent nos pays depuis environ vingt-cinq ans et avec les transformations radicales qu'ils vivent – depuis celles engendrées par les technologies d'information et de communication jusqu'à celles produites par l'élargissement de leur caractère pluriculturel –, ces traits caractéristiques de la situation actuelle développent, tant chez les individus que dans les collectivités, un sentiment croissant d'incertitude: incertitude face à l'emploi dont on en sait jamais si on en aura un et si on

le gardera lorsqu'on a la chance d'en avoir un; incertitude face au couple
que menace sans cesse la rupture; incertitude face à un environnement
dont la dégradation inquiète de plus en plus; incertitudes multiples de la
vie quotidienne face à la violence dans les villes, à la drogue, aux délits
sexuels, ...; incertitude enfin face à la nécessité de remise en question
récurrente qu'imposent les changements technologiques, la succession
accélérée des modes en tous domaines, le caractère inédit de nombreuses
situations qui rendent désuets des modèles hier pertinents. Tous ces
aspects se confortent pour laisser l'homme démuni et pour faire croître
en lui un sentiment d'insécurité constante et de risque permanent.
Comment s'étonner dès lors de le voir puiser dans le réservoir de
pratiques disponibles, pour tenter tout au moins de se réconforter et de
trouver le courage d'affronter ses peurs et les situations problématiques
qu'il vit. Car – il convient de le rappeler – plus souvent qu'il n'en attend
une résolution 'magique' de ses problèmes, l'homme moderne cherche
dans les pratiques de religion populaire la force d'être l'acteur de son
destin – ce qui, une fois encore, nous ramène à l'importance qu'il
accorde à son agir, à ses choix et à son expérience personnels.

Il est encore deux aspects de la société contemporaine qui nous
paraissent contribuer à rendre compte du pourquoi de la résurgence de la
religion populaire. Le premier d'entre eux consiste en ce que l'on appelle
généralement aujourd'hui la globalisation, c'est-à-dire – pour prendre
une définition parmi les multiples existant – "l'accélération croissante de
l'interdépendance concrète globale et de la conscience de ce que le
monde est un tout"[13]. Ce processus de globalisation suscite tout en même
temps des résistances diverses, résistances qu'il convient d'entendre à la
fois comme une opposition à une tendance du système à
l'homogénéisation et comme l'expression d'une conception du monde en
tant qu'il est fait "d'une série d'entités et de modes de vie culturellement
égaux et relatifs"[14] ce qui provoque l'émergence d'affirmations
identitaires particularistes de types divers. À la recherche des formes
d'expression, de représentation et d'ancrage, celles-ci vont notamment
s'exprimer à travers le recours à certaines formes de religion populaire.
Il en va ainsi par exemple d'affirmations identitaires régionales ou
nationales – et il convient de ne pas confondre nation et État[15] – ou
encore professionnelles. N'assiste-t-on pas, en effet, à un regain des
cultes adressés à des saints liés de façon privilégiée à une ville ou à une
région, ou à une des multiples figures de la Vierge, associée à un lieu

---

13. R. ROBERTSON, *Globalization. Social Theory and Global Culture*, London, Ed.
Sage, 1992, 8.

14. *Ibid.*, 102.

15. J. HABERMAS, Confèrence faite à Bruxelles en 1992. Texte photocopié.

spécifique? Certains pèlerinages et certaines dévotions n'unissent-ils pas de façon récurrente les membres de certaines professions qui, à côté d'une éventuelle expression religieuse, trouvent là un moment et un lieu pour affirmer les particularités de leur métier et les liens qui par là les unissent? Ainsi en ce qu'elle stimule les particularismes, 'la circonstance globale' favorise-t-elle une revalorisation de tous les modes d'expression de ceux-ci et, notamment, de certaines pratiques de religion populaire.

C'est aussi en ce sens que paraît jouer une autre caractéristique de monde contemporain – à savoir l'importance que celui-ci accorde à la consommation, aux images et aux spectacles. Il n'est sans doute pas utile d'expliquer longuement ce point: nous savons combien les objets participent à notre vie et à notre identité, au point de parfois prétendre dire celle-ci lorsqu'il sont utilisés comme expression d'un statut social effectif et plus souvent souhaité[16]. Nous savons aussi combien les images sont présentes dans nos vies – sur l'écran de nos téléviseurs et de nos ordinateurs, dans les innombrables livres et magazines qui prolifèrent sur le marché, sur les murs de nos villes saturés de publicité, … Nous savons enfin combien les spectacles en tous genres représentent désormais une part croissante de l'économie capitaliste qui multiplie les 'fêtes' – souvent batardisées[17] –, les foires, les expositions, les championnats, les jeux, … La religion populaire se trouve volontiers en affinité avec ces traits contemporains. La consommation – de statues, de médailles, de bougies, … mais aussi de nourriture et de boisson – en représente une composante éprouvée et participe pleinement à sa logique. Il en va de même pour les images: statues et images pieuses, mais aussi photos qui témoignent de la présence sur le lieu sacré; images que l'on emporte dans la mémoire et qui entretiennent le lien au sacré; images aussi des livres, des films … qui évoquent l'existence de ces lieux, de ces objets et des ces pratiques. La dimension spectacle et fête participe elle aussi pleinement à diverses manifestations de la religion populaire, à travers les grands rassemblements que celle-ci suscite, à travers le décor et la mise en scène qu'elle suppose. L'aspect festif se retrouve en outre dans le fait que certaines de ces pratiques coexistent et même s'intègrent avec des pratiques de vacances et de voyages – les itinéraires touristiques incluant fréquemment des haltes plus ou moins longues dans des lieux sacrés et le 'tourisme religieux' constituant une branche très dynamique de ce secteur économique en pleine croissance. Sur ce plan encore, la religion populaire semble se trouver en affinité avec le monde contemporain ce qui permet sans doute de mieux comprendre sa

---

16. J. BAUDRILLARD, *Pour une critique de l'économie politique du signe*, Paris, Éd. du Seuil, 1972.

17. VILLADARY, *o.c.*

résurgence et l'autonomie de ses développements par rapport à la religion institutionnelle, au contenu du croire qu'elle énonce et aux prescriptions éthiques qu'elle formule.

À ces divers aspects de la société actuelle qui permettent de saisir la logique dans laquelle s'inscrit la religion populaire aujourd'hui, nous pourrions encore ajouter un élément: le 'bricolage', qui caractérise nombre de domaines de la vie contemporaine et, parmi eux, le religieux. Nous l'avons dit: les pratiques de religion populaire ne s'inscrivent en effet pas dans un corpus cohérent de croyances et ne revoient à aucune dogmatique intégrée. Comme telles, elles s'offrent au choix des pratiquants et s'accommodent sans difficulté du voisinage de pratiques exotiques et de dévotions hétérogènes, empruntées à des contextes historiques et géographiques les plus divers. Et s'il s'y trouve une cohérence, c'est l'individu-pratiquant qui la conçoit par et pour lui-même, sans recours à une quelconque légitimation externe et sans prétention de faire école.

Conclusion

La résurgence des pratiques de religion populaire ne présume aucunement de la redécouverte du sens qui leur était attaché et que d'aucuns voudraient leur voir signifier. Cependant, ces pratiques semblent participer à ce qu'Ariès appelle "la stratégie globale de l'homme"[18], non plus cette fois "contre la nature et sa sauvagerie" mais bien contre le mythe de la toute-puissance technique et scientifique, de la maîtrise absolue, de l'homogénéité démocratique et de la rationalité tous azimuts. Face à celui-ci, l'homme continue à se vivre soumis aux forces obscures d'Eros et de Thanatos, confronté à l'échec et à la violence et sans cesse ramené à "l'expérience du problème qu'il est pour lui-même"[19], problème qui s'est fait d'autant plus aigu que l'individuation s'est accrue. Quoi d'étonnant dès lors à ce que nombre de rites se voient aujourd'hui réappropriés ou inventés en vue de tenter soit d'exorciser ces difficultés qu'aucune rationalité moderne n'a réussi à réduire, soit d'affirmer l'existence de relations à d'autres qui font sens et par rapport auxquels la fragilité des liens est d'autant plus éprouvée?

Loin dès lors qu'ils ne faille voir d'emblée dans les pratiques de religion populaire une dégradation du religieux, il convient sans doute d'y lire la quête inconsciente d'un dépassement de l'immanence dans tout ce

18. ARIÈS, 598.
19. M. GAUCHET, *Le désenchantement du monde. Une histoire politique de la religion*, Paris, Éd. Gallimard, 1985, 299.

que celle-ci a d'éphémère et d'incertain. Ainsi ces pratiques seraient-elles appel de continuité et de durée, témoignage de relations dont elles manifestent l'importance au-delà de leur fragilité.

En pèlerinage avec des malades

Antoine RUBBENS

Dans son livre *Une enfance gantoise* Suzanne Lilar raconte l'excursion annuelle avec sa maman à la grotte mariale d'Oostakker-Lourdes. Elle nous fait part de ses souvenirs et impressions. "Toujours nous y retrouvions le même petit peuple d'éclopés (culs de jatte, manchots, goitreux) et d'anormaux reconnus de loin à leur gesticulation saccadée. J'aimais énormément ce spectacle, non par dépravation, mais par curiosité de toutes les formes de la vie, par avidité de découvrir celles qui généralement se dérobent à la vue et dont ici l'on faisait ostentation. Mon goût flamand de la difformité s y donnait libre cours. Autre chose me satisfait dans cet étalage: j'y voyais le contre-pied d'un monde que l'on me montrait trop arrangé, trop joli. Tout ce que l'on croyait devoir m'épargner se trouvait par la présence de ces estropiés et de ces demeurés remis en place. Un ordre quelque part se recomposait, le difforme et le bizarre venant occuper leur rang à côté de la beauté" (*o.c.*, 76-77).

Depuis l'époque de la jeunesse de Suzanne Lilar, la société a fort évolué et elle a fait des progrès sensibles pour intégrer les handicapés. Mais même encore maintenant, c'est plutôt rare qu'on les voit en grand nombre dans les rues de nos villes. Ce fut pourtant le cas lors de la manifestation nationale du 28 septembre 1997 à Bruxelles où des malades, des handicapés et des bien-portants ont manifesté à l'initiative des Mutualités chrétiennes contre l'augmentation excessive des coûts des soins de santé à charge des malades chroniques.

Endroits privilégiés

Les lieux de pèlerinage restent jusqu'à nos jours des endroits privilégiés où les malades et les handicapés peuvent se présenter sans trop de difficultés. Ils savent qu'ils y sont attendus et accueillis. Il n'est donc pas étonnant de les voir nombreux à Lourdes, à Banneux et aux lieux de pèlerinage plus modestes près de leur maison. Pue de temps après les apparitions à Bernadette Soubirous, des malades sont déjà allés à Lourdes. En Belgique chaque année plus de 35.000 personnes partent en pèlerinages organisés à Lourdes.

À Banneux, Mariette Béco a rapporté les paroles de la Vierge, qui lui disait le 11 février 1933: "Je viens soulager la souffrance". Quelques semaines plus tôt, le 19 janvier 1933, la Vierge lui avait déjà dit: "Cette source est pour toutes les nations". Lors de son voyage apostolique en Belgique en mai 1985, le pape Jean Paul II a prié à Beauraing et à Banneux. Surtout à Banneux, il s'est adressé aux malades et il leur a parlé du sens chrétien de la souffrance. Il les saluait en disant: "Voilà plus de cinquante ans que non seulement les malades, mais le peuple immense des pauvres d'aujourd'hui – il y a tant de manières d'être pauvre! – se sentent chez eux à Banneux. Ils viennent chercher ici le réconfort, le courage, l'espérance, l'union à Dieu dans leur épreuve. Ils viennent louer et invoquer ici la Vierge des Pauvres, sous le vocable particulier et très beau de Notre Dame des Pauvres. Ils sont à bon droit convaincus qu'une telle dévotion correspond à l'Évangile et à la foi de l'Église; si le Christ a défini sa mission comme l'annonce de la Bonne Nouvelle aux pauvres, comment sa Mère ne serait-elle pas accueillante aux pauvres?"

De chaque lieu de pèlerinage peut en effet resplendir un rayon de la parole réconfortante de Jésus: "Venez à moi, vous tous qui peinez et ployez sous le fardeau, et moi je vous soulagerai. Chargez-vous de mon joug et mettez-vous à mon école, car je suis doux et humble de coeur, et vous trouverez soulagement pour vos âmes" (Mt. 11,28).

Procession de confiance

Des ex-voto des nombreux lieux de pèlerinage témoignent de la confiance et de connaissance des malades et de leurs proches. Cette procession d'intercession et de confiance continue. À Laarne, la paroisse où j'habite, il existe un groupe local de *Ziekenzorg-C.M.*, comme c'est d'ailleurs le cas dans mille autres endroits en Flandre. Ce groupe paroissial organise chaque année une excursion à un lieu de pèlerinage. Ce voyage d'un jour crée ou renoue des liens, car malades et organisateurs se mettent en route vers une même destination où ils partagent ensemble une même foi. Un autre groupe paroissial, composé surtout de pensionnés, part chaque année à Lourdes. Un tel pèlerinage renforce encore plus ces liens.

Ensemble avec des croyants, venant d'autres pays et cultures, les pèlerins sentent qu'ils appartiennent à une plus grande communauté. Il perçoivent avec joie qu'ils ne sont pas seuls à témoigner de leur foi. Ils marchent dans les traces de générations antérieures. Le pèlerinage est un phénomène universel. Jésus s'est fait pèlerin lui-même. Il a participé aux pèlerinages de la Galilée vers Jérusalem. Mais Jésus a toutefois souligné la relativité de chaque pèlerinage, surtout dans son entretien avec la Samaritaine au bord du puits de Jacob.

La femme voulait entraîner Jésus dans une discussion sur la valeur des lieux de culte. Jésus répondit: "Femme, crois-moi: l'heure vient où vous n'irez plus ni sur cette montagne ni à Jérusalem pour adorer le Père... L'heure vient – et c'est maintenant – où les vrais adorateurs adoreront le

Père en esprit et en vérité" (Jean 4,21 et 23).

Les pèlerinages sont fort liés à la foi populaire. Dans l'accompagnement spirituel des pèlerins, il est bon sans doute de se rappeler la conversation de Jésus avec la Samaritaine et de retenir son avertissement. Mais en même temps nous ne pouvons pas oublier que Jésus avait un grand respect pour la foi de chaque personne. Aussi il n'a pas non plus repoussé la femme, qui voulait toucher la frange de son manteau (Luc 8,44).

Entraide

Depuis un demi-siècle les Mutualités chrétiennes partent en pèlerinage avec des malades. Le 3 août 1947, vingt mille mutualistes, parmi lesquels deux cents malades, quatre cents handicapés, se réunissaient à Scherpenheuvel (Montaigu), le célèbre lieu marial du Brabant pour le premier pèlerinage national. Cette rencontre a donné l'élan à une attention plus vive pour les malades dans l'action mutualiste de base. Des groupes d'entraide et de solidarité locale ont été formés par le Service d'*Aide aux malades*. Des bénévoles font des courses pour les malades, ils sont prêts à les conduire chez leur médecin ou à la clinique. Du côté néerlandophone, *Ziekenzorg* s'est organisé au niveau local avec le but de visiter les malades à domicile, de créer des lieux de rencontre et surtout avec la ferme volonté de travailler à l'intégration des malades dans la vie socio-culturelle.

Il existe depuis cette époque la Journée des malades au niveau paroissial ou au niveau d'un secteur. Bien souvent, c'est un lieu marial qui les accueille. Je donne pour exemple les rencontres annuelles du Brabant wallon, où les malades sont invités par alternance, soit à Ittre, soit à Basse-Wavre.

Le premier pèlerinage des Mutualités chrétiennes avec des malades vers Lourdes a eu lieu en 1949. Il s'était associé à celui de Jette. En 1950, le pèlerinage mutualiste se faisait avec le Pèlerinage de Printemps de Leuven. Depuis 1951 le pèlerinage de *Ziekenzorg* se fait dans le cadre des pèlerinages LOB (Ligue Ouvrière Belge). C'est, en effet, sous le label LOB-Malades que *Ziekenzorg* est connu à Lourdes à côté de LOB-familles et LOB-retraites. En 1997, *Ziekenzorg* a organisé six pèlerinages en avion et quatre en train. Au total l'organisation a amené 3413 personnes à Lourdes, dont 2298 malades et accompagnants et 1115 bénévoles.

Aide aux Malades, le service francophone des Mutualités, collabore avec les *Familles Populaires* (MOC et Vie Féminine). Au début, ces pèlerinages se faisaient exclusivement par les chemins de fer qui transportaient malades et personnes valides. L'accompagnement était pris en charge par des bénévoles et des permanents des Mutualités chrétiennes. La Fraternelle Joseph Cuypers animait ce groupe des bénévoles. Depuis 1984, les Service d'*Aide aux Malades* amène aussi des pèlerins malades par avion à Lourdes. En 1997, le Service a assuré deux pèlerinages vers ce grand lieu marial des Pyrénées avec 230 malades et 127 bénévoles.

Lourdes

"Je vis la cité sainte, la Jérusalem nouvelle qui descendait du ciel d'auprès de Dieu". Cette chanson est souvent chantée à Lourdes et elle exprime très bien les sentiments de joie des pèlerins, surtout malades, pour qui cette cité céleste est descendue à Lourdes. Ils aiment d'y aller, même si le voyage est difficile. Ceux qui vont en avion doivent en général se lever très tôt. Pour les malades grabataires et les grands handicapés, un voyage en train de nuit est très lourd. Les pèlerinages sont aussi chers pour des gens qui doivent vivre d'un revenu de remplacement ou d'une petite pension.

Le programme est chargé à Lourdes. Il faut déjà du temps pour soigner les malades le matin. Il y a la visite à la grotte, la cérémonie d'ouverture, le chemin de croix, une célébration pénitentielle, une veillée mariale, l'onction des malades, la participation à la procession du Saint Sacrement et la procession aux flambeaux. Et le moment du départ arrive trop vite.

Chaque lieu de pèlerinage a son message. Celui de Sainte Thérèse à Lisieux est autre que le message de Lourdes. On doit le découvrir et y être attentif. Le conseil pastoral de Lourdes présente chaque année un thème, qui tient compte de la spécificité du lieu et du message de la Vierge Immaculée à Bernadette, mais aussi de l'actualité pastorale. Au seuil du Grand Jubilé de l'an 2000, le Conseil de la Pastorale de Lourdes a choisi les thèmes proposés par le pape Jean Paul II. Chaque pèlerinage peut adopter ces thèmes ou en choisir d'autres. *Ziekenzorg* et *Aide aux Malades* choisissent leurs thèmes indépendamment l'un de l'autre. Mais on retrouvera bien sûr dans ces deux organisations des accents communs, liés à leur insertion dans un mouvement social.

Le groupe d'animation pastorale francophone est allé à Lourdes les années précédentes avec des thèmes comme: Prendre des risques (1993); Familles, chemins d'amour (1994); Osons des chemins d'espérance (1995); Ensemble, reprenons souffle (1996); Renaître dans le Christ (1997).

Avec la participation de tous

Les célébrations à Lourdes gagnent en profondeur et en qualité si tous peuvent y participer activement et surtout lorsque les malades eux-mêmes sont invités à faire une lecture, à formuler des intentions de prière à partir de leur vécu et avec leurs mots ou exprimer un témoignage. Dans les hôtels, où séjournent les malades, un bénévole ou un malade est attentif à la dimension pastorale. On attend surtout de ces personnes qu'elles puissent engager d'autres pèlerins à l'animation pastorale du pèlerinage. En général, une soirée est prévue dans les hôtels pour une mise en commun en carrefour et pour un temps de réflexion.

Les malades apprécient si l'oeil a quelque chose à regarder dans les célébrations. D'où l'importance de travailler avec des symboles et des couleurs.

Le moment le plus impressionnant d'un pèlerinage avec des malades est celui de la célébration de l'onction des malades. Les malades qui demandent ce sacrement se savent entourés par un bénévole, une infirmière, un médecin, éventuellement un membre de leur famille. La dimension communautaire de ce sacrement y reçoit toute sa dimension. C'est la Seigneur lui-même, qui, par ce sacrement leur rend visite, les réconforte, les guérit intérieurement et les soulage. C'est lui, qui, par ce sacrement confie aux malades une mission, qui s'exprime déjà simplement dans le rappel qu'une société qui ne prend pas soin de ses malades est elle-même malade.

L'huile, l'eau, la lumière, le rocher sont des symboles importants de Lourdes. Le cierge que nous recevons et que nous faisons brûler, la petite pierre d'une mosaïque, le chaînon d'une chaîne, une carte de voeu sont parmi les objets tous simples que nous apportons comme souvenir précieux à la maison et qui aident à entretenir un lien d'amitié. La convivialité est une des valeurs majeures d'un pèlerinage et d'un séjour avec de malades.

Les malades et bien portants peuvent donner suite à l'appel prononcé lors de la neuvième apparition d'aller boire à la source et de s'y laver. L'eau de Lourdes n'est pas une eau magique. Aller sa baigner dans cette eau est une acte d'humilité.

À Lourdes, les malades veulent s'approcher de la grotte, la toucher de leur main. C'est l'expression que notre être s'engage dans la prière. Un grand avantage des lieux de pèlerinages est précisément que le pèlerin peut exprimer sa foi sans trop s'occuper du regard des autres et des qu'en dira-t-on.

L'équipe de Capharnaüm

Les malades, qui ne peuvent pas se déplacer indépendamment, ont besoin de l'aide d'autres personnes. Celles-ci doivent être attentives au désir du malade d'aller prier seul à la grotte et parfois aussi d'aller faire une course en ville. Le bénévole et le malade ne voient pas toujours ces lieux de la même façon. Leur attitude envers la foi et ses expressions de dévotions sont différentes. Un jeune de vingt ans ne comprend plus le sens d'une procession avec le Saint Sacrement. Un lieu de pèlerinage a besoin d'une catéchèse. Malades et bénévoles peuvent se porter mutuel-

lement dans la foi. Ils sont alors proches de cette petite équipe de Ca-
pharnaüm, où quatre porteurs amenaient le paralysé près de Jésus au
milieu de la maison. Tous étaient sous l'impression de la grande foi de
ce paralysé en la personne de Jésus, qui lui disait: "Lève-toi et marche"
(Marc 2,11).

Influence des pèlerinages

Les pèlerinages des Mutualités à Lourdes sont à l'origine des séjours de
vacances pour malades en Belgique. Après un pèlerinage, les malades se
sentaient comme les disciples de Jésus, qui devaient descendre du mont
Tabor après avoir été témoins de sa transfiguration. Les premières semaines de vacances pour malades ont eu lieu, en 1959, à l'Institut Christ
Roi des Frères de la Charité à St-Job in 't Goor. Plus tard les Mutualités
chrétiennes ont acquis le couvent des Pères Picpus à Zandhoven, l'ont
aménagé et agrandi pour le rendre accessible aux malades et handicapés.
Sept jours de vacances à Hooidonk-Zandhoven ou dans la maison de
vacances et de convalescence de Ter-Duinen-Nieuwpoort et de Spa-
Nivezé ou dans un autre centre permettent aux malades de briser
l'isolement, dans lequel ils se trouvent bien souvent.

En 1997, *Ziekenzorg* a organisé des séjours pour 14.479 malades et
4.549 bénévoles. Du côté francophone, 1.234 malades, accompagnés par
589 bénévoles ont participé à des séjours de vacances en Belgique. Ces
séjours sont marqués par une grande convivialité: ils sont l'expression
d'une solidarité vécue. L'animation pastorale y a aussi sa place. Il allait
longtemps de soi qu'un prêtre fasse partie de l'équipe accompagnante.
Comme sa présence devient plus rare, l'équipe reste toutefois sensible à
ne pas oublier une dimension pastorale et à organiser des célébrations.

Quelques initiatives méritent une mention spéciale. Jusqu'en 1992, le
Service *Aide aux malades* organisait à Beauraing, près du sanctuaire, une
semaine qui mettait surtout l'accent sur l'aspect religieux en favorisant
l'esprit de retraite. Depuis 1996, pareille semaine se tient au Château de
Chaytifontaine à Banneux. Elle a comme objectif de conduite en pèlerinage des personnes qui ne peuvent plus se rendre à Lourdes de par leur
âge, leur handicap ou leur situation précaire. En août 1997, cinquante
trois personnes y ont participé. Elles ont visité, prié aux sanctuaires et
assisté aux processions. Au cours du séjour le sacrement de l'onction des
malades a été célébré. Les divertissement ne manquaient pas, par
exemple une excursion au Bon Vieux Dieu de Tancrémont et la dégusta-
tion de tartes!

Ziekenzorg organise chaque année à Hooidonk-Zandhoven pendant
l'Avent et la Semaine Sainte un séjour de réflexion. Aux temps forts de
l'année liturgique, les thèmes suggérés par *Vivre ensemble, Entraide et
Fraternité* et ceux du *Carême de partage* donnent suffisamment matière

à la réflexion. Les malades de longue durée, qui chez soi ont rarement la possibilité d'assister aux offices, apprécient beaucoup les célébrations de la Semaine Sainte. Le Jeudi Saint avec le lavement des pieds et le Vendredi Saint avec la vénération de la Croix, célébrés avec des malades, sont des cérémonies très impressionnantes.

Les années précédentes, Mgr P. Schreurs, évêque de Hasselt, et Mgr P. Van den Berghe, évêque d'Anvers, sont venus témoigner du sens de la Semaine Sainte dans leur vie. Pendant la veillée pascale, les vacanciers sont allés de Zandhoven à la cathédrale d'Anvers pour y chanter de tout coeur l'Alléluia. Oui, le Christ a vaincu la mort!

Est-ce que tout ceci fait partie de la nouvelle évangélisation? Dès qu'une parole de l'Évangile peut pénétrer dans notre coeur, l'annonce de l'Évangile se réalise. Si nous partageons le petit peu d'Évangile que nous comprenons avec d'autres, la Parole se répand. Là où des gens se rassemblent autour de l'Évangile, l'Église se manifeste. Mais nous percevons de suite une autre question: que vais-je faire, une fois de retour chez moi? Comment partager la joie de ce que j'ai vécu dans un pèlerinage, un séjour, une rencontre internationale?

Ce qui reste d'un pèlerinage et d'un séjour n'est souvent qu'un souvenir. Mais ce souvenir peut être une force pour l'avenir. De Mgr Coppens, mon professeur d'exégèse à Leuven j'ai retenu cette parole: "Il ne faut jamais renier dans les ténèbres ce qu'on a vu dans la lumière".

La dévotion à la Sainte Vierge à Kortenbos
Un exemple concret de la religion populaire
en relation avec la liturgie

Bernard V. FETS

1. Origine et histoire

La petite localité de Kortenbos (1200 habitants), est un arrondissement de Saint-Trond, ce qui n'a pas toujours été le cas. Le fait précisément que Kortenbos a successivement été transféré à plusieurs communes, a influencé le développement du lieu de pèlerinage. De plus, Kortenbos se trouve sur une ancienne voie de communication entre l'actuel Limbourg néerlandais (Maestricht) et le 'midi', c'est-à-dire le nord de la France. Un point de rencontre de différents peuples et cultures, caractéristique de tant de lieux de pèlerinage.

C'est en 1636 que la dévotion à la Vierge Marie à Kortenbos a été mentionnée pour la première fois. Une veuve pieuse, Elisabeth van Oeteren, avait reçu une petite vierge en terre cuite d'un père franciscain de Saint-Trond. Elle habitait dans son domaine, situé sur le territoire de Kortenbos. Elle fit ériger la statuette sur un vieux chêne, dans l'espoir que la Sainte Vierge accorde sa protection à ces lieux troublés. La statuette originale ressemble beaucoup à celle de Foy-Notre-Dame (aux environs de Dinant). Un pèlerin l'a peut-être rapportée de là. Très vite on a fait mention de guérisons et d'autres faits inexplicables (miracles) en relation avec la statuette de la Mère de Dieu à Kortenbos. La Vierge Marie fut vénérée alors sous le vocable de 'Guérisseuse des malades' ou de 'Délivrance des malades' (*Salus infirmorum*).

À cette époque Kortenbos appartenait à la paroisse de Kozen, fondée des siècles plus tôt par l'abbaye des prémontrés d'Averbode. Le curé d'alors, Paul van Hove, prémontré d'Averbode, commençait à se préoccuper de ce qui se passait dans ce petit coin de sa paroisse. Il écrivit une lettre à son père abbé dans laquelle il l'informait sur les guérisons inexplicables, les miracles et les faveurs obtenue par l'intercession de la Vierge Marie. Mais en plus, il demanda à son supérieur de l'aide: des religieux en vue de secourir les pèlerins ainsi que le soutien nécessaire en vue de construire une église. L'aide fut accordée et la première pierre de l'église actuelle fut posée en 1641 par le curé van Hove lui-même. L'abbaye d'Averbode envoya en plus des architectes et d'autres artisans d'art. les franciscains de Saint-Trond, eux aussi apportaient leur pierre à l'édifice, leur influence ne sera d'ailleurs jamais tout à fait absente à Kortenbos. Il est bien connu que tant les prémontrés que les franciscains ont joué un rôle assez important lors de la contre-réforme dans les Pays-Bas espagnols (la Belgique actuelle). Kortenbos fut, tout comme Montaigu, un des hauts-lieux du renouveau catholique en Belgique au 17e siècle. En témoignant la maître-autel de la basilique avec son tableau typique de la Vierge Marie, 'Guérisseuse des malades', ainsi que les dix confessionnaux, incorporés de façon artistique aux boiseries.

2. Kortenbos, un lieu de pèlerinage aujourd'hui: quelques constatations

2.1. S'il est vrai que beaucoup de pèlerins font des pèlerinages vers des lieux célèbres (Lourdes, Compostelle), en vue d'obtenir une faveur concrète, cela est encore plus vrai, à mon avis, pour les lieux de pèlerinage plus modestes. À Kortenbos, depuis toujours, les pèlerins viennent implorer la guérison de leurs maladies corporelles. D'où le vocable: 'Délivrance des malades'. Dans les documents et récits relatifs aux guérisons, il était surtout question de rhumatismes et de 'mauvaises jambes', des maux toujours fréquents dans cette région. Mais des 'difficultés psychologiques' aussi sont mentionnées. Les 'pensées sombres' sont souvent l'indice de problèmes sous-jacents.

2.2. Ce qu'on vient de dire se traduit bel et bien dans les intentions formulées par les pèlerins, soit en groupe, soit individuellement et de façon anonyme: guérison d'une maladie, réussite d'une opération chirurgicale, solution d'un problème familial (de meilleures relations familiales). Les intentions formulées par les pèlerins trahissent souvent des souhaits plutôt matérialistes tels que réaliser des bénéfices lorsqu'ils font un héritage, ou gagner le loto... Et enfin il y a les intentions classiques: obtenir de bons résultats lors d'un examen, trouver un emploi, faire un bon voyage. Il est rare qu'on trouve des intentions écrites qui expriment la gratitude pour une faveur obtenue ou qui soient plutôt optimistes. Presque jamais on une demande une prière pour la paix, pour l'Église universelle, pour les jeunes églises ou les missionnaires.

2.3. Très vite après la naissance du lieu de pèlerinage, on a organisé des processions au départ des paroisses environnantes. Elles avaient lieu dans le but concret d'implorer l'intercession de Notre-Dame de Kortenbos en vue de protéger la population de la peste, de la guerre ou d'autres fléaux. Quelques paroisses ont conservé cette tradition. Surtout au mois de mai. Une des conséquences des processions paroissiales est que beaucoup de ces gens – habitant dans les paroisses environnantes – considèrent la paroisse de Kortenbos comme leur paroisse alternative. Ils fréquentent l'église de Kortenbos tout au long de l'année, mais ils n'ont pas de lien avec la communauté paroissiale de Kortenbos, ni avec leur propre paroisse d'origine dont ils fuient les activités pastorales spécifiques.

2.4. Beaucoup de gens qui viennent à Kortenbos, désirent garder l'anonymat. Même s'il y a beaucoup de pèlerinages de groupes organisés (paroisses, groupes socio-culturels), il est frappant de constater combien de personnes individuelles, de couples et de petits groupes viennent prier dans l'église de Kortenbos. On peut dire que l'église, étant ouverte tous les jours de l'année et durant toute la journée, n'est jamais vide. (Il faut savoir qu'à l'heure actuelle, il s'avère difficile de laisser les églises paroissiales ouvertes). Il serait risqué toutefois d'organiser une célébration liturgique dans l'après-midi du 15 août (l'Assomption) par exemple, en raison de l'afflux des pèlerins ce jour-là. Ce n'est pas vraiment ce que souhaitent la plupart des pèlerins. Ils fréquentent l'église de Kortenbos comme ils veulent, tout en gardant l'anonymat si c'est possible, à leur rythme et avec leurs problèmes et intentions.

Les responsables pastoraux de Kortenbos sont donc invités à chercher un équilibre adéquat entre la prière silencieuse et les célébrations communes.

2.5. Comme les autres lieux de pèlerinage, Kortenbos offre aux pèlerins une bonne part de nostalgie et de liturgie traditionnelle. Surtout au mois de mais: la procession mariale, l'adoration du Saint-Sacrement (communément appelée 'salut'), bénédiction des enfants, bénédiction des voitures et des bicyclettes, pèlerinage des cavaliers, etc.

Nous sommes confrontés au défi captivant de donner aux pèlerins un message qui dépasse leurs problèmes et besoins personnels, individuels. Les thèmes de la liturgie dominicale (p. ex. les dimanches du temps pascal) ou la 'lectio continua', auxquels la réforme liturgique du Concile Vatican II a prêté tant d'importance, n'intéressent que trop peu les pèlerins moyens. Il y a par exemple une forte demande de neuvaines mariales (les premiers neuf jours du mois de mai) alors que la neuvaine de Pentecôte – si recommandée par l'Église – reste sans écho. L'Église universelle a entamé l'année du Saint-Esprit. Les commissions diocésaines de liturgie ont élaboré des suggestions à cet effet. Elles ont rédigé des textes appropriés, notamment pour la neuvaine de Pentecôte de 1998. Cette neuvaine tombera cette année dans les derniers jours du mois de mai. Comment procéderons-nous, où est-ce qu'on mettra l'accent? Qu'est-ce qui doit prévaloir?

3. Défis et questions

3.1. Il reste captivant de découvrir les motivations profondes des pèlerins qui se rendent dans des lieux de pèlerinage tels que Kortenbos. Quels sont les petits ou les grands problèmes qui les préoccupent? Quelles sont leurs souffrances? Est-ce qu'ils viennent aussi pour remercier Dieu, pour exprimer leur joie? Il incombe au pasteur d'écouter, d'essayer de comprendre, de consoler, de prier avec les pèlerins.

3.2. La restructuration de la pastorale paroissiale (un seul curé responsable de parfois trois paroisses, fédéralisation de paroisses, ici et là des activités qui concernent plusieurs paroisses), ainsi que la rationalisation, surtout des célébrations eucharistiques ont eu pour conséquence que les fidèles, devenus eux aussi très mobiles, sont moins liés à leur paroisse. Les lieux de pèlerinage (à Kortenbos, l'église est aussi église paroissiale) offrent aux fidèles des célébrations qui conviennent davantage à leur propre rythme. En même temps ils ont fait un pèlerinage. En outre ils assistent à des rites et des cérémonies qui n'existent plus dans leurs propres paroisses. Ils ont le sentiment – à tort ou à raison – qu'on les écoute et qu'on les accueille davantage alors qu'ils gardent l'anonymat. Il est remarquable qu'on trouve la même attitude chez les jeunes. Ici la question s'impose si un lieu de pèlerinage renforce le lien avec la communauté ecclésiale ou s'il constitue au contraire un obstacle. Autrement dit: les lieux de pèlerinage, le culte des saints en général et de la Vierge Marie en particulier, favorisent-ils ou bien entravent-ils la nouvelle évangélisation telle qu'elle a été conçue dans nos diocèses?

3.3. Comme on le sait Thomas a Kempis n'aimait pas trop les pèlerinages, tels qu'il nous les décrit dans son 'Imitation de Jésus Christ'. J'aimerais donc formuler la question suivante: un pèlerinage est-ce un défi de vivre mieux sa foi et de rendre témoignage à l'Évangile, ou est-ce plutôt un moment de repos dans la vie de tous les jours exprimant les sentiments religieux latents qui sommeillent dans mon coeur aussi?

Il est clair qu'au pasteur incombe une responsabilité énorme. Il doit tenir compte de ce qui vit dans tout coeur humain, en fondant la dévotion et la religion sur le message biblique qu'il doit actualiser dans le monde d'aujourd'hui. Le schéma qui voici nous permet de résumer ce que nous venons de dire. Il n'est pas exhaustif et il est susceptible d'interprétations différentes.

Pastorale - Liturgie	*Pèlerinage*
transmission de la foi	religion
symbolique (l'essentiel)	allégorique (le secondaire)
biblique	dévotionnel
communauté	individu

Conclusion

Le curé de Kortenbos est responsable d'une communauté paroissiale et en même temps il est recteur d'un lieu de pèlerinage. Une situation donc privilégiée, à première vue en tout cas! Des problèmes très divers appellent son attention et les chrétiens d'aujourd'hui lui exposent leurs problèmes et besoins. Il est fasciné parfois de la façon dont les pèlerins à Kortenbos attendent des réponses de son part. le curé de Kortenbos invitera les pèlerins à transmettre dans le monde d'aujourd'hui la sollicitude de Dieu pour les hommes et il veillera à ce que cette sollicitude pénètre dans le coeur de chaque pèlerin, sur l'intercession de la Sainte Vierge. Le recteur de Kortenbos devra apparemment réconcilier des intérêts opposés, ce qui ne doit pas l'inquiéter pour autant! Il suffit de viser toujours à un bon équilibre et à une pastorale bien réfléchie.

Youth, Liturgy
and Postmodernity

Stijn VAN DEN BOSSCHE

This contribution is composed of three parts.[1] First an encompassing framework about postmodernity is offered. Second, the postmodern young is considered and how they deal with religiosity and the Christian tradition. Third, the implications of the first two parts for liturgical celebration with young are brought to light. Finally, a few open questions from postmodern youth pastoral to the liturgy conclude the contribution.

But then what about popular religion, the theme of the liturgical congress that this periodical has given an account? In the traditional meaning of the term, popular religion can be circumscribed as a particular religious tradition, in this case Christian faith, that functions as a cultural religion, but at the same time is mixed in a 'popular' way with religiosity as an attempt to master contingency. In this sense, popular religion is completely absent among postmodern youth.[2] Indeed, among young people there is no longer any prevailing religion present, even if they are *also* underhand with scraps from Christianity. If we therefore understand 'popular religion' without the encompassing framework of a particular religious tradition, such as a prereflexive religio*sity*, which took hold in a certain people – whereby the latter concept must again be understood as the way of dealing with the questions that flow from the contingency of existence – then it seems to be the case that the 'popular religion' of

1. This contribution takes as its point of departure the Flemish pastoral situation, and was originally written in Dutch. Therefore also many references are to Flemish literature. To facilitate use of these references, Dutch quotations in (both) the text and footnotes have been translated into English.

2. We found only one reference to popular religion in the context of youth ministry. Martin Klöckener briefly refers to the *'Volksfrömmigkeit'* ... to ascertain that it no longer exists among youth. See M. Klöckener, "Die entfremdete Beziehung zwischen Jugendlichen und Liturgie', *Liturgisches Jahrbuch* 39 (1989) 228-259, here p. 236. Further support to our hypothesis can be found in the *Lexikon für Theologie und Kirche* (Freiburg im Bresgau, 850, s.v. 'Volksfrömmigkeit'), which already pointed out in 1965: "Die Volksfrömmigkeit ist zur Zeit in einer Krise, da deren Ausprägung meist auf das Mittelalter oder die Barockzeit, bäuerliche oder bürgerliche Lebensstrukturen zurückgeht und dem heutigen Weltbild und Lebensgefühl widerspricht. Neue Frömmigkeitsformen bilden sich in der pluralistischen Gesellschaftsordnung nur schwer."

present-day youngsters is the postmodern religiosity.[3]

1. Postmodernity as a cultural framework

Let us commence our reflection with a brief overview of what postmodernity stands for.[4] We advance one dictum of our postmodern era, which is very revealing for the theme of youth and liturgy. At the same time, we also want to consider something: postmodernity means neither the absence of religiosity, nor the return of the Christian.

1.1. Postmodernity: freedom predetermines rationality

Postmodernity begins at the end of the era of metaphysics as foundational thinking. The traditional foundational thinking of our culture must be located self-evidently within Christian tradition: to the premodern Westerner, reality was founded in the God of the Bible. Modernity was characterised as the era in which humans discover and live their autonomy. There, religion was dethroned as the sacred canopy above society. In modernity, critical rationality wants to found itself. Descartes' *"Cogito, ergo sum"* as the one and only premise that cannot be doubted, remains exemplary here, but one can as well think of the rise of the positive sciences and the history of technological revolution, or even of the renaissance with its rediscovery of non-Christian antiquity.

But this attempt of man to found himself has failed. The modern grand narratives which promised universal salvation, have become perverted and brought the earth to the edge of destruction. In its attempts toward universality and unity from the ego, modernity came to exactly the opposite: plurality, fragmentation and irreducible mutual difference, and this among individual as well as among cultural *cogito's*. A foundation of being within thinking no longer appears possible: "Because modernity has not succeeded in delivering convincing proof of a universal foundation for experience and understanding, it imparted the idea to us that

---

3. An echo of this transition from traditional popular religion to non-tradition bound religiosity of the culture might be heard in the expression 'religious popular culture' which different speakers during the congress preferred to 'popular religion', see e.g. in this journal the contribution of P. Post, "Religious Popular Culture and Liturgy: An Illustrated Argument for an Approach". This shift confirms our assumption that youth is merely in the vanguard of the whole pastoral (r)evolution, and that popular religion vanishes together with cultural Christianity.whether in the long term a popular religion can develop within a minority Christianity, remains an open question even after this congress.

4. For a more elaborate discussion, see the contribution in this journal of L. Leijssen, "Religion populaire et postmodernité".

such a foundation possibly could not be there at all. For this observation of the crisis in contemporary rationality there has also been found a name in the meantime: postmodernity."[5]

In his own terminology, the Catholic French philosopher Jean-Luc Marion likewise recognises this impossibility to found being rationally, which brings him to the following observation: "Through this we probably experience a radical reversal of the relation between freedom and rationality."[6] Throughout the entire metaphysical tradition, the generally accepted and hence collective rationality has determined freedom. Whoever has not submitted to the traditional norms, has been considered ab-normal. But today there is no longer an absolute or generally accepted norm available: *anything goes*. This reverses the relation between rationality and freedom: rational is what we choose in all freedom to consider rational. The only thing we have left is our freedom to choose. This freedom is not yet particular, since as preceding each and every rationality, it is still without any qualification with respect to content: "Freedom is not one of the possibilities, but more radically the possible par excellence, because it opens up the horizon of all possibles."[7]

How all this alters the status of reason (it does not necessarily imply complete relativism), we cannot elaborate here in detail.[8] We do want to briefly consider the question of what faith and reason have left in common under the described postmodern condition. If faith is only a non-foundable possibility that is left to our freedom, are we then handed over to a new fideïsm? To a certain degree, yes. If metaphysics has become implausible and had to cede place, then only a reflexivity *"from faith to faith"*[9] remains, a new fideïsm in the sense that our faith ultimately re-

---

5. J. Bloechl - S. Van den Bossche, "Postmoderniteit, theologie en sacramentologie. Een onderzoeksproject toegelicht," *Jaarboek voor Liturgie-onderzoek* 13 (1997) 21-48, 23 (our translation). At the same time it may become clear how closely postmodernity bears resemblance to modernity. Descartes' *'cogito, ergo sum'* as the only undoubtable stand that survives *'le doute méthodique'*, is in fact already an articulation of the idea that the freedom of the ego determines rationality. Modernity wanted to universalise this 'cogito', and in this way made autonomy a grand narrative. Postmodernity is the discovery of the failure of this project, and so a 'back to square one'. See e.g. W. Welsch, *Unsere postmoderne Moderne*. Acta humaniora (Weinheim, 1987).

6. J.- L. Marion, *Prolégomènes à la charité* (Paris, 1986) 62 (our translation). See also the whole chapter 'La liberté d'être libre', p. 43-68. For a broader elaboration of the same subject matter see Id., *Dieu sans l'être* (Paris, 1991).

7. Marion, *Prolégomènes*, 63 (our translation).

8. For the consequences for the problematic of truth, see e.g. L. Boeve, "De weg, de waarheid en het leven. Religieuze traditie en waarheid in een postmoderne context," *Bijdragen* 58 (1997) 164-188.

9. See J.-S. O'Leary, *Questioning Back. The Overcoming of Metaphysics in Christian Tradition* (Minneapolis-Chicago-New York, 1985) passim.

ceives its truth from faith.

To rationally account for our faith would thus mean: to phrase as rationally as possible, not why we believe (something), but *what we already believe*[10]. And whenever we reconsider our Christian tradition in a nuanced way, we notice that this has in fact always been the case.[11]

As a result, for Marion the rational clarification of faith means that faith must be clarified time and again so that within a certain juncture of time it refers to the Mystery. The Mystery must as it were be presented to reason, without the Mystery becoming accessible to reason. This is the necessary function of apology in theology[12], and at the same time its failure, because apology can never escape the domain of reason. And reason can only cover the domain accessible to it: to place one in front of the option of faith. If one does not 'make the leap', then reason is completely powerless.[13] For freedom precedes rationality.

In short: a rational wording of faith remains important, but is always an expression of what is already believed. When applied to liturgy, this makes it clear that liturgy can never convince or prove its being correct. Still it must be as liturgically-'rational' as possible: i.e. it must bring into presence the Mystery.

1.2. Postmodernity: a specific (non-)filling-in of religiosity

On the one hand, modernity initiated in society a process of functional differentiation in the diverse spheres of action, whereby the religious was moved from the centre of culture tot its periphery, yet was not abolished.[14] On the other hand, perhaps most of all, the grand narrative of technology periodically gave the impression that secularised humankind would one day be able to do without religiosity, that this sphere of action would thus disappear. Nothing could be less true![15] Now that it has be-

---

10. L.-M. Chauvet, *Symbol and Sacrement. A Sacramental Reinterpretation of Christian Existence*, transl. P. Madigan and M Beaumont (Collegeville: The Liturgical Press, 1995) 2.

11. See e.g. Marion, Dieu sans l'être, 50.

12. See Marion, *Prolégomènes*, 69-88.

13. Ib., 81.

14. See e.g. L. Boeve, "Initiatie en traditie in een postmoderne samenleving. Een theologische verheldering," *Verbum* 64/7-8 (1997) 128-135, here 130; Id., "Erfgenaam en erflater. Kerkelijke tradities binnen de traditie,' in *Traditie en initiatie. Perspectieven voor de toekomst*, ed. H. Lombaerts and L. Boeve (Leuven, 1996) 43-77, here 50.

15. A striking example of this can be found in the picture *Dekalog I* of the Polish director K. Kieslowski, where the computer seems to obtain command over life and death, but in doing so pitifully fails. About this see S. De Bleeckere, *Levenswaarden en levensverhalen. Een studie van de decaloog van Kieslowski* (Leuven, 1994) 11-20.

come clear that the grand narratives are not capable of installing the Kingdom of God in a secularised version, religious fever is back in abundance: "Perhaps nowhere else but in postmodernity is there so much yearning for presence [of the sacred], but there is also the realisation that to the degree that one thinks oneself able to capture a present meaningfulness, the very registration of it immediately announces the postponement of a nearby fulfillment."[16] Whatever emerges within historical reality, can never signify radical alterity or absoluteness. Postmodern religiosity is therefore a hunger that refuses to be satisfied: it must by no means adopt a narrative structure. Or put differently: life hankers after more than historically given life, but no God announces himself, who transcends existence, who is an Other. This has led Johan Baptist Metz to the following slogan for our contemporary culture: "Religion ja, Gott nein."[17] The religious is doing well, but this does not announce better times for (Christian) faith in God, as sometimes seems to be hoped for in circles of ecclesial policy and elsewhere.[18] Conversely, the new traditionalism and the so-called 'wild religiosity' suffer the same disease: they both seek identity without alterity, as has shown L. Boeve[19], and must therefore be placed over against Christian faith in God rather than to be integrated in it.

16. G. De Schrijver, "Sacramentaliteit van het bestaan in de overgang van premoderniteit naar moderniteit en postmoderniteit," *Hedendaagse accenten in de sacramentologie*, Nikèreeks 32, ed. J. Lamberts (Leuven-Amersfoort: Acco, 1994) 17-64, 53 (our translation). The article has been published in English in G. De Schrijver, "Experiencing the sacramental character of existence: transitions from premodernity to modernity, postmodernity, and the rediscovery of the cosmos," in *Current issues in sacramental Theology. A Tribute to Cor Traets*. Studies in Liturgy, ed. J. Lamberts (Leuven: Peeters, 1994, 13-27. Unfortunately this very quotation was mistranslated (p.21), so that in the English version it becomes incomprehensible.

17. See J.-B. Metz - T.R. Peters, *Gottespassion. Zur Ordensexistenz heute* (Freiburg-Basel- Wien, 1991) 22-24.

18. See e.g. J. Vrancks, *Het onverwachte perspectief: gesprekken over kerk en zingeving* (Leuven, 1995).

19. See Boeve, *Initiatie en traditie*, 134; Idem, "Religieus benji-springen. Jongeren en transcendentie-ervaringen in de postmoderne cultuur," *Tijdschrift voor geestelijk leven* 52 (1996) 111-124.

2. Postmodern youth, religiosity and Christianity

2.1. Postmodern young people and their religiosity

2.1.1. Postmodern youth: an analysis

How is all this embodied in a postmodern youth? As an eye-opener we
first describe the transition from *generation X* to *generation Y*. We examine some excerpts from a short, but very revealing article *in Weekend
Knack*[20]. Generation X[21] was the generation of relativism, and was thus
described as "doom-mongering, apathic, ironic and fretful". Generation
Y seems to be the generation of young people for who even relativism
demands too much commitment: "After X comes logically Y, in the
American press loudly welcomed as *Generation Why?*, because of their
refusal to be classified anywhere (...) 'They come across respectably.
They are so very conformist that it seems as if the generation gap no
longer existed', says *Gerry Lybeer*. But the gap is larger than ever, because they live in their own, specific world. Reacting against has been
replaced by closing oneself off. (...) It becomes clear that the Y-generation is not what it seems to be. Conformism is rather a carefully con-
structed strategy of survival, a pragmatic solution in order not to become
cynical." Generation Y "shops in *the supermarket of styles*", is "*post-
fashion*" (fashion is still too binding) and "*post-tribe*" (also the self
chosen tribal culture of the *peer group* is trapping), and goes in for "*style
surfing*" (life becomes an Internet). Thus Y only radicalises X; its new
conformism veils radical cynicism. The article concludes with a quote
from Douglas Coupland, whose book *Generation X* gave this phenomenon its name: "The most important about X they never understood,
namely that it has nothing to do with age, but is a way of perceiving the
world."

In what way does postmodern youth perceive the world?[22] The first

---

20. See L. Kemps, "Generation Why?," *Weekend Knack* of 3/9/97, 41-42 (our translations).

21. See D. Coupland, *Generation X. Tales for an Accelerated Culture*, 1991.

22. For a more exhaustive account see S. Van den Bossche, "Jeugdpastoraal – een
oriëntatie," *Collationes* 24 (1994) 285-312; Id., "De kerk: uitverkoop of herinrichting?,"
De steen is weggerold. Verrijzenis en verzoening vandaag (Antwerpen, 1997) 107-121,
here 111-115. Here we put together the essentials, and add recent literature. A number of
characteristics of postmodern youth will be recognised in L. Voyé, "Effacement ou
relégitimation de la religion populaire', in this journal. There is also a very good description from a free-thinking perspective, in K. Raes, "Waarden van en waarden in het
uitgaansleven van jongeren. Instant sex, fast drugs en black sabbaths?," Id., *Het moeilij-
ke ontmoeten. Verhalen van alledaagse zedelijkheid* (Brussel, 1997) 189-212.

observation of contemporary youth shows above all a growing uncertainty. No single tradition or value, no life perspective still stands unshakeably upright.[23] This is true for youth and for their identification figures such as parents and educators. There is no longer a generation gap, because there is no delimited pubertal crisis as search for identity left: the search has become permanent...

The cause of this uncertainty lies in the complex plurality of lifestyles and truths which are poured out over the young. There is no longer an identity against which to react (e.g. the educational project of a Catholic school), there is only the search for a non-available identity, and the other side of this, the 'to each his/her own truth' or 'anything goes'. In other words: freedom defines rationality, which remains constantly aware of its own uncertainty.[24]

23. R. Rezsohazy summarises the inquiries, which he has done every five years since 1977, as follows: "greater autonomy of individuals and the lack of coherent systems, carried across from one to another generation". See R. Rezsohazy, "Analyse van het verschijnsel: de waarden van jongeren, *Nieuw tijdschrift voor politiek* (uitg. Cepess) 1/1 (1997) 9 (our translation).

24. See about all this Ph. Van Meerbeeck, "De ontredderde jeugd: een getuigenis," *Nieuw tijdschrift voor politiek* (uitg. Cepess) 1/1 (1997) 11-17. Van Meerbeeck's evidence from psychiatric praxis is very depressing. Although his tone is a little irritating, herein we hear the indignation of a doctor who observes mentally what others describe from the observations of weekend accidents. To help the reader sense the seriousness of the problematic, we relate some pointed quotes (italicisation and translation are ours). First about young from what was called above the Y-generation, and their parents: "We see parents who are late adolescents, who keep a young look for themselves, because they have difficulty with aging, and *teenagers who have become hyper-conventional,* who do the best they can to be integrated. And the parents say: he is not rebellious enough, he is far too listless, he does nothing at school, he has no interests, he keeps hanging in front of the television, he does not have a single passion. We face demoralised teenagers, who have no plans, who care about nothing. And for these reasons the parents consult us." (p.12) And further on concerning identification figures and uncertainty: "The father is completely outstripped. He is good for nothing anymore. There are women who love each other and let themselves be inseminated by the same nonymous donor. There are thus two small children that differ one year in age, who have two mummies who sleep together. Imagine their children at the age of fourteen. They surely are going to have some identity problems. But the adult world does not care about this. Ask the people who employ insemination, and *they will tell you that those harmful consequences have not been proved scientifically.*" (p.16) Finally a last quote about freedom and rationality: "And the parents, they still remain in the sphere of influence of their generation for which it is '*Forbidden to forbid*'. Parents can undergo a late puberty regarding their child's love life. There are parents who take *the right to freedom*. Now that you are grown up, I leave with my secretary, my co-worker. The adolescent is really in a competitive position, and sometimes the father leaves with the girlfriend of his daughter, and the mother is inconsolable and weeps in the arms of her son, saying: "Daddy has gone, all men really are pigs, they only think about sex." And the father says: "Your mother is frigid, she never wants, and I, you must understand, I feel a need to ..."." (p.17)

The straightforward consequence of this is that young people harbour a deep distrust of Big Truths. They look at them like hair-restorers for bold men: if one of these would really work, the others would have disappeared from the market a long time ago...[25] Rather than to hand themselves over to one tradition of meaning, lifestyle or fashion, they combine in their individual way of life all sorts of fragments, in an always provisional and incomplete way, to an unfinished entity. In sociological jargon: they create a bricolage- and collage-identity.[26] Several authors furthermore point in this context to the increasingly *harmonic* unification of *contradictions* within the one collage (but what does unity mean in a collage?), because of the relativity of each point of view, but also because of the contradictions between the discourses of the different spheres of life.[27] Meanwhile all this does not seem to bring forth an integrated life.

In its ongoing effects on daily life, the postmodern attitude can then develop in two directions. At its best, it is a non-totalitarian, searching dealing with truth and meaning, in the line of politically responsible deconstructionism of philosophers like Derrida and Lyotard. The other possible direction, however, is a relativism that merely abandons the search for truth and depth, and delivers itself to the narcissist aesthetics

25. See H. Barz, "The Pursuit of Happiness. Empirische Befunde zur Religion der unglaübigen Jugend in Deutschland," *Praktische Theologie* 29/2 (1994) 116. This article is a recapitulation of Barz's extensive research on these themes in three volumes: H. Barz, *Religion ohne Institution? Eine Bilanz der sozialwissenschaftlichen Jugendforschung. Mit einem Vorwort von Georg Schmid. Teil 1 des Forschungsberichts "Jugend und Religion"* (Opladen, 1992); Id., *Postmoderne Religion. Am Beispiel der jungen Generation in den alten Bundesländern. Mit einem Vorwort von Thomas Luckmann. Teil 2 des Forschungsberichts "Jugend und Religion"* (Opladen, 1992); Id., *Postsozialistische Religion. Am Beispiel der jungen Generation in den neuen Bundesländern mit einem Vorwort von Shmuel N. Eisenstadt. Teil 3 des Forschungsberichts "Jugend und Religion"* (Opladen, 1993). For critical reflexions on the radical conclusions of Barz, see A. Schöll, "Alltagsreligiosität von Jugendlichen. Kritische Anmerkungen zur Studie "Jugend und Religion" von Hainer Barz, *Praktische Theologie* 29/2 (1994) 117-134.

26. See R. Englert, "Sakramente und Postmoderne – ein chancenreiches Verhältnis," *Katechetische Blätter* 3/96, p. 155.

27. See a.o. M. Bouverne-De Bie, "Hoe paradoxaal is de leefwereld van jongeren," XXX, *Jongeren en cultuur in beweging* (Leuven, 1996) 147-160, passim; M. Elchardus, *Een jeugd uit uitstel geboren. Een exploratie van de cultuur van de postadolescentie, Jongeren en cultuur in beweging*, 9-43, here 36-38; R. Mokrosch, "Natürliche Religion im Alltag Jugendlicher und Erwachsener? Gedanken im Anschluss an Paul Tillichs Begriff der ontologischen Angst, *Natural Theology versus Theology of Nature?*, ed. G. Hummel (Berlin-New York, 1994) 271-284, here 272-277.

of what 'works' (just for a little while): the emotion, the kick.[28]

Yet there is another pernicious side effect: the world as global market, or the commodification of all life spheres[29], that also pervades the life world of youth. Economy, no longer in service of a societal project[30] and hence left to itself, starts functioning as a parasitical grand narrative, and sweeps along all and everything in the whirl of making money to spend money. Behind the many possible choices of the supermarket lurks manipulated consumption, to which youth appear not to remain insensitive.

We might sum up this short overview with a witticism: in postmodernity everybody becomes young. Youth starts at an ever earlier age, continues always longer, and starts again as a 'second youth' after a short period of adulthood. Key elements in our culture are uncertainty and the search for identity, the difficulty to choose[31], and postponed or avoided commitment.

2.1.2. Contemporary youth: probably postmodern, certainly post-Christian

In all fairness, we have to add to this analysis an observation of a somewhat different colour: some social scientists appear to be slightly more reserved in their conclusions than are philosophers and theologians or psychiatrists. Statistical reality is as always more grey than in bright clair-obscure observed tendencies. M. Elchardus, for example, does not admit the predicate postmodern for contemporary youth, and thinks that a new category such as post-adolescence can already explain many of the evolutions.[32] J. Kerkhofs likewise points out continuity in the midst of all the discontinuity.[33]

It would take us too far afield to start balancing their findings over

28. Concerning this, see H. De Dijn, "Postmodernisme, zingeving en jongerencultuur, in Id., *Hoe overleven wij de vrijheid? Modernisme, postmodernisme en het mystiek lichaam* (Kapellen-Kampen, 1993) 37-52. Also L. De Cauter, *Archeologie van de kick. Verhalen over moderniteit en ervaring* (Amsterdam-Leuven, 1995). The example of the kick-culture seems to be the soap opera, and in its more perverse shape the reality-show.

29. Concerning this, see L. Boeve, "De godsdienst van de markt: religie in de postmoderne cultuur," *Wereld en zending* 25 (1996) 138-147.

30. See F. Fukuyama, *The End of History and the Last Man* (New York, 1992).

31. See J. Dumon, "Geloven in Jezus Christus en levenskeuzen," *Collationes* 27 (1997) 299-323.

32. See Elchardus, "Een jeugd uit uitstel geboren," 38. One must notice however that Elchardus refers to postmodern*ism* as a philosophical-societal current, a notion far more strictly to be determined than the notion postmodern*ity* as used in the congress, which rather tries to typify our culture as a whole in its historical evolution.

33. See J. Kerkhofs, "Wat vinden jongere generaties van waarden?," *Jongeren en cultuur in beweging*, 45-57, here 51-53.

against those of philosophers and theologians – and anyway it does not look like there is a real contradiction.[34] R. Rezsohazy finds a middle course: "The personally designed value systems do not cause too much trouble as long as life does not throw extraordinary challenges. But they risk to start staggering when the life's routine becomes interrupted. (...) The young loses his bearings, he loses North, he does not know which way to turn. Desperation."[35]

Nevertheless, all authors agree on one thing: on the level of religion and (certain subsectors of) ethics, there is clearly a breach with the past. This agreement raises two considerations.

First a warning light appears for the theologian if these very two life spheres appear to be liable to change more than the others. This is a sign of something! For options about meaning and ethics always used to procure – at least prereflexively – 'a way, a truth and a life' on basis of which the individual builds his/her life, notwithstanding all functional differentiation. But if in this field a breach occurs, one can expect the other life spheres to follow in the long term the religious-ethical mental change.

And this pattern can be recognised in concrete youth work. If sexual ethics are left out of consideration (a domain where our western-Christian tradition bears historical wounds), it is indeed not so easy to name concretely where the prevailing portrayal of humankind of the traditional Christian youth work statistically (because there clearly are excrescences) evolves away from the Christian portrayal of humankind – and besides, one does not feel a need to provide culpabilising moral hints of that kind. Now this persuades some to keep calling this youth work Christian, even 'Church', based on orthopraxis.[36] The evolution towards the postmodern paradigm is however very clear on the level of faith and Church commitment, and hence on the level of the global basic meaning giving attitude that colours youth work with a contemporary touch. In a painful way this shift is expressed in the increase of suicide and suicidal behaviour among the young, and in the way other youth react to it.[37]

---

34. We observed a similar apparent contradiction also a few years ago; See Van den Bossche, "Jeugdpastoraal – een oriëntatie," 292-293.

35. See Reszohazy, "Analyse van het verschijnsel: de waarden van jongeren," 9 (our translation).

36. See about this: Van den Bossche, "Jeugdpastoraal: een oriëntatie," 300-302.

37. See Van Meerbeeck, "De ontredderde jeugd," 13: "Suicide among the young today has taken new proportions. There is an epidemic of suicide. (...) And then everybody goes to the funeral of one of them, and afterwards they say: 'in fact he has right, and I would do the same thing as he'." Also see Raes, "Waarden van en waarden in het uitgaansleven van jongeren," 201: "Already before I made – in imitation of Susan Sontag – the link between this awareness of radical 'futility' and the dominant presence of the

The Christian clearly does not hope for the portrayal of humankind of our culture to evolve away from the Christian portrayal of humankind, because then the conflict between culture and faith will begin in earnest. Of course, determining the concrete future remains a matter of reading tea-leaves, but we do take seriously the warning, only 100 years ago, of Friedrich Nietzsche, the father of all deconstruction, who confirmed that he was narrating the history of the coming two centuries![38] Therefore, in our view, postmodernity is not an experiment of thought, but the major pastoral challenge western Christianity faces.

The second consideration can then be formulated far more compactly. Even if the discussion remains open in how far the postmodern paradigm has found entrance among the young, it is still certain, also statistically, that they have become post-Christian[39] and that their meaning-giving system is not Christian popular religion, but the religiosity of postmodernity. Quod erat demonstrandum.

We do not want to conclude this section about postmodern youth and their religiosity without calling to mind that while postmodern religiosity does hamper the choice for faith, it does not make it impossible. In postmodernity, Christian faith is reminded in a radical way of its particularity, but remains possible from the freedom of rationality. Consequently, among today's generations of young there is a minority of Christians for whom the identity of their faith takes on a growing importance.[40] They are no longer Christians-by-birth, as in the time of popular religion, but Christians-by-option or by conversion.

colour black in a lot of subcultural clothing, just like in a lot of rock music where the themes of death, suicide and futureless violence – whether or not connected to drug use – are constantly brought under attention. (...) From this angle one must situate the strikingly high number of suicides among young people less than twenty-five years old. These numbers have doubled in ten years time, and constitute the second cause of death after traffic accidents in this age category. A world in which one has the experience of being rejected is a world one will also reject oneself, because it has nothing to offer."

38. F. Nietzsche, *Wille zur Macht, Vorrede*, §2, as quoted in Marion, *Prolégomènes à la charité*, 131.

39. See I. Verhack, "'God' in de 'eerste post-christelijke generatie'. Indrukken opgetekend bij de monniken van Tibériade," *Communio* 1995/6, 401-410, who commences his article as follows: "Sociologists agree that we face the first *post-Christian* generation, almost two thirds of the 18 to 24 year olds now.", with reference to Bruno Chenu, quoted in E. Poulat, *L'ère postchrétienne. Un monde sorti de Dieu* (Paris, 1994) 221.

40. In this connection, it deserves notice that, at the K.U.Leuven, the number of students who add a degree in theology to their profane studies, is on the rise. Probably once again the growing importance of choice plays a role here: whoever in his/her search gradually opts for the Christan faith as a narrative from which he or she can live, likes to explore the identity of that faith more thoroughly.

2.2. Religious questions of postmodern youth, and Christian answers

2.2.1. Ancient questions

The deeper and by their nature religious questions of the young are the same questions that have always been questions to humankind, and globally probably always will be: if no knowledge is universal, then ignorance is. P. Van Meerbeeck describes this as follows: "At the university 600 young enter the first undergraduate in psychology, although there are only few perspectives. But they think that there they will learn something about themselves, about the main questions of humankind, about memory and the sexual, about love, about death."[41] Indeed, in the end also contemporary young want to be somebody and to belong to somebody. To probe with them into the real questions, all of which have something to do with 'l'amour et la mort', therefore is not so very difficult.

2.2.2. Christian faith versus postmodern religiosity

After our earlier descriptions however, it must be clear that the Christian answer to those questions is not very evident nowadays. At least two reasons for this can be forwarded.

First, the postmodern religiosity of the young can be defined as an immanent religiosity[42]. As we explained before: there is 'something more' (Religion ja), but this more cannot be filled in by an alterity (Gott nein). Insofar as the nostalgia for the more-than-historical rises from the feeling that all that is given is historical and relative, how could one then accept that the awaited absolute alterity manifests itself in any historical-particular religious tradition? The postmodern religious sense is pre-

---

41. Van Meerbeeck, "De ontredderde jeugd," 15.

42. See Kerkhofs, "Wat vinden jongere generaties van waarden?," 55; Barz, "The Pursuit of Happiness," passim; U. Schwab, "Perspektiven evangelischer Jugendarbeit," *Praktische Theologie* 29/2 (1994) 147-159, here 156-158. It is striking that a non-religious author makes exactly the same observations about what he then calls 'neo-paganism'. See Raes, "Waarden van en waarden in het uitgaansleven", 206: "This is not a faith with a strong moral foundation – as is characteristic of the Judeo-christian tradition – nor is it a faith into transcendence, but a faith in the functioning of immanent powers of all sorts, that stands squarely on the 'legitimate' and widespread scientific world view, although it often calls upon a pseudo-scientific jargon (think about the success of *The X-files*). (...) Whatsoever, characteristic of this neopagan culture is that it stands not only squarely on each kind of normative authority, but also on the humanistic reliance in the 'autonomous person' who has liberated himself from a 'self-indebted tutelage' (Kant). It believes in the power of irrational forces *outside* human, but yet *inside* the world."

cisely the antithesis of the religious message of a religion of revelation[43]: this says "Gott ja, Religion nein", this latter in the sense of Bonhoeffer, whereby the given autonomy of historical reality must be recognised. Any way of faith surrendering by definition rules out the postmodern religiosity of longing for what is absent: the pearl one was in search of is now found. But this works also the other way around: the degree of someone's affective recognition of the postmodern religious sense is inversely proportional to his/her being approachable for religious revelation. In this way it becomes very difficult to believe in a personal God, whose being personal precisely pertains to radical alterity and an absolute transcendence over against the ego[44], a God who moreover reveals himself as alterity within history. The *faith in God* has become a particular option that cannot be founded.

But this self-revealing personal God also qualifies himself in Christian terms. God is not just an Other. It is likewise difficult for postmodern young to accept the totalitarian claim the biblical God makes on the life of his creatures. He is a jealous God, He wants to be the Lord, the First. To have a preference has become very difficult in postmodern times of (not) choosing. According to the famous Flemish mystic Jan van Ruusbroec it is precisely only this that God asks from human: his preference.[45] To believe for the Christian means to make the biblical God, as He lets himself be known in many ways and especially in his Son, the First in ones life. And this is also the position Jesus claims: "I am the Way, the Truth and the Life" (John 14: 6a). Has there ever been a culture more in search for the truth than ours, for what is real life, and for a way that one can go? But precisely because all of this is unclear, it is unclear also why Jesus Christ may apply this to his person. Experience teaches us that this choice for Jesus is very difficult for the postmodern young, even when they voluntarily attended some kind of authentic Church for a long time. We can conclude that even as a particular option the *Judeo-christian* faith is not the most evident way to believe for postmodern youth.

---

43. See Bloechl-Van den Bossche, "Postmoderniteit, theologie en sacramentologie," 30: "Radical postmodernity, as we can say now, stands or falls with the sturdiness of its two pillars: historicism and 'the death of God'. We can also add to this that it defines itself as a world view precisely by denying the content of Christian faith."

44. For more on this theme, see the thematic issue "God, geen persoon?," *Collationes* 26/2 (1996) passim.

45. See D.A. Stracke a.o., *Jan Van Ruusbroec. Van den gheesteliken tabernakel.* Tweede aangevulde en verbeterde uitgave (Tielt, 1946²) 9, line 26.

2.2.3. Christianity from an analogical to a contrasting relation toward culture

Only when both these difficulties are pushed aside, underestimated or overlooked[46], can one see a real chance for Christianity in postmodernity. Rudolf Englert, for example, asks how far the current social and personal non-identity, which arouses again a sense for the *sacred*, also testifies to a sensibility for the *sacramental* dimension of reality.[47]

This phrasing of the question of course sounds very promising. But the distinction between sacrality as more than historicity and sacramentality as encounter with a loving alterity must then remain clear. In Englert's position, this distinction seems to blur. This becomes apparent when to 'the worn out sport shoe' – that among the young enjoys a high symbolic value, and represents the lived life, hence becomes sacral – is also attributed a sacramental character.[48] This bears witness to what one might almost call a guilty naiveté. Naiveté in the sense of the story in which the religious teacher tells about something brown that jumps through the trees and gathers nuts. The teacher asks what this could be. Somewhere in the back of the classroom a sceptical child answers: "According to all logics this should really be a squirrel. But you shall see: to her it will again be Jesus Christ..."[49] Or like a youth one day complaining to us: "Sir, they pushed faith down our throats." In other words, a clearance sale to a basically modern-metaphysical distortion is of no avail to Christian faith, certainly not at the moment when such metaphysics with its universal presumptions is as good as dead.

The naiveté in addition becomes guilty, since it loses sight of any critical pedagogical disposition. When grunge-idol Kurt Cobain kept wearing ripped and soiled jeans once he had become a mega-star, to identify with the poor young from the American slums where he had also grown up, this carried indeed a valuable symbolic. But when rich European young thoroughly destroy their new jeans, until the new has gone and they bear the rips, in order to be admitted to the adored grunge peer-group, then the rich symbol has been degraded to an instrument of

---

46. Both of course refer to each other: love can be defined philosophically as the acceptance of absolute alterity.

47. Englert, "Sakramente und Postmoderne," 157.

48. Ibid., 158. Further on, this author talks about 'sacraments of daily life' as there are the first sigaret in the morning, the fresh shower, or the news late at night. Although at the end of his argument Englert shortly indicates that the Christian sacraments grant a character of promise to people's dreams of happiness and change reality 'realsymbolisch' [Rahner], there is still no report of the particular Christian narrative.

49. For the joke and commentary see W.A. De Pater, "Het postmoderne nog eens uitgelegd, *Nederlands theologisch tijdschrift* 1996/3, 177-202, here 188.

postmodern collective narcissism.[50]

From this example it may become clear that the theologian who wants, at any price, to push Christianity in the young's sport or other shoes, and thereby passes over the freedom of their rationality hideously, in the end risks losing contact with both the young and Christianity.

Still, one must not exaggerate. In the above example things go wrong because an analogy between Christianity and culture (sacramentality and sacrality) is replaced by an identification of both. This does not render all analogies worthless. W. de Mahieu, for example, makes a more nuanced distinction.[51] He distinguishes in the context of youth pilgrimages the analogical approach, where resemblance is sought between daily life and the pilgrimage, from the contrasting approach, where the experiences of the pilgrimage contrasting with daily life, question that daily life.[52] We could also call this a modern versus a postmodern approach. In modernity, faith recognises itself in the rationality of life, and has at the same time a correcting function: is it (only) analogous to life. In a postmodern setting, faith appears as an alternative rationality which, if one enters it (literally in a pilgrimage), that is, if one freely *opts* for it, changes the rationality of life radically. One returns "completely changed", even if not all recognition of former life is absent.[53] To recall the image of the supermarket once more: in the supermarket of religions, in order to attract attention one must highlight the distinction between oneself and the other, not the resemblances with what is displayed on the other shelves.

De Mahieu recognises that both approaches have their opportunities and need not exclude each other, and that even the analogical approach is

---

50. See De Dijn, "Postmodernisme, zingeving en jongerencultuur,' 44. Throughout his contribution, Englert seems to accept rather uncritically that one can create one's own symbols oneself.

51. W. de Mahieu, "Pelgrimeren, vandaag nog?," *Communio* 1995/6, 428-436; About the novelty of faith, see also J. Dumon , "Weerstanden in de jongerenpastoraal," *Collationes* 24 (1994) 313-333.

52. We continue here following de Mahieu's terminology. One could, however, argue that we deal rather with the part of resemblance (instead of analogy) and contrast, and that the correct relation between faith and culture is that of an analogy, that typical comparison where the contrast always remains larger than the resemblance. In this sense the fourth Latheran Council formulated the analogical relationship between God and the world: "...*inter creatorem et creaturam non potest tanta similitudo notari, quin inter eos maior sit dissimilitudo notanda*." (Denzinger, 1974, 262, nr. 806). For the quotation and a larger section about analogy, see L. Aerts, *Gottesherrschaft als Gleichnis? Eine Untersuchung zur Auslegung der Gleichnisse Jesu nach Eberhard Jüngel.* Europäische Hochschulschriften, Reihe XXIII, Theologie, Bd. 403 (Frankfurt am Main - Bern - New York - Paris) 110.

53. de Mahieu, "Pelgrimeren, vandaag nog?," 428.

more frequently applied. Yet he considers the contrasting approach more fundamental, and certainly in the contemporary context his assessment would seem correct. The acceptance of the particularity of its discourse opens for the Church better perspectives to relate to a culture that in its religiosity has bade farewell to its Christian past. The approach of recognition is then replaced with the approach of confrontation, the paradigm of cultural religion or popular religion withdraws for the model of the possible conversion.

An example may help clarify this contrasting approach. The English author Aidan Chambers wrote a postmodern, religious novel for the young[54], which is in itself already a risky enterprise. Whether Chambers wrote a piece of art we must not discuss here, but his pastoral intuition has not failed. He portrays the love between the unbeliever Nik and the Christian Julie. In their conversations the theme of faith occurs regularly. One could expect now – in a modern perspective – that the Christian Julie would try to explain her faith to Nik in terms as universal as possible, whereby the emphasis would mostly be on the humanitarian character of Christianity. Nothing of the kind, however, occurs: Julie's favourite text appears to be the gospel of John. Nik is allowed to attend a Church service, but must keep silent while Julie is meditating. Julie is as much in love with Nik as he with her, but she does not want to sleep with him just like that: she has problems with that as a *believer*. Later on Nik also meets "the old Kant", an older dominee whose character is absolutely unsuitable to sharing his faith with (young) people, but whose clumsy efforts make him appear to be a real man of God. After a terrorist attack, Nik catches his breath in a Benedictine convent, where during the completely unfamiliar periods of 'silentium' he wrestles with his (un)belief... Christianity is not reduced here to universal reason, but is hinted at from the outside and handled in its mystical-ecclesial and ethical particularity, by a young man for who secularisation is so self-evident that he no longer asks any questions about the past. In thus unfolding his story, Chambers has found great insight into fruitful contemporary youth ministry.[55]

Let us round off this section about postmodern youth, religiosity and Christianity with a confession: notwithstanding the confrontation with Julie, the dominee and the Benedictines, Nik does not convert to Christian faith, and this could very well be the most probable outcome of the story. In other words, if the contrasting approach is expected to have

54. A. Chambers, *Now I Know* (London, 1987).

55. In all fairness, we must mention that Chambers has not been that appealing among the young themselves... What was meant as a novel for youth appears to have in fact fascinated the youth minister more than the young.

power of persuasion again just like that, then the contrast itself is lost sight of, and this approach has been exchanged again for the analogical one. No pastoral approach can override the freedom of rationality and the contrasting relationship of Christianity toward contemporary western culture. The acceptance of the postmodern perception of reality seems a *conditio sine qua non* for Christianity to gain a viable place in contemporary western culture as an option. It cannot, however, function in a strategy of massive re-evangelisation of the European continent. We want to stress this, because precisely at this point an ambiguous logic is often employed in pastoral work, whereby the recognition of particularity is instrumentalised as part of a universally pointed strategy of persuasion: if we again dare to proclaim the gospel unabridged, then it will appeal to (all) people... For example, after the unmistakable and very delightful success of the Catholic World Youth Days in Paris (August 1997), the acute French cardinal Lustiger let himself be seduced to the enunciation that youth no longer attended Mass because their parents did not teach them to do so any more[56], that is, because they did not introduce the particularity of their tradition in education. First of all, this is definitely untrue. Many parents put considerable effort into stimulating their children to attend Sunday Mass. And the untruth of the statement proves its mistake: this 'sunday-culture-contrasting' gesture of the parents could not possibly be sufficient to persuade their children. An American archbishop, also in his euphoric evaluation of the World Youth Days, was talking about a new French Revolution, this time a revolution of Love.[57] As if a few high days of Christian identity, that were indeed very graceful to Christian young people, could have so persuasive an impact that they could alter the heavy crisis among French youth, a crisis about which all kinds of socially responsible people have been working so hard to address...

---

56. See *Weekberichten C.I.P. Vlaanderen* van 3/9/97, 15: "'These soundings tell us that the young do not go to Church anymore', says Lustiger. 'But I answer to this that they never went there. These soundings tell us that the young do not recognise themselves in the values of the Church anymore. I answer to this that they simply do not know them, because no one taught them these values. Let us listen to the questions they ask, even if they do not find the good words anymore because we did not hand these over to them. In fact these Youth Days tell more about the elder than about the young, who could not leave Church because they never entered it. In a way the uncertainty of the young only mirrors the failure of their parents'."

57. Ibid.: "The US archbishop Francis Stafford, president of the Pontifical Council for the Laity, spoke about 'a second French Revolution, a revolution of Love'."

3. Postmodern youth and Christian liturgy

Christianity in postmodernity should only try to be what it is as authentically as possible, and offer to culture what it understands from its faith. It can never convince rationally, because it has a particular position, that in fact contrasts the cultural narrative of pluralism rather than being analogous to it.

Youth ministry, however, neither can nor should claim a private ecclesiology: it must not escape to the cultural position of Christianity.[58] Pastoral attentiveness to the young must not forget about the gospel. In Dietrich Bonhoeffer's words: not youth, but Jesus Christ is the future of the Church.[59]

Only now can we apply the relation between Christianity and religiosity of the postmodern young to liturgy. The problem of youth in the Church then in fact does not so much concern liturgy, and liturgy cannot solve this problem.[60] No liturgical adaptation can persuade the young, if they do not opt for its "rationality". All liturgy can do is be itself in an authentic way. As this last point is itself a theme for an entire article in liturgical science, we will confine ourselves here to a clarification of the formulation of the problem, partly also from our pastoral experience with youth, and conclude with some open suggestions and questions, the elaboration of which we gladly entrust to the liturgists themselves.

3.1. Youth liturgy in an analogical approach?

3.1.1. The analogical model of conservatism

So far we have not given too much attention to the conservative model, because our topic was postmodernity, liturgy *and youth*. Here we do want to emphasise briefly that conservative thinking is also an analogy thinking that risks dilution in an identification of historical reality with an alterity becoming present symbolically-sacramentally. In conservatism, identity is sought for via identification of the traditum or the solidified teaching with faith as the perception of a Mystery. Again there is no contrast between faith and culture; the contemporary culture is merely replaced by the culture of the past. As a result, in strict conservatism no 'and youth' is dealt with. There is only the closed identity of the doctrine, which then appears to stand out for alterity no more than the

---

58. See O. Fuchs, "Jugend und Liturgie im Horizont der Evangelisierung," *Liturgisches Jahrbuch* 37 (1987) 156-187, here 157.

59. D. Bonhoeffer, *Gesammelte Schriften III* (München, 1960) 292-293.

60. Fuchs, 158.

complete adaptation. Just like modernist faith, conservative faith does not drink from the Mystery that no one can ever appropriate; it cherishes itself in the closed system of doctrine and truth-at-hand. In conservative liturgy, then, there is no hermeneutical relationship between the young and the liturgical event: there is only the living of the identity of closed rubricism.[61]

It can therefore suffice to notice that the only attraction of conservative faith and liturgy, which is very big for a small group of the young, departs from its given certainty or identity.[62] A number of young people grasp for faith in a severe theistic-causal and ontotheological image of God, pushing aside any question of theodicy. In the liturgical domain O. Fuchs speaks about 'liturgical hares' (the term comes from the young) who contribute in leaving everything like it used to be."[63] We personally remember a young man asking the bishop why communion on the tongue had been dropped... Some conservative young people favour the restoration of Latin in liturgy. This is exactly the reverse phenomenon of what is going on in the success of the Gregorian chants of the monks of Los Silos, and yet the same. In both cases identity is sought via the Latin, respectively where this Latin stands for the rock-solid certainty of tradition, and where as an art it keeps bearing a sacrality that is exotic-esoteric, gorgeous, but for the young is stripped of every tradition of revelation.

3.1.2. Also the progressive-analogical liturgical model at the end of its rope

In the meantime, the most prominent analogical-liturgical model is that of adaptation to the present. All too often youth liturgy seeks to convince in a metaphysical way, or to adapt so that its (supposed universal) rationality might persuade the freedom of the young to enter this (in fact self-willed) rationality. Nevertheless, especially in liturgy, the place par excellence where space must be left for the Mystery, strategies of plausibility do not work. They even make the liturgy less attractive[64] since they rob it of its symbolic particularity. Liturgy must be authentic, if it wants to confront the young with the option of faith.

A young person once gave us, in all seriousness, this definition of the ideal class-mass: "It is a mass at which you should no longer see in any

---

61. See Boeve, "Religieus benjispringen?" , 113-114.

62. About this, see P. Stappaerts, *God tussen kerk en discotheek. Jongeren en geloof* (Leuven, 1993) passim.

63. Fuchs, 187.

64. Ibid., 162.

way that it is a mass." Maybe this class-mass offers a nice spectacle – what is not at all self-evident. But it certainly does not offer the Mystery of Eucharist. Still this unorthodox definition shows where the (sport) shoe is pinching. In a postmodern context, Christian liturgy can no longer orient itself to recognition-from-life.[65] This is the impasse of the liturgical strategies of the grand narrative: they are in search of a new rationality that can persuade freedom. And the more alienated young appear to be from Christian liturgy, the more metaphysically the whole game is played: what is celebrated must at any cost be founded from life, from the supposed universal ànd at the same time Christian rationality, so that the young will enter the celebration. The result is the well-known "too many words", often accompanied by social, political and lately also ecological, moralising.

All this becomes most clear in the search for a "new language" and the creation of "new symbols".[66] Who does not remember a celebration like the one where the Good Samaritan becomes the driver of a small Volkswagen, who stops at the accident, after two hurried miscreants, the levite-in-BMW and the priest-in-Mercedes drove by... When the infantile character of such 'retranslations' comes to light[67], then 'extra-biblical texts' become the gospel. The better(?) chansonnier is promoted to be psalmist, and Kahlil Gibran supplies the meaningful reading for the wedding celebration. At her funeral, Lady Di's brother serves a political pamphlet for a homily, and luckily the good parish priest and his flock do not always understand the text of the favourite song that is played – electrically – as a communion chant at the funeral of the teenager that was killed in a weekend accident.

Also rites and symbols are strangled in clarification, are given a new interpretation or are replaced. In a modern baptism the newborn was "anointed, because life is like an engine that can not run without oil", this to the stupefaction of the grand-uncle missionary on holidays from a 'traditional' culture. The altar becomes an advertising panel for all kinds of charity. Polystyrene foam at each empty wall yells out the Good News.

We apologise for this somewhat cynical outburst; in fact we strongly believe in the encounter with the fifth gospel and in new symbols in which Christian salvation can be light up. But then these should be authentic references to the *Christian* mystery, and not rationalisations of

---

65. Ibid.

66. Fuchs, 158 indicates, in contrast to such trials, that the crisis is not liturgicogene or bibliogene, but ecclesiogene!

67.. In a homily it was noted, probably rightly, that the Good Samaritan should have been a wealthy man to have been able to do what he did...

different sorts. Later on we will come back in the interrogative mode to the difference between these, which is not always so clear. But a liturgist can probably easily show why liturgy is the place par excellence where rationalisation makes the living of the faith mystery impossible.

3.1.3. Should we go on "offering" liturgy in our Christian institutions for youth?

In the Flemish context, where 70 percent of all children and young go to Catholic schools, and where 20 percent of all children and youth join a Catholic youth movement (the last being a quasi-monopoly!), the preceding unavoidably poses the question to the place of liturgical moments in these pedagogical – and, nowadays, no longer considered as 'pastoral' in the strict sense – contexts.[68] In connection with this we can only make a plea for a free choice of option, growing with growing age.

For every liturgy integrated in pedagogical structures is situated a priori in the logics of a very strong analogy. It integrates a faith celebration in an evident way in the process of becoming human. Not by coincidence in the case of the Mass that should not look like a Mass, we deal with a *class*-Mass! In contexts of this kind, liturgy faces a true dilemma: cultural adaptation or Christian implementation. It is simply no longer possible "just to offer" Christian liturgy, as it is often formulated, to young people who do not opt for it. Confrontation is possible only when freedom lets itself be confronted![69]

But still another reflection merits our attention. Quite quickly, and sometimes rashly, it is said that if such is the situation, then we must celebrate with the young in alternative ways (time of reflection, prayer service...). Two risks are then present, wherein alternative efforts often go wrong.

First, such alternatives are usually understood as standing in a cate-

---

68. The standpoint Martin Klöckener takes, seems too easy to us, and certainly does not reflect the trials that are made in Flanders. He takes it for granted that for far most young the alienation of liturgy can be reduced to the alienation of faith and Church itself, which is of course correct. But from this he concludes: "Diese grosse Gruppe von Jugendlichen kann hier vernachlässigt werden; auf sie müsste zunächst im vorliturgischen Kontext der Evangelisierung eingegangen werden."; see M. Klöckener, "Die entfremdete Beziehung zwischen Jugendlichen und Liturgie," *Liturgisches Jahrbuch* 39 (1989) 228-252, here 230. With such a statement one deprives liturgy of its missionary opportunities. We will rather make a plea for a context of voluntariness, that allows liturgy to act missionarilly.

69. Here the whole question of growing in opting personally should of course be dealt with. The accompaniment of this growth is done particularly in the family as home Church. About this, see Van den Bossche, "De kerk: uitverkoop of herinrichting", 116-119.

chetical or initiation process: the young are "not up to the Eucharist", because of its high Christian identity; but in a low-Christian celebration with more liturgical space for creativity they must then be able to enter. Here, however, the freedom of postmodern rationality is once more sidestepped: the faith-initiating process with the young can only start after an option on their part, and not before it. That option needs not be an option of faith of course, but it should at least be an option to give this process a chance. One can "go and get the young where they are" only if they *want* to come along. The low-Christian profile approach one thinks one may still impose smells of recuperation all the more as it appears more clearly as Christianity-in-disguise! As such, a prayer service or low-Christian reflection time with the class comes to face the same dilemma as a eucharistic celebration. These ways rather belong in a catechetical-initiating process with volunteers – who are then in fact either unbaptised or baptised catechumens – who indeed often are not up to eucharist yet, or have aversions left that have been built up during former obligatory presence in front of the altar.[70]

There remains, of course, a general-religious celebration that requires no narrative tradition: to celebrate life is in itself valuable, also loose of a Christian interpretation. We do not want to object the importance of such a celebration, but practice points out that carrying out this kind of celebration is extremely difficult, and this is the second risk of alternative celebrations. An explanation for this difficulty we seek in the specificity of postmodern religiosity. An immanent religiosity that wells up from the lack of transcendence in the perception of reality, can well express itself in symbols, but whether it can be seamlessly turned into a religious celebration, is not that evident. Religious celebration is connected with the readiness to let the transcendent dimension of life come to the fore, and that does not work out when there is no such dimension...[71]

From our work in the field we see only two contexts where the young, from their own perception of reality, with all immanent religiosity, sense

---

70. In any case, non-eucharistic celebrations are of course valuable in themselves, and much speaks for it that not always and everywhere eucharist is celebrated, but other liturgical ways of praying from the tradition are rediscovered. See about this e.g. R. Sauer, "Die Chance des Jugendgottesdienstes für das Gottfeiernlernen," in Id., *Die Kunst Gott zu feiern* (München, 1996) 253-263, here 260, who mentions possibilities like: "Früh- und Spätschichten, Liturgische Nacht, Wortgottesdienst, Bussgottesdienst, Meditationsgottesdienst, Jugendkreuzweg, Wallfahrt, Emmausgang, Taizé-Gebet, ökumenische Gottesdienste, Stundengebet."

71. On the used terminology of course questions can be raised. We do not enter the discussion whether an immanent, i.e. atheistic religiosity is ever possible. We only want to emphasise that 'general-religious celebrating' is most of the time, and to our sense correctly, filled in by standing still consciously before a transcendent dimension of reality, and that this very sense of general transcendence is no longer evident.

something of transcendence, and hence want to celebrate in a religious way. To be clear: we then deal with collectively shared cultural values, and not with the foundation of transcendence in humanity itself.

The first context is that of death as the most radical question of life.[72] On the occasion of a deceased class mate, the whole group wants to reflect on this; during the midday break the chapel becomes crowded, where a picture of the deceased is exposed and quiet music plays, and available meditative texts are read with attention. The longing for more than the life that broke down here breaks open the lack of transcendence into a question and a possibility. All this is very meaningful, and a witnessing Christian interpretation among other narratives must certainly not be lacking; this is a real pluralism of identities, and here hides an apologetic[73] chance for Christian conversion or a spark of what was present but only slumbering. Nevertheless, such an event does not allow for a recuperation of the present young for Christianity. Over against the feeling of 'there is something more' also stands a '(t)here is nothing more'. For many, the further dealing with the death will consist of wanting to forget as soon as possible; life goes on, dead people do not come back, and when going out the next Saturday night, conversation about the deceased is taboo. And this is no cynicism but a closed awareness of immanence.

The second context for celebrating life is that of the group sense that is boiling over. Emile Durkheim, father of the sociology of religion, situated the origin of religion in the totemisation of the group sense. It should not then be surprising that a celebration during holiday camp succeeded so well, and was "completely different" from that in the parish. A successful bivouac asks for celebration! But again, whether the perception of this celebration was Christian, is far from clear. Even when the ritual form of the camp celebration was the Eucharist, most of the young will barely have thought about a connection with the Pascal mystery (even if it is again possible that the eyes of some open up for faith here). Eucharist has functioned then as the most convenient ritual – for until today it is part of the culturally prevailing tradition, and to invent new rituals is not easy at all – to celebrate camp life. Out of group feelings of this kind leaders of the local youth movement, who normally do not show any ecclesial tendencies, come and ask the amazed parish priest whether their group may grace the weekend liturgy on the occasion of their annual start.

72. About this, see D. Hutsebaut, "Jongeren en hun omgaan met dood en rouw," Id., *Een zekere onzekerheid. Jongeren en geloof* (Leuven, 1995) 145-206.
73. We are aware of the unfriendly undertone of the term. With apologetics we here mean again, as before, the border area between ratio and faith.

When the young are together for a pedagogical and not for a pastoral reason, so as young and not as searching Christians, we seldom see other contexts than death and the strong group sense, that ask for celebration themselves.[74] To snub leads to accidents in this matter. One can ask this to teachers who in September 1997, the year of the Holy Spirit in the run up towards the third millennium, had to try to blow (eventually also non-eucharistic) new breath into the traditional 'Mass of the Holy Spirit'. What sense a reflection on the Spirit which is meaningful for Christians was assumed to have for postmodern young, is totally unclear. And in the general, human sense we should note that a group-spirit may be boiling at the beginnings of September among decision makers, that teachers can be enthused with team-spirit, but at the same time, that the beginning of the school year creates no special religious experience for the young, gladly not of death, but neither of the group, or not to such a degree that the new year recalls transcendence and asks for religious celebration. As a result, this celebration appears to be a poisoned gift for the pastoral committee of the school.

3.2. Youth liturgy in a contrasting approach

3.2.1. A liturgy rooted in the Mystery

We have already mentioned that in conservative liturgy no 'and young' is taken into account, because this liturgy considers itself responsible only towards the *traditum*. Although we have many questions about this proceeding, we must here follow the option to a certain extent: authentic youth liturgy is a liturgy that does not neglect the young, but can relativise them, precisely because it knows itself to be, as a celebration, called by the Mystery.[75]

---

74. If one does not limit the view to the young, then of course there are more moments in postmodern life that ask for celebration. Sociologists even warn us that the sacraments could start leading their own life around these moments, separate from any Christian tradition. See e.g. K. Dobbelaere, J. Kerkhofs a.o., *De versnelde ommekeer. De waarden van Vlamingen, Walen en Brusselaars in de jaren negentig* (Tielt, 1992) L. Leijssen, K. Dobbelaere, M. Cloet (red.), *Levensrituelen: Het Vormsel.* Kadocstudies 12 (Leuven, 1991); Id., *Levensrituelen: Geboorte en Doopsel.* Kadocstudies 20 (Leuven, 1996).

75. Fuchs, "Jugend und Liturgie," 160, nuances this point: "Auch wenn die angesprochene Kontinuität nichts mit Rubrizismus und Ritualismus zu tun hat, sondern gerade um der Erlebbarkeit willen als eine höchst plastische Vorgegebenheit aufgefaßt werden muß (in der die kreative Teilnahme der Beteiligten zum Zuge kommen darf), haben die Vorhaben einer notwendigen Öffnung und Veränderung liturgischer Vollzüge doch ihre unveräußerlichen Grenzen, damit die Liturgie der Kirche nicht ihren Charakter verliert, ein in seiner Inhaltlichkeit ganz spezifisches und in seiner geschichtlichen Veränderbarkeit relativ beständiges Symbolgeschehen zu sein und zu bleiben."

The paradox is that such a liturgy to the young appears to be more attractive than the all-too-adapted kind. O. Fuchs emphasises that he does not make a plea for a market-oriented liturgical offer, but that "also strictly from the intention of effect one can be thoroughly deceived with the opinion that something new, strange, not easy to understand and mysterious, could not be as appealing and attractive to the young as something relatively rapidly understandable and comparable to their life. Both categories have in any case, as for their potential effect, an ambivalent character. I recall here only the many youth religions and esoteric groups, who precisely with their numinosities exercise a fascinating power on young people. The enculturation of alternative messages has then opportunities to succeed when in the mediation process the tension between innovation and assimilation is and remains being upheld."[76]

Thus only a Church community praying in an authentic way is capable of offering good youth liturgy, even if it is not specifically oriented to the young. Miles away from the definition of a good class-mass stands an other statement of a girl about the Eucharist. We went with a group of eighteen year old volunteers to the Trappist abbey of West-Vleteren. After the weekday Eucharist in the abbey one of the participants uttered: "This was the nicest Mass I ever attended." Now this Trappist abbey clearly has no tradition of youth liturgy... but the liturgies there, as in many abbeys, breathe authenticity! Again and again this has struck us in youth ministry: whenever the young (opt to) step into the offered authentic liturgy[77], the alienation from the Christian tradition often appears to be present, but not problematic. For example, they are completely unfamiliar with the liturgy of hours, but most of the times they find it fascinating.

So too, when the young want to believe, the irrelevance of the problematic of language sometimes is perplexing, with all ambivalence of the term. On Palm Sunday 1996 we were among 7,000 French students at the end of their annual pilgrimage from Paris to Chartres, who wholeheartedly sung the Hail Mary in the small streets of Chartres. And we asked ourselves whether we were really the only ones who had a few translation questions about this text, and felt a little embarassed about the staring gazes from the surrounding house blocks... Yet all the stronger was the impression the whole event of this journey made on us, where texts of Augustine and Henri Nouwen were put together in the pilgrims' booklet, and where the students in the Eucharist of Palm Sunday wel-

---

76. Ibid., 162 (our translation).

77. A growing number of abbeys do not accept complete class groups any longer, because the aimed at experience of the abbey becomes impossible when a part of the young present made no option for it.

comed with sincere joy their contemporaries who were going to be baptised and/or confirmed at the Easter Vigil. Here Church was growing, out of the Church grew liturgy, and in the strength of this liturgy Church grew again.

From this last example one must thus not deduce that we make a plea against any adaptation of the tradition in youth celebrations. But rather this adaptation must be performed in order to light the mystery, and not to imitate the daily life of the young. In our diocese of Gent we had the chance to cooperate to diocesan prayer services for young. The liturgy of these biblical vigils is very simple. It rests on a lot of communal chant, especially with songs from Taizé, supported by a choir and an orchestra of young people. Texts from the bible are read, there is a short interpretation and a longer period of silence, intercessory prayers are said. There is attention for symbols, candle light, bodily expression. The celebration lasts for something more than an hour, so longer than a usual weekend Eucharist. What is called here a youth liturgy, is in fact the chaining of some basic moments of Christian liturgy. These celebrations have relative success among the young: on the countryside they meet some 80 to 150 participants, in the city of Gent the number varies between 250 and 400, up to 700 when on Good Friday the bishop presides in the cathedral, in a youth vigil around the cross set up along the same pattern.

We must, however, warn here again that such an approach cannot circumvent the free option of the young. It did not work out when the leaders of a local youth movement – with the best of intentions – decided to plan such a vigil as a group activity, and came with the whole group in uniform: the freedom of these young had not been respected. Who thinks of this consideration as irrelevant, can always try to sing one of the famous Taizé songs with a complete class. Everything the richness of these songs consists of, from the singing in parts with its almost orthodox particularity, via the biblical text, to the repetitive character, is experienced as soft and boring by those who do not opt for its "rationality".

3.2.2. The crucial question: where is the celebrating community?

Above we have sufficiently emphasised that the crisis in youth pastoral is not bibliogene or liturgicogene, but ecclesiogene. It is this last we want to highlight here: without any doubt the crucial problem for youth liturgy is the lack of a Church community! This problem can hardly be overestimated. For how to celebrate without a celebrating community? Once more we concur with what Fuchs writes about this: "An attractive parish can open up avenues to a relatively traditional liturgy; and an attractively shaped liturgy becomes empty in the long term, if no social relationships in the community are linked to it."[78] And the importance of a Church community increases along with the decreasing ability of the young to think it present in a liturgy where it does not or insufficiently come into visibility: "The burden of the problem is carried by the ecclesial social forms, in which the liturgy is embedded. They manifest or hide its plausibility. This counts even more in the context of a growing neocatechumenal situation, where less and less preexisting knowledge about these things can be reckoned upon."[79]

All too often we have had to hear this at the end of an initiative with the young: "Here I experienced something, but now... In our parish there is nothing..." No reproach should be made to existing parishes: nobody can build a community without people being there. Consequently we believe that the first question about youth liturgy is a question about the restructuring of the parishes, whereby liturgists and others should mark the boundaries inside which one can only speak in a meaningful way about a celebrating Church community.

It is in this context that the ambivalent trial of a separate youth liturgy is entered. In youth ministry the tension territorial-categorial is always strongly present. In fact, one can assume that a flourishing Church community does not need any separate youth ministry! In other words, youth ministry must work additionally, and can not aim at complete Church building.

The same is true for youth liturgy: where it replaces the parish by, for example, adopting a weekly schedule, it often has counter-productive results. Experience teaches first that in the labourious struggle to reach the young it runs the risk even far more than a territorial parish that faith gets replaced by a social-moralising or Church-political alternative. We know examples where in the end the liturgical activity was cancelled, because it appeared to be the least relevant part of all that was done. We know examples where under the denominator 'young' all possible utterings of (therefore not less legitimate) Church dissidence gathered, with the result that youth, for whom 1968 is completely history, stayed away in the end.

But even if such things do not happen, the flow to the larger Church community remains very problematic. In an authentic youth Church, after six years the first weddings had passed, and the first baptism took place. One can not blame the young people, who found in this youth Church the way to personal faith experience and Christian marriage, for continuing to hang around this new type of community. Often the transi-

---

78. Fuchs, "Jugend und Liturgie," 158 (our translation).

79. Ibid., 173 (our translation); see also Klöckener, "Die entfremdete Beziehung," 242-243, on the alienation of – as well believing – young from the parish.

tion to elsewhere is practically impossible, because there is so little elsewhere! But in fact such youth Church can evolve into a personal parish. And in the meantime the nearby territorial parish feels stabbed in the back by this initiative. Even if it gives the best it can, it can never concur with a youth parish: over 80% of the members in a normal parish are more than 50 years old, all classified by the young as grandmothers and grandfathers...!

Finally, over against all risks of and objections to categorial youth liturgy stands the massive fact of the ongoing disintegration of the parishes and the unpropitious perspectives of their vitality. Already now it seems to be the case that the young find faith via a 'believing peer group', whether connected to the parish or not, rather than via the life of the parish community itself. We therefore share the ambivalent feelings we met in several authors about separate youth liturgy.[80]

3.2.3. Concluding questions about authentic youth liturgy

As a supplement to the reflections about authentic liturgy and the ecclesiogene nature of the problems described, in which a few questions for liturgical science have already arisen, we would like to conclude by formulating some further questions about authentic youth liturgy: how does youth liturgy arrive at an authentic reference to the Mystery of Gods love for humanity, in word, symbol and rite?

If faith is essentially an act of encounter between identity and alterity, if the experience of God for which liturgy creates space, consists in the experience of His immanence and His transcendence to reality, then it should not be surprising that this tension comes to the surface in each youth liturgy. All of our questions circle around the same tension, between on the one hand the Mystery, and on the other hand contingent reality, diachronically as cultural traditum or synchronically as a specific contemporaneous perception. We have nothing else than both these aspects of historical reality, and how is one to judge where, and where not, each of them becomes transparent to the Mystery?

First diachronically, alterity is never at hand: it always occurs via historical tradition. Which traditum (still) refers to God, and which is enclosed in itself? Here imports the cultural determination of tradition,

---

80. Fuchs, *Jugend und Liturgie...*, 177, makes a plea for "eine generationenübergreifende Pastoral und Liturgie". R. Sauer has a chapter on *Die Chance des Jugendgottesdienstes für das Gottfeiernlernen* in Id., *Die Kunst Gott zu feiern. Liturgie wiederentdecken und einüben* (München, 1996) 253-263, but at the same time warns against "Gettobildung" (p. 262-263).

its historically conditioned character.[81] Klöckener points to the deficit in the relation between searching-believing young and liturgical tradition as a culture.[82] He distinguishes as aspects of this problem the statute of liturgy as 'provisional result of historical development', and the relationship of the young to the world of signs and symbols of liturgy, to liturgical language (yes, after all relativisation of this trouble!), to liturgical music, to liturgical space.

On the other hand, God is synchronically immanent and transcendent to each contemporaneous perception of life. On the anthropological level, Klöckener discerns as aspects of the problematic of alienation – again among searching-believing youth – the search for identity of the young and liturgy, their longing for a liturgy near to life, their sense of community and the liturgy, their creativity and preferential love for the new and the liturgy.[83]

Both problem areas can be recognised all too clearly, including in Flanders. In concretely celebrating with the young these notions translate into areas of tension between subjectivity (the sensitivity of the young and the belief in Gods immanence among them) and objectivity (the tradition, which is in fact a collective subjective look at reality, but other than in such shapes we do not experience God's alterity). We just enumerate some similar tension areas, about which questions arise again and again, and whereby the definitive correct answer probably does not exist.

- Do we celebrate 'in one or another house', where the life of the young is enacted, or in a sacral space? Must discontinuity between activity and prayer be encouraged, or must both overflow into each other? And which space is sacral for the young?
- How do we deal with word and Word? When must we speak just human language, and when is hieratic language symbolically stronger?

81. This becomes quite manifest in Anthony De Mello's story about the guru's cat: "When the guru sat down to worship each evening the ashram cat would get in the way and distract the worshippers. So he ordered that the cat be tied during evening worship. Long after the guru died the cat continued to be tied during evening worship. And when the cat eventually died, another cat was brought to the ashram so that it could be duly tied during evening worship. Centuries later learned treatises were written by the guru's disciples on the essential role of a cat in all properly conducted worship." See A. De Mello, *The Song of the Bird* (Anand, 1982) 79.

82. See Klöckener, "Die entfremdete Beziehung," 244-249.

83. Ibid., 237-241. The other two levels where Klöckener observes the alienation between young and liturgy, more or less coincide with both our previous points 3.1.1. and 3.1.2.: he mentions the level of faith (relation towards God - towards H. Scripture - towards the handed-over faith teaching of the Church - towards handed-over forms of spirituality, popular piety and prayer) and the level of the interpersonal relationships (to the parish and the priests).

Rubrics or creativity? For example, we notice that young priests increasingly opt for an 'offical' canon again, also in youth celebrations.

- The same evidently counts for symbols. Which kinds of bread and wine can serve as species (to leave out of consideration wilder experiments)? What about liturgical garments and objects?

- And again the same questions rise about rites. Are rituality and expressivity each others antipode? And where do they cancel each other out?

- What role must be accorded to intelligibility and ratio in liturgy, that in the end lights the Mystery in its essential non-intelligibility (again the success of Los Silos)? Why does Christian faith have its own narrative?

- What is the importance of creating atmosphere? Liturgy does not rely on the kick, but rather on the 'boringness' coming into real experience. In Taizé, one senses very well that some young stick in a kind of overheated sphere. All the more, one senses the authentic living of many others, and of the monks themselves.

As one runs through this incomplete list of questions, it appears likely to be true of all times, and not limited to youth liturgy and the subjective needs that play a role there. We personally would rather put subjectivity one step below objectivity, because Christians celebrate something that does not belong to them. But this does not make attention for the subjective pole unimportant!

We conclude with ten points of orientation that Martin Klöckener works out for whoever wants to celebrate liturgy with the young tomorrow[84]: adaptation by reduction of the full measure of liturgical prescriptions – the necessity of lots of kinds of liturgy – linking the structure of history of salvation and the anthropological structure in liturgical celebration – tie in with already given time rhythms – respect for freedom and bondage in liturgy – wholesome living intellectual and with the senses of liturgy – proclamation of the Holy Scripture – time for coming to oneself and silence – critical integration of the new spiritual song – liturgical formation of the young.

Each of these points of orientation – which in the elaboration can receive a postmodern accent – poses a question from youth ministry to liturgical science, whereby 'youth' in fact stands for the need for catechetical-initiation potential of liturgy. But in a postmodern age this question, too, concerns not only the young.

---

84. See M. Klöckener, "Auch morgen mit Jugendlichen Liturgie feiern. Orientierungspunkte für den Gottesdienst mit jungen Menschen," *Trierer Theologischer Zeitschrift* 99 (1990) 296-313.

'Popular Religiosity and Liturgy'
Need and Opportunities for Evangelization

Jozef LAMBERTS

Almost twenty years ago, more precisely in 1978, during a congress of Italian professors of liturgy on 'liturgy and popular religion', the noted Benedictine Pelagio Visentin from the abbey Santa Maria di Praglia in Bresseo (Padova) gave a lecture on 'Liturgia e religiosità popolare: due mondi ancora lontani?'[1]. Visentin asked this question fifteen years after the promulgation of the *Constitution on the Sacred Liturgy*. This constitution indeed gave little attention to popular religiosity and the interest of liturgists during the sixties and the beginning of the seventies was confined to the implementation of liturgical renewal. They did this through the composing and translation of the typical editions of liturgical books, the realization of the liturgy as 'the summit and fount of Christian life' by the active participation of the faithful as the crowning of the efforts done by the Liturgical Movement[2]. The discussion on popular religiosity likewise began in Western Europe at the beginning of the seventies, although not immediately among liturgists. Gradually the liturgists also came to remark the great distance between the liturgy as conceived by the council and popular religiosity. I think that in the meantime, notwithstanding the many studies on this topic, both worlds have not been brought in a closer connection in Church praxis.

1. A Re-reading of Sacrosanctum Concilium 13

When one says that the *Constitution on the Liturgy* gave little attention to the question of popular religiosity one refers to its article 13. This

---

1. Pelagio Visentin, "Liturgia e religiosità popolare: due mondi ancora lontani?," *Liturgia e religiosità popolare. Proposte di analisi e orientamenti. Atti della VII Settimana di studio dell'Associazione professori di liturgia, Seiano di Vico Equense (Napoli): 4-8 settembre 1978.* Studi di liturgia 7 (Bologna: Edizioni Dehoniane, 1979) 217-246.

2. Jozef Lamberts, "Active Participation as the Gateway Towards an Ecclesial Liturgy," *Omnes Circumstadstantes. Contributions Towards a History of the Role of the People in the Liturgy Presented to Herman Wegman,* ed. Charles Caspers and Marc Schneiders (Kampen: Kok, 1990) 234-261.

article indeed deals with the *pia exercitia*, or popular devotions as one aspect of popular religiosity. Here we read:

> Popular devotions of the Christian people are to be highly endorsed, provided they accord with the laws and norms of the Church, above all when they are ordered by the Apostolic See. Devotions proper to particular Churches also have a special dignity if they are undertaken by mandate of the bishops according to customs or books lawfully approved. But these devotions should be so fashioned that they harmonize with the liturgical seasons, accord with the sacred liturgy, are in some way derived from it, and lead people to it, since, in fact, the liturgy, by its nature far surpasses any of them.

1.1. A Rejection of Popular Devotions?

Particularly the last sentence gave the impression that the council was holding back in regard to popular devotions. Insofar as the liturgy "far surpasses any of them", how can one then pretend that they "are to be highly endorsed"? Do we not have then to speak instead about condoning and at the same time trying to replace them as much as possible by the true liturgy? During the first years after the council many priests have put aside, neglected or even forbidden popular devotions such as benediction, stations of the cross, the recitation of the rosary, Angelus, Marian devotion during the month of May, devotion to the Sacred Heart, visits to the Blessed Sacrament, holy hour devotion, novenas, processions, pilgrimages, blessing, etc. At the same time, admirable efforts have been undertaken to allow the official liturgy of the Church, the 'ecclesial liturgy', to regain its central place. But one probably also forgot that when one calls the liturgy, most of the time reduced to the eucharistic celebration, the 'summit', there must be something else of which it must and can be the summit. One apparently believed in a kind of utopia that once the liturgy could be celebrated in the vernacular, simplified, and with the active participation of the faithful, they would no longer have need for popular devotions.[3] In this way a vacuum was created. As it may be evident now, we lost the healthy balance between liturgy *stricto sensu* and popular religiosity.[4]

1.2. The Context

It was certainly not the aim of article 13 of the Constitution to exclude

---

3. Balthasar Fischer, "Relation entre liturgie et piété populaire après Vatican II," *La Maison-Dieu* 170 (1987) 91-101, 98.

4. Anscar J. Chupungco, *Liturgical Inculturation: Sacramentals, Religiosity, and Catechesis*, Collegeville, 1992, 96.

popular devotions. We therefore need to replace this article within its context. This context is primarily the goal of the first chapter of the Constitution, namely to indicate the general principles for the reform and promotion of the liturgy. And in the context of articles five to thirteen to highlight the nature of the liturgy and its importance in the Church's life. Article 7 solemnly declares that the liturgy is to be considered:

> an exercise of the priestly office of Jesus Christ. In the liturgy, by means of signs perceptible to the senses, human sanctification is signified and brought about in ways proper to each of these signs; in the liturgy the whole public worship is performed by the Mystical Body of Jesus Christ, that is, by the Head and his members. From this it follows that every liturgical celebration, because it is an action of Christ the Priest and of his Body which is the Church, is a sacred action surpassing all others; no other action of the Church can equal its effectiveness by the same title and to the same degree.

In this line article 13 rightly concludes that such a liturgy by its very nature far surpasses popular devotions, but it does not thereby say that they consequently should be worthless. Moreover, article 9 states that the liturgy does not exhaust the entire activity of the Church. And article 12 points to the fact that

> the spiritual life is not limited solely to participation in the liturgy. Christians are indeed called to pray in union with each other, but they must also enter into their chamber to pray to the Father in secret.

It would probably be better to make a distinction between liturgy *stricto sensu* and worship as a broader circumscription, or between 'official liturgy' and 'popular liturgy'.[5] One is organized and demanded by the authority of the Church to be observed by all, the other which is varied, indeterminate, and variable arises from the people.[6] Sometimes they simply operate side by side. So people in the south of Spain celebrate with much enthusiasm and involvement the *semana santa* in the street, while the clergy is celebrating the official liturgy in almost empty churches.[7]

---

5. See Jozef Lamberts, "'Who Are Our Guests? Some Considerations About Liturgy and Popular Catholicism," *Questions Liturgiques. Studies in Liturgy* 74 (1993) 65-88. Luis Maldonado, "Liturgia, sacramentos y religiosidad popular," *El Vaticano II, veinte años después*, ed. C. Floristan and J.-J. Tamyio (Madrid: Ediciones Cristiandad, 1985), 235-270, esp. 261-263.

6. Salvatore Marsili, "Liturgia e non-liturgia,"*La Liturgia, momento nella storia della salvezza*. Anàmnesis. Introduzione storico-teologica alla Liturgia 1, ed. Burckhardt Neunheuser (Turin, 1974) 150-158, 151.

7. Maldonado, 263.

1.3. An Important 'Declaratio'

The context becomes even more obvious when we know that the goal of
the preparatory commission was to read the articles 11-13 (in the original draft: articles 7-9) as a whole, as it was written in the commission's
'Declaratio':

> The general goal of this part is to solemnly confirm the doctrine of the encyc-
> lical *Mediator Dei* on the relation between liturgy and the spiritual life of
> individuals. More specifically it deals with the possibility, even the fundamen-
> tal necessity, of a cooperation between participation in the liturgical celebra-
> tions and honest devotion: two things which touch the individual. The aim is,
> once the opposition is taken away, to point this way to the advantage of the
> liturgy. One even aims at the unity of spiritual life. That is why one says that
> the full participation in the liturgy presupposes the exercise of devotion and
> the Christian virtues in the individual's entire life, so also outside of the lit-
> urgy. This way it must be apparent that the commendation of the liturgy does
> not hinder but rather demands an intense care for spiritual life also outside of
> the liturgical actions, with all the ascetic means from Christian tradition. The
> popular devotions in general, such as the stations of the cross, the rosary, and
> others are to be highly endorsed, as Pope Pius XII has stated in his encyclical
> *Mediator Dei*. The goal of this section however is to deal with popular devo-
> tions in their relation to the liturgy as this is done in the Instruction of the
> Sacred Congregation of the Rites on 3 September 1958. Now we have agreed
> about the possibility and necessity of the unity between liturgy and popular
> devotions, we have to reach a harmonious union. So we have to instruct the
> faithful about the predominance of liturgical prayer and the liturgical as re-
> gards the other forms of devotion. One can easily see this necessity in the
> practice of those popular devotions, which divert from the liturgical cycle or
> are even in flat opposition to the liturgical cycle. So for instance with some
> feasts of the saints which clash with the most solemn feast of the liturgical
> year (e.g. the procession in honor of saint Anthony on the feast of Pentecost)
> or with novenas which are given such an importance over the liturgical feasts
> that the remembrance of the liturgical season is no longer obvious. To abolish
> such forms of devotion in such a way that there remains only the liturgical
> celebration is certainly wrong. But the pastors of souls must exert themselves
> to teach the faithful that they have first of all to celebrate the liturgical life of
> the Church, in connection with the mysteries and the seasons of the liturgical
> year, this before all other kinds of devotion. They have to liberate the faithful
> from all which still tastes of superstition in these forms of devotion. Here we
> especially refer to the number of days during which one has to say specific
> prayers, and to the shape of these prayers, etc. This sometimes seems to pro-

voke many problems.[8]

This 'declaration' sheds some light on the goal of articles 11-13 and more particularly of the latter. Article 11 says that all must be done to ensure that the faithful take part in the liturgy as it is defined fully aware of what they are doing, actively engaged in the rite, and enriched by its effects. Article 12 states that the spiritual life is not limited solely to participation in the liturgy. Article 13 consequently wants to point to the relation between this liturgy and popular devotions. The 'declaratio' clearly refers to the encyclical *Mediator Dei* of Pope Pius XII in which articles 170-183 discuss how to deal with popular devotions in a pastorally justified way.[9] Also against this backdrop, according to article 13 of the Constitution, it is obvious that popular devotions may not be rejected, but must be brought back to their correct proportions, while some conditions are set. What is striking at first is that one speaks about "highly endorsed" (*valde commendantur*) and "a special dignity" (*speciali dignitate*). In addition to ecclesiastical recognition, these conditions include that they should relate to the liturgy, harmonize with the liturgical seasons, and lead the people to a more intensive celebration of the liturgy. Important elements are given here, which must be taken into account in each form of liturgical pastoral care in the domain of popular religiosity.

1.4. A Broader Vision of 'Liturgy'

An important factor indeed is ecclesial awareness, which is supposed to be present in a paramount way in what we have called 'ecclesial liturgy', but therefore is not absent in each form of 'popular liturgy'. Is it still completely correct to call it liturgy when a priest is celebrating the eucharist with only three faithful and to deny it the *pia exercitia* where many people are gathered together in faith even when this is not always in the presence of an ordained minister? What gives us the right to continue to call the previous 'clerical' liturgy really liturgy although an essential aspect, namely the 'active participation' of all the faithful, is obviously absent? Even when originally the monks were not priests they prayed together the divine office. Nobody will deny that this was a liturgical celebration where "the Church is unceasingly praising the Lord and

8. "Excerptum ex 'Declarationibus' additis Schemati a Commissione Praeparatoria parato, quod affertur ad meliorem intellegentiam nn. 7, 8, 9 Schematis," *Emendationes*, Caput I, nos. 1-9 (Vatican City, 1962) 11.

9. Jozef Lamberts , "Un anniversaire important: 'Mediator Dei et hominum' 50 ans depuis sa parution," *Questions Liturgiques - Studies in Liturgy* 78 (1997) 131-147.

interceding for the salvation of the whole world" (SC 83).

Next to the full 'ecclesial liturgy' there are other kinds of liturgy, including 'popular liturgy', which are not less liturgy although they lack something of full theological, ecclesiological significance, experience and manifestation. This way, already participating in the liturgical sphere, they can also be approaches to and preliminary exercises for the moments when the *ecclesia* is fully aware of being convoked by the Lord, stimulated and unified by the Spirit, in the grateful celebration of the mysteries of salvation. In this way, popular devotions can receive an intermediary function, in a certain sense be ways unto salvation, ways along which the Lord will reach his people. Here we need to reflect on the adage *'per Mariam ad Jesum (et cum Ipso, et per Ipsum et in Ipso ad Patrem in virtute Spiritus Sancti)'*.

2. Popular Religiosity and 'Evangelization'

2.1. Need of Evangelization

What we can deduce from the preceding reflection is the need of 'evangelization' or maybe better of a 'new evangelization'.[10] We need to meet the people in those ways where they experience the sacred, the transcendental reality and try to celebrate it in their own way, in order to bring them to the Holy One and to encounter Him in an salvific way and to celebrate this in a liturgy which is fully ecclesial. In other words, we need to find those avenues along which people who are at home only with popular religiosity may begin to feel at home with the Church's official liturgy.

Indeed, popular devotions are rooted in Christian tradition, a number of which are a Christianization of pre-Christian customs, but that have received from the Gospel a proper meaning. Here we should remember the 569 mission given by Pope Gregory the Great to bishop Augustine of Canterbury on the occasion of the Christianization of the Anglo-Saxons to keep what was not in contradiction with the Gospel.[11] At the same time, also because of the changing situations of life and time, popular devotions also need a revision, a critical evaluation from the Gospel. That is why we must try to let the Gospel speak in whatever form of popular devotion, and especially to interpret it through homily and preaching on behalf of the seeking people in their particular situation.

---

10. *Liturgia ed evangelizzazione nell'epoca dei Padri e nella Chiesa del Vaticano II. Studi in onore di Enzo Lodi*, ed. Ermenegildo Manicardi and Fabio Ruggiero (Bologna: Edizioni Dehoniane, 1996).

11. Beda Venerabilis, "Historia ecclesiastica gentis Anglorum," *PL* 95, 57-58.

2.2. 'Evangelii nuntiandi'

In the 1975 apostolic adhortation *Evangelii nuntiandi* Pope Paul VI already wrote on evangelization in the modern world in connection with the third general meeting of the Synod of Bishops.[12] Here we find the important sentence:

> the Church is continuously to be evangelized in order to keep its freshness, power and ardor in proclaiming the Gospel.[13]

Evangelization would thus seem to be an ongoing task for those who are already evangelized or have become Christians. In other words: evangelization is not only proclaiming Christ to those who do not know him, but also a permanent re-reading of the 'signs of the time', the re-thinking of our human existence in the light of the Gospel. Consequently, Pope Paul VI links this approach of evangelization with the role of the sacraments and with popular religiosity.

[47].... Evangelization thus exercises its full capacity when it achieves the most intimate relationship, or better still a permanent and unbroken intercommunication, between the word and the sacraments. In a certain sense it is a mistake to make a contrast between evangelization and sacramentalization, as is sometimes done. It is indeed true that a certain way of administering the sacraments, without the solid support of catechesis regarding these same sacraments and a global catechesis, could end up by depriving them of their effectiveness to a great extent. The role of evangelization is precisely to educate people in the faith in such a way as to lead each individual Christian to live the sacraments as true sacraments of faith – and not to receive them passively or to undergo them.
[48] Here we touch upon an aspect of evangelization which cannot leave us insensitive. We wish to speak about what today is often called popular religiosity. One finds among the people particular expressions of the search for God and for faith, both in the regions where the church has been established for centuries and where she is in the course of becoming established. These expressions were for a long time regarded as less pure and were sometimes despised, but today they are almost everywhere being rediscovered. During the last Synod the bishops studied their significance with remarkable pastoral realism and zeal. Popular religiosity of course certainly has its limits. It is often subject to penetration by many distortions of religion and even superstitions. It frequently remains at the level of forms of worship not involving a true acceptance of faith. It can even lead to the creation of sects and endanger the true ecclesial community. But if well oriented, above all by a pedagogy of

---

12. Paul VI, "Adhortatio apostolica Evangelii nuntiandi," *AAS* 63 (1976) 1-76.
13. No. 16.

evangelization, it is rich in values. It manifests a thirst for God which only the simple and poor can know. It makes people capable of generosity and sacrifice even to the point of heroism, when it is a question of manifesting belief. It involves an acute awareness of profound attributes of God: fatherhood, providence, loving and constant presence. It engenders interior attitudes rarely observed to the same degree elsewhere: patience, the sense of the cross in daily life, detachment, openness to others, devotion. By reason of these aspects, we readily call it 'popular piety', that is religion of the people, rather than religiosity. Pastoral charity must dictate to all those whom the Lord has placed as leaders of the ecclesial communities the proper attitude in regard to this reality, which is at the same time so rich and so vulnerable. Above all one must be sensitive to it, know how to perceive its interior dimensions and undeniable values, be ready to help it to overcome its risks of deviation. When it is well oriented, this popular religiosity can be more and more for multitudes of our people a true encounter with God in Jesus Christ.[14]

2.3. The Influence of 'Liberation Theology'

The increased interest for popular religiosity the Pope is referring to, is mainly the result of the second conference of the Latin American Bishops (CELAM) at Medellín in 1968. The goal of this meeting was to open up new avenues for the realization of the resolutions of Vatican II in the Church of Latin America. The idea of the Church as 'people of God' seemed to be particularly important. Document number six of Medellín deals with popular religiosity in the perspective of popular culture, more specifically the subcultures of the marginal rural and urban groups. To opt for these people is also to opt for a double movement of liberation: liberation from socio-economical oppression and liberation from religious ignorance by the proclamation of the true Gospel in respect to their idiosyncracy so that this may be experienced in their own popular way.[15]

Some liberation theologians look toward a further association with popular religiosity to find the language and the symbols there for initiating the process of real liberation. But speaking about language and symbols not only leads into the domain of preaching the Gospel but also of liturgy where these narratives and songs must receive the possibility of resonation, where these symbols and rites may have their founding,

14. English translation in *Origins. NC Documentary Service* 5 (1975-76) 459-468, 466.

15. The fact that 'liberation' from an 'oppressing' religiosity is necessary, is demonstrated by the well known example that people in Latin America do celebrate Good Friday, but do not really know Easter. This fact also shows the way people have identified the suffering Jesus with their own suffering situation. As a result the proclamation of resurrection means that one starts a process of real liberation and 'resurrection' for this people.

changing, and stimulating significance.[16]

During their 1979 meeting at Puebla, the CELAM edited another important document: 'Evangelization today and in the future of Latin America'.[17] Here it is clearly stated:

> We have to encourage a mutual and enriching exchange between liturgy and popular devotions, so that the yearning expressed in prayer and charisms, which is present in our countries today, may be channeled with lucidity and prudence. On the other hand, popular religiosity, with its abundance of symbols and expressions, can share its creative dynamism with the liturgy. With due discernment such a dynamism can help to incarnate better in our culture the universal prayer of the Church.[18]

3. Popular Religiosity and Inculturation

3.1. Within the Context of the Inculturation of the Liturgy

The latter text leads us immediately to the issue of the inculturation of the liturgy, where the expressions of popular religiosity may play an important role. Without using the term 'inculturation', articles 37-40 of the *Constitution on the Sacred Liturgy*, under the title 'Norms for Adapting the Liturgy to the Culture and Tradition of Peoples', already posed the question. While the term 'aptatio' is used there, the fourth instruction for the correct implementation of the *Constitution on the Sacred Liturgy*, dealing with the articles 37-40, was entitled: 'The Roman Liturgy and Inculturation'.[19] This was the topic of the preceding colloquium of the Louvain Liturgical Institute.[20] The question we must now further reflect on is about the relation between inculturation and the different forms of popular religiosity.[21] Indeed, the issue at stake is not alone how the liturgy may be celebrated in different cultures as such, but also in the popular culture, the culture namely of the broader popular strata, which does not always mean the culture of the poor in a particular society. The question is how the different forms of popular religiosity

16. About the encounter between popular culture and evangelization see for instance: L. Schuurmans, "Nuances in de bevrijdingstheologie," *Wereld en Zending* 6 (1977) 304-318.

17. *La evangelización en el presente y en el futuro de América Latina. Documento de Puebla*, Buenos Aires, 1979.

18. *Id.*, 167-168.

19. "De liturgia romana et inculturatione," *Notitiae* 332 (1994) 80-115.

20. *Liturgie et inculturation. Liturgy and Inculturation.*Textes et Études Liturgiques XIV, ed. Jozef Lamberts (Leuven: Peeters, 1996).

21. Chupungco, 95-133.

and popular devotions may be recognized as liturgy in the broad sense of the word. Moreover, how may specific aspects of popular religion enrich liturgy, without of course transforming the liturgy into a form of popular religiosity?

3.2. The Input from Popular Religiosity

To start with the latter, we could point to the spontaneous, festive, joyful, expressive, creative, immediate, profoundly human characteristics of the forms of popular religiosity and especially to those involving the entire group.[22] These are elements which could fertilize our liturgy, which speaks about 'active participation' but is very often experienced as cerebral, verbal, and distant.

We could say that Vatican II has restored the classical liturgy, but that all the work is not yet completed. If the liturgy wants to really be the affair of the faithful people, a second movement needs to be started, by which those elements could be integrated.

The promoters of the Liturgical Movement, such as Lambert Beauduin, Pius Parsch and others, from their social concern, have cultivated some values of popular religion like pilgrimages, Marian devotion, etc. But this did not go hand in hand with an appreciation of popular religiosity as a whole and of what they interpreted as devotions the people were using because they were alienated from the true worship of the Church through the clericalization of the liturgy. In other words, the people must in a certain sense be liberated from these popular devotions, which are only a substitute for the true devotion which is to be found in the liturgy. That is why this liturgy must be made more understandable for these faithful (through the introduction of the vernacular, first seen as a translation of the extant liturgy) and by creating room for a real active participation of the faithful (especially through holy communion, giving the liturgical responses and acclamations, through the fulfilment of some ministries). This vision on liturgy, at the outset popular, unintentionally introduced a new elitism into what was intended to be the worship performed by the entire people of God, which is gathered together *hic et nunc*.

The result was a 'limited' liturgical movement, mutilated on the domain of popular inculturation. We now need a reclaim-movement in this domain. The liturgy, provided its essential elements are present and kept intact, "may be expressed in forms which the people of God, under the guidance of their pastors, consider more appropriated to their historical,

22. C. Valenziano, "La religiosità popolare in prospettiva antropologica," *Liturgia e religiosità popolare* (as in note 1), 83-110, 95.

cultural, and psychological situation".[23]

Some expressions of popular religiosity could play here an important role. Here we think about the language as well as about the rites the liturgy uses. The language of the official liturgy is sober, direct, and linear, addressing the intellect, mostly formulated in a rather theological manner. The language of popular religiosity is discursive, florid, pictur-esque, vivid, and appeals to sentiments and emotions.[24] Both languages could be complementary to one another and this way appeal to the entire human person. Also in its ritual shape popular devotions are character-ized by a direct engagement of the faithful, like the communal recitation of the rosary, the communal moving forward in processions, on the Way of the Cross, etc. The official liturgy however clearly defines the role of each one, especially of the ordained ministers. Here also one could look for a better harmonization, which does not mean that popular devotions may be intermingled with the liturgy, as Pope Paul VI stated in his 1974 apostolic exhortation *Marialis cultus*.[25] The richness of language and expressions, which we can find in popular religiosity, without changing the fundamental content of the liturgy, may contribute to the realization of a fully inculturated, recognizable, lively celebration by the entire local manifestation of the people of God.[26]

4. A Critical Approach

When we speak about changes for a further inculturation of the liturgy from the richness which we can find in popular religion, we must ap-proach them at the same time with a sufficiently critical attitude.

4.1. The vision of Robert Pannet as Example

It was Robert Pannet who became the great advocate of 'le catholicisme populaire' in France since 1974, a year after Serge Bonnet had drawn attention to the problem from a sociological point of view.[27] Pannet wanted to highlight the living religious values as they were present in wider popular groups in France and which have often been slighted as

---

23. Marsili, 156.

24. Chupungco, 113.

25. Paul VI, "Marialis cultus," *AAS* 66 (1974) 113-158, no. 31.

26. Concrete examples, although from his own cultural background, are given by Chupungco, 126-133.

27. Serge Bonnet, *A hue et à dia. Les avatars sous la Ve république* (Paris, 1973). Robert Pannet, *Le catholicisme populaire. 30 ans après 'La France, pays de mission?'* (Paris, 1974).

"formalistic or sociological Christendom". This popular catholicism according to Pannet is culturally rather than socio-economically defined. Such people act more emotionally than rationally, more impulsively than reflectively, more practically than on principle. They participate very little or even not at all in the established culture, even on an ecclesial level, because this is usually dominated by the middle class.[28] Their thinking and acting, however, is greatly impregnated by the age-old Catholic influence, in such a way that culture and religion are extremely interrelated. This is clearly expressed by the 'rites of passage': birth, holy communion, marriage, funeral as important familial events are celebrated by these 'chrétiens festifs' by setting them in a religious context.

For them religion needs to confirm the values and promises which they cherish within their familial sphere: warmth, affection, tenderness, recognition, safety, joy. In this context, religion plays for them a stabilizing role rather than being mere routine. Religion should act upon sentiments rather than to hold up a certain doctrine: it should give them the feeling that they belong to the group. Furthermore, religion has to give them a moral framework, an ultimate scale of values, which does not mean a morality of duties as is evident in the way they deal with conjugal morality for instance. Eventually, religion has for them an utopian character, fostering their deep belief that everything has its ultimate meaning.

Pannet also thinks that refining is necessary, but he warns not to reject the good with the bad. We are not really aware of the deeper values as they are living in popular religiosity, which we have to 'evangelize' rather than eliminate.

A serious question is indeed whether the renewed liturgy has not deprived the popular faithful of their familiar symbols (Christmas crib, the cross, the rosary, Mary and the saints) in such a way that they remain empty-handed. Several forms of popular devotion (the way of the cross, benediction, processions) are almost entirely left out. Did we not create a vacuum in this way? Pannet warns of the risk that when the Church in her liturgy looses touch with popular religiosity, people may fall victim to experts in superstition, sects or dubious 'apparitions', etc.

Since the end of the sixties the Church in France has given stricter requirements for receiving the sacraments, especially infant baptism and marriage. The aim was to react against sacramental automatism and to promote more authentic celebrations of faith. A book such as Pannet's,

---

28. One can feel here the influence of the Marxist Antonio Gramsci, who had a considerable influence on Italian theological reflection on the subject of popular religiosity during the seventies. See B. Hein, "Antonio Gramsci und die Volksreligion," *Volksreligion - Religion des Volkes*, ed. Karl Rahner e.a. (Stuttgart, 1979) 156-164.

however, questioned the norms which were used. Although they are not present in the eucharistic celebration on the Lord's Day, at the key moments of their lives they feel their relationship with the Church. They want to celebrate their faith although they do not find the words to express it. Then they expect the Church to help them in the expression of faith and to celebrate these particular moments.

4.2. Critical Evaluation

The question however remains: is this sufficient? The stricter requirements for the reception of the sacraments were accompanied by a 'pastorale de cheminement', a pastoral approach of preparation.[29] Perhaps, this pastoral approach was not really on people's level. We need a basic catechesis which is very close to people's lives and gives them the possibility to express their own feelings.

Although Pannet's plea for popular religiosity may be valuable and revealing, he disregards an important factor which true religion must have in one's life. This is the change of life, the conversion, the ethical consequence, the call for responsibility in this world. Indeed, liturgy as anamnesis, as celebration of Christ's redemptive work in the name of God, not only demands our praise and thanksgiving, but places us in an analogous situation, asks for our cooperation in the salvation of all human beings, asks for our 'diaconia'.[30] This dimension we do not find in popular religiosity, which risks degenerating into a kind of 'opium for the people'. So we think that a liturgy which seeks to welcome popular religiosity must be aware of this danger. For instance, on the occasion of a pilgrimage we may not only confirm people in their need, but also invite them to a reorientation of their lives and to real commitment. But

29. Already in 1951 the French episcopate had decided to recommend a careful delay in infant baptism: *Directoire pour la pastorale des sacrements*, 1951. On 6 December 1965 new instructions were published, which advised that at the occasion of their children's baptism parents should receive catechetical instruction in order to know their responsibility and to choose in complete freedom for infant baptism: *Commentaire du document épiscopal "La pastorale du baptême des petits enfants"* (Neuilly-sur-Seine, 1966). In the debate in France, where some defended a 'baptême par étapes' or even a postponement with a 'rite d'acceuil', Pannet was involved: Robert Pannet, *Baptisez-les! Contribution au débat pastoral sur le baptême des petits enfants. Avec la collaboration de Georges Lagrange, Antoine Renéaume. Préface de Hans Urs von Balthasar* (Paris, 1981). About the current situation in France: Commission Épiscopale de Liturgie, *Pastorale Sacramentelle. Points de repère. Commentaire et guide de travail. I: Les sacrements de l'inititiation chrétienne et le mariage*. Liturgie 8 (Paris: Les Éditions du Cerf, 1996).

30. Jozef Lamberts, "Liturgie: tussen anamnese en diaconie," *Jaarboek voor Liturgie-onderzoek* 5 (1989) 109-131.

this can only succeed from a process of liberation by which people may really say, sing, and celebrate their narratives, songs, and symbols, carefully preserved through generations, but by which at the same time they are called to takes steps toward the utopian realization of what is expressed by these narratives, songs, and symbols.

5. Touchstones for a Positive Engagement with Popular Devotions

By way of conclusion we would like to propose some basic conditions, characteristics or touchstones for a pastorally justified way of engaging with popular religiosity and especially with popular devotions.[31]

5.1. Oriented toward Christ

The first condition is that popular devotions are ultimately to be oriented toward Christ, must lead people to Him, and in every case they may not divert them from Him. Through Christ, God came to liberate people in the full sense of the word. He is 'the' Sacrament of God. All further sacramentality derives its sense and power from Him. The sacramentality which is emanating from Him may have far reaching 'offshoots', but there where these offshoots reach the concrete man or woman they also need to be ways which lead them to Christ.

Pastors and pastoral workers must have a feeling for the specific situation of the popular faithful in order to find with them the way which leads them to Christ. The far reaching 'offshoots' can take different shapes: places of pilgrimage can evoke a 'memorial' of the experience of the 'sacred' which once took place there and re-present it in its meta-dimension; 'saints' may show the faithful, as well as call and encourage them, how they can follow the Lord in the analogous situation in which they live; relics can lead them to the saints and through them to the Lord; respecting its paschal structure, the Way of the Cross can become in and with Christ "a paradigm for each human existence on the way unto its total incarnation"[32]; blessings may help people not only to ask for favors but also 'to say good' (bene-dicere) to God, to praise and glorify Him[33], etc.

'Christocentric' does not mean that we have to banish all saints, replacing them with Christ. That way we would confuse the faith of many

---

31. Jozef Lamberts, *Op weg naar heelheid. Over bedevaart en liturgie*. Nikè-reeks 39 (Leuven-Amersfoort: Acco, 1997) 107-115.

32. Leonardo Boff, *Via-Sacra da Ressurreiçao* (Petrópolis: Editora Vozes, 1983) 14.

33. Jozef Lamberts, "Werken met het Benedictionale: een uitnodiging tot huisliturgie," *Tijdschrift voor Liturgie* 72 (1988) 200-218.

people. What we have to do is to demonstrate the link between this particular saint and Christ, how he or she tried to concretize living with and from Christ since this is expected of each Christian. We have to show and to let it be felt how this saint was in his/her own way a witness to the Lord and of the new way of life that becomes possible in the power of the Holy Spirit in the consistent following of the Lord. This way we bring people to Christ through the saint in whom they have experienced the 'sacred' in a concrete way.

Magic or superstitious practices will probably always remain a danger, especially when the way along which the Lord will reach them is long, or when we perhaps obscure the face of the Lord who is beckoning them, or even worse when we stand before Him in such a way that people who are searching for salvation risk losing their way.

5.2. Interpreted from Scripture

The christocentric dimension presupposes that Scripture must hold an important place in the different forms of popular religiosity. A Way of the Cross, a procession or a pilgrimage must be for people a chance to rediscover God's self-revelation as it reaches us even today through Scripture: the God of the Covenant, who will come to us in a liberating and salvific way. The Word of God must resound in such a way that it can become for the searching man or woman a word of encouragement, conversion, renewal, call, challenge, or meaning.

It is important to realize that also in Scripture God's self-revelation takes different shapes and occurs through a slow, gradual process.[34] Before letting the scriptural word resound, this challenges us to create room for the narratives of searching people so that the Divine Word may really be proclaimed as a message of Good News for them. It incites us to concretize this Word for people in search for salvation through preaching and homily.

At the different rituals, for instance a pilgrimage, preaching can have an important place where word, symbol and symbolic act can interact. There is, for instance, a liturgical celebration at the grotto of Lourdes where the reading from Scripture helps people to see the analogy between the water at Lourdes and the water which bubbled up for the Hebrews from the rock (Ex 17:1-7) or was streaming from the temple (Ez 47:1-12), or the spring of water which the Lord let welling up in us to eternal life (John 4:14), reminding them of their own baptism.[35]

---

34. See *Dogmatic Constitution on Divine Revelation 'Dei verbum'*, nos. 2-4, 14-17.

35. André Cabes, "La pastorale liturgique à Lourdes," *La Maison-Dieu* 170 (1987) 102-118, 104.

5.3. *Leading to the Liturgico-Sacramental Celebrations*

It is also important that through their popular devotions people should be brought to a more intense celebration of the liturgy *stricto sensu* and especially of the sacraments. The setting of some of these devotions within a service of Word and prayer can make them authentic liturgy. Already in the first centuries, the eucharistic celebration took a central place in the pilgrimages. This can also be found in the medieval pilgrimage literature, and is still the case in Lourdes for instance. Here, as in other places, according to an old tradition the sacrament of penance has an important function. Here people sometimes confess again after a long time and experience the liberating and reconciling grace when they may believe in an understanding and forgiving God. Also in Lourdes the communal celebration of the anointing of the sick since 1967 has helped many people, both sick and healthy, to rediscover the proper meaning of this sacrament.

5.4. *An Ecclesial Experience*

Each form of popular religiosity should contribute in its own way to the rediscovery and the re-experience of our being 'ecclesia'. Especially in the important places of pilgrimage, one can experience how the people of God is indeed composed of men and women from all nations, how through the diversity of races and peoples true catholicity is manifested and experienced.

An important experience of this being Church together is had by pilgrims in their processions. To stride along or to 'proceed' (procedere) religiously, communally and solemnly is not only a universal phenomenon, but is from the beginning an integral part of the Christian pilgrimage.

Not only during pilgrimages, but also at the occasion of other expressions of popular religiosity many people have the experience that the distance between people, the distinction between poor and rich, between the different races, between the classes, seems to vanish. This spontaneous experience of 'communitas' can probably lead to the experience of the christian 'koinônia'. It is here where those elements which make the Church cooperate, namely preaching (kerugma), liturgy and community (koinônia). It would be a good thing when this also leads to the fourth of these elements, which is diaconia.

5.5. *Stimulation for a Revision of Life*

The revision of life, or what we may call the ethical consequence, also belongs to the true liturgical celebration as an anamnesis of the Lord's paschal mystery. Insofar as we may rank the expressions of popular religiosity among a broader scope of liturgy, this ethical consequence also applies to them. Moreover, it is an important standard of value. Pastoral care in the context of the new evangelization, as we have discussed, should play an important role in this domain.

After all, we must evaluate 'popular religiosity' in a more positive way, as is still often done. When we are not ready to do something serious with the expressions and experiences of popular religiosity, they will indeed remain nothing more than 'popular religiosity' and one will continue to speak about them in an even more denigratory way. But in this case one should not be astonished or scandalized when people, who for whatever reason no longer feel at home in our liturgical celebrations *stricto sensu*, but who are present in places of pilgrimage, in processions, and other expressions of 'popular religiosity' are 'welcomed' by experts in superstition or fall victims to sects and dubious 'apparitions'.